TANTRA
The Yoga of Love and Awakening

TANTRA
The Yoga of Love and Awakening

A Personal Guide to the
Tradition, Philosophy and Practice of Tantra

Ramesh Bjonnes

HAY HOUSE INDIA
Australia • Canada • Hong Kong • India
South Africa • United Kingdom • United States

Hay House Publishers (India) Pvt. Ltd.
Muskaan Complex, Plot No.3, B-2 Vasant Kunj, New Delhi-110 070, India
Hay House Inc., PO Box 5100, Carlsbad, CA 92018-5100, USA
Hay House UK, Ltd., Astley House, 33 Notting Hill Gate, London W11 3JQ, UK
Hay House Australia Pty Ltd., 18/36 Ralph St., Alexandria NSW 2015, Australia
Hay House SA (Pty) Ltd., PO Box 990, Witkoppen 2068, South Africa
Hay House Publishing, Ltd., 17/F, One Hysan Ave., Causeway Bay, Hong Kong
Raincoast, 9050 Shaughnessy St., Vancouver, BC V6P 6E5, Canada
Email: contact@hayhouse.co.in
www.hayhouse.co.in

ISBN 978-93-81398-46-3

Printed and bound at
Rajkamal Electric Press, Sonepat, Haryana (India)

CONTENTS

CONTENTS

Part III
Tantric Sex, Healing and Ethics

The most beautiful thing we can experience is the mysterious. It is the source of all true art and all science.

– Albert Einstein

INTRODUCTION

Huston Smith, popular scholar and author on religion, terms yoga as 'the most protracted human effort to explore the limits of consciousness'.[1] Today the world over, there is a resurgence of interest in this time-tested human practice. Indeed, according to a market study by *Yoga Journal* in 2005, around 16.5 million people practised yoga regularly in the United States alone, and an additional 25 million wanted to try the practice within the next year. Millions more Americans perform some kind of Eastern meditation – Buddhist, Zen or Hindu.

This growing interest in Eastern wisdom represents a hunger for a spirituality that is transformative and authentic, a desire for spirituality with soul. While most people familiar with yoga know it was developed by Indian sages in ancient times, few are aware of its spiritual roots in the wisdom tradition of tantra. In this book, you will venture into the dynamic and enchanting world of this yogic path. You will learn how this holistic practice and wisdom philosophy can be a guide in cultivating yogic awareness, sacredness and love in everyday life.

Posture yoga is practised for its profound ability to enhance physical well-being, but the essential purpose of this practice is much more than achieving optimum health and fitness. In fact, yogic exercises also have a spiritual benefit: By increasing our flexibility, improving our posture and circulation, and especially by balancing our hormone secretion, they help us become more relaxed and peaceful. Combined with meditation, yoga exercises help us better realize our full human potential. The spiritual meaning of the word yoga is union. The word tantra signifies the path of spiritual expansion and liberation that ultimately leads to the state of yoga, to spiritual union with our inner self. To be in harmony with our inner self, even in the midst of the chaos of daily life, is the real goal of tantra.

Towards an Integral Yoga Movement

Even in the trendiest and most body-centred yoga studios in the world, people are now incorporating many aspects of this holistic and integral lifestyle. Hatha Yoga, the most popular form of physical yoga, is based on thousands of years of yogic experiments, and was further refined and written down in the *Hatha Yoga Pradipika* text by tantric yogis during the Middles Ages. And Bhakti Yoga, the yoga of devotion – the singing of devotional bhajans and kirtans – is another popular form of tantra that crystallized during the time of the great sage Krishna (circa 1500 BC), but the roots of this spiritual tradition go even further back into antiquity. This form of ecstatic, trance-induced spirituality has been widely practised in India for thousands of years. Kirtan and bhajan concerts have become a familiar attraction at thousands of yoga studios and retreat centres, even in the West, thanks to musicians such as Grammy-nominated kirtan singer Jai Uttal and popular chant-master Krishna Das.

There is a new movement among yoga practitioners today, a movement away from just focusing on yoga as a set of physical exercises towards a practice that integrates body, mind and spirit. Many of these contemporary experiments in holistic spirituality represent a return to the original roots of yoga, to the spirit of tantra. What I will outline in this book, then, is a programme for bringing the essence of tantra back into our lives and into our practice of yoga.

Tantra and Veda: The Two Spiritual Rivers of India

India is home to many sacred cultures. People have long believed that all these traditions originated from one main spiritual river, namely the vedas. Most students of yoga have been taught that all the profound, spiritual and medical wisdom teachings of India – including yoga, ayurveda and tantra – are smaller offshoots from the mighty vedic river.

Broadly speaking, however, the lush, prehistoric landscape of India contained two separate rivers, one vedic and one tantric. The vedic stream supplied the world and the Indian continent with philosophy and religious rituals, while the tantric stream supplied yogic practices and tantric meditation. Through the parallel flow, as well as the commingling of these two rivers, the rich cultural and spiritual heritage of India became a reality.

Tantra has not only shaped the world of yoga and ayurvedic healing, but has also influenced a whole tapestry of wisdom traditions throughout the world, including Buddhism, Zen, Hinduism and Taoism. Even many elements in Greek and Celtic culture and mythology can be linked to tantra, including the Cult of Dionysus. According to French author Alain Daniélou, there was once an ancient, tantra-oriented civilization that stretched from the River Ganges to Spain. Daniélou reminds us that the Greeks referred to India as the 'sacred homeland' of Dionysus, and that the historians of Alexander the Great saw the Indian Shiva and Greek Dionysus as similar gods. Moreover, some writers suggest that figures found among artefacts of the Celts of Northern Europe resemble the tantric god Shiva.

Beyond Sex Tantra

Historically, there have been many branches and schools of tantra that are varied in worldview and practice. In its inner essence, however, tantra represents a life-affirming, body-mind-spirit tradition that includes the practice of physical yoga exercises, devotional dancing, mantra meditation, chanting, breathing exercises, visualization techniques, sacred cosmology and even alchemy and holistic medicine. This comprehensive tradition is often referred to as 'tantra yoga'.

Yet, most Western books on this subject today inform us that tantra is simply some form of esoteric sexual practice, and in India many people think of tantra as an occult practice which deals mostly with spells and magic. In reality, most of the writings on sex-tantra in the West have been lifted straight from the pages of the *Kama Sutra*, a Hindu text on lovemaking, which is neither part of tantric nor yogic literature. Not surprisingly, more and more people are searching for a more authentic and holistic experience of tantra. This search was reflected in the article 'Tantric Sex' in *O: Oprah Magazine*, where its 14 million readers learnt that Western tantra has been 'overly sexualized'.

Spiritual tantra is about finding balance in all aspects of our lives. In its essence, it is about seeing and realizing that everything we do can become a sacred, spiritual act, including sex. As yoga writer Vimala McClure reminds us, tantra is not just the yoga of sex; tantra is the 'yoga of everything'. So, while tantra broadly represents the various, ancient yogic paths and their particular history, the practice of tantra – a Sanskrit word that literally means *the practice that leads to spiritual liberation* – can also be characterized as the universal quest for union with God, with Spirit, or with the Beloved. Irrespective of religion, this inner spirit of tantra is reflected in all genuine *spiritual practices*. For, the essence of tantra is not based on religious dogma or superstitious beliefs; it is rooted in spiritual practice as an inner, transformative experience. Hence, the spiritual essence of tantra is universal mysticism, the practice of personal, spiritual transformation found in all sacred traditions.

Throughout human history, there have been largely two approaches to religion: one which out of fear and reverence prayed to the forces of the universe, and one that out of curiosity and awe sought to observe, understand and surrender to the mysterious universe we live in. The first approach led to the formation of religious rituals and prayer, such as those found in the early Rig Veda, and the second enterprise led to practices such as contemplation, meditation and yoga postures. Tantra's life-affirming, love-centred and practical approach to life and the world around us epitomizes this second approach. Some scholars even believe tantra represents the most sophisticated and comprehensive path of personal transformation ever conceived.

In most books and magazine articles on yoga, we learn, mistakenly, that tantra is a fairly recent spiritual path that branched out from the much older vedic tradition. However, studies have since shown that it was not just the vedas, but also tantra that provided the underlying cultural, philosophical, scientific, medical and spiritual currents in Indian society. As Daniélou reminds us in his award-winning book *A Brief History of India*, the tantric teachings were the spirituality of people in large parts of the world for thousands of years.

And what was this spirituality based on? For the general population, it was based on the dual worship of the Mother (goddess) and the Father (god), in India popularly known as Shakti and Shiva. For the yogis in deep meditation, these symbolic expressions were experienced as the dual aspects of Brahma, of cosmic consciousness. They represented the archetypes of unity in diversity. Thus, the yogis embraced both unity and duality, both wholeness and opposites. They realized that these opposites dissolved in Brahma, and that the inner essence of all life and all things was bliss and love. Because, to them, the underlying cause of reality, the all-pervading Brahma, was both blissful and loving. They also recognized that this blissful reality can be realized in this very lifetime through the practice of yogic exercises and meditation. That is why tantra is often called the path of ecstasy, or the path of love.

The Essence of Tantric Spirituality

One common vision held by all schools of tantra is the notion that everything is 'divine' – that every form, particle or atom of this universe has an inherent capacity to reveal the 'divine'; that everything is, at its core, God. Another fundamental aspect of tantra is that we must engage in a sustained spiritual effort, or *sadhana*, in order to realize this inherent divinity. In order to experience sacredness in everyday life, we must practice spirituality – yoga, meditation, prayer and chanting – diligently. As the ancient yogis would say, daily spiritual practice is essential in achieving results on the path of tantra.

While the practice of tantra is commonly found in all the various schools of yoga, the philosophy of tantra differ somewhat from the two other major schools of Indian yoga philosophy, namely the 'Classical Yoga of Patanjali' (commonly known as Ashtanga Yoga) and the 'Advaita Vedanta of Shankaracharya'. As a so-called dualist,

Patanjali believed that the spiritual realm was not embedded in our worldly existence; rather, that it is separate from it. On the other hand, both tantrics and vedantists are non-dualists – they both believe in the oneness of existence – however, where the tantrics see the world as 'divine', the vedantists see it as an illusion.

It is perhaps this holistic and practical attitude – that Divinity is everywhere and that sacredness can be realized anywhere – that makes tantra so appealing to contemporary spiritual seekers. Indeed, according to several prominent yoga teachers quoted in *Yoga Journal*, tantra is the 'next step in America's spiritual evolution'.

The Tantric Renaissance

Thousands of years after the dawn of tantra, when many of its teachings had been integrated into the vedic, or Hindu religion, it resurfaced with great cultural and spiritual esteem. It was during this tantric renaissance, between AD 500 and AD 1200 that the age-old tantric teachings were first written down on books made of palm leaves. Both Buddhism and Jainism were greatly influenced by tantra during this period, and Tibetan Vajrayana Buddhism, for example, is a version of tantra. In the words of philosopher Ken Wilber, 'the great flowering of the non-dual Tantra especially occurred ... in India, and from there it spread ... to Tibet, China, Korea, and Japan.'[2] It was also during this prolific period that Hatha Yoga was further developed and systematized by tantric yogis. In other words, many of the yoga exercises practiced by millions of people in yoga studios today have their roots in tantra. Many meditation and visualization techniques taught in Buddhist monasteries and retreat centres all over the world today are also various expressions of tantra.

Lord Shiva and Shrii Anandamurti: Two Giants of Tantra

Two of the most familiar gods in Indian mythology, Krishna and Shiva, were also most likely historical personalities that influenced Indian history as well as the practice of yoga and tantra. Although many scholars consider them only to have been mythological figures, Georg Feuerstein writes in his esteemed *The Encyclopedia of*

Yoga and Tantra that it is 'probably unwarranted'[3] that some scholars doubt the existence of Krishna, who, as a great king and sage united India around 1500 BC.

The idea that mythological figures and ancient gods and goddesses once were historical figures, is understood in academia as euhemerism, the theory that myths are narrative accounts of historical events. Shrii Anandamurti subscribed to this theory regarding Shiva and Krishna, and he described them as 'mythologized historical figures'. The historical Krishna is, of course, most famous for being the voice behind the spiritual wisdom of the Bhagavad Gita. There is perhaps less agreement about the existence of the illustrious Shiva, but according to tantric oral history as well as the insightful writings of the renowned Indian sage Anandamurti (1921–90), both the early origins of yoga and ayurveda can be traced back to this ancient tantric teacher. Like other self-realized yogis, Anandamurti's enlightened mind was permanently embedded in divine love and bliss. There was also something radically unique about this yogic master: he had the uncanny ability to reveal information – whether historical, scientific or spiritual – without the need to study or refer to books or academic journals. His expansive mind could penetrate all of life's mysteries and reveal the inherent reality of material, psychic as well as spiritual phenomena. Hence, he was not only a master of tantric spiritual science; he was also well-versed in the material sciences, in philosophy and in history, even though he never formally studied any of these subjects.

Moreover, Anandamurti, who had no guru of his own, was allegedly born as an enlightened master. Over time, I would personally witness some of his occult powers and receive numerous glimpses into the depth of his spiritual wisdom. Relying on his tantric insights, as well as the written and oral history of India, Anandamurti revealed Shiva as a historical personality, spiritual teacher and pioneer of arts and medicine. Shiva's existence, previously hidden behind layers of myths and vedic biases, has thus come to life through his insightful discourses and writings. Through his work, the biographical outline of history's earliest tantric master has become a tangible reality. According to Anandamurti, Shiva founded and systematized tantra more than 7,000 years ago. Not surprisingly, Shiva has been considered the 'king of yogis' by the people of India for thousands of years. Many ayurvedic physicians are also fond of referring to him as 'the first ayurvedic doctor'. In support of this sentiment, Anandamurti claimed in his writings on tantra that Shiva systematized a version of ayurveda called Vaidya Shastra from its scattered roots among the early vedic shamans and seers. Shiva is also said to have invented the musical octave based on the sounds of seven different animals. This ancient Indian octave – Sa-Re-Ga-Ma-Pa-Dha-Ni-Sa – was constructed by using the first letters of these animal names in Sanskrit. Moreover, he and his wife, Parvati, advanced the first *mudras*, the poetic and spiritually significant hand and foot gestures that Indian classical dance is based on.

Tantra is thus the perennial wisdom of yogic and mystic sages. It can be considered the earliest form of yoga, and it is as relevant and effective today as it was when it was developed at the dawn of human civilization. When contemporary sage Eckhart Tolle encourages us to cultivate 'the power of now', he is, in his own profound way, simply retelling an old tantric tale. For Shiva, the enlightened Buddha of his time, instructed his students to live in the present. By introducing yogic exercises and meditation practices in a systematic and holistic way, Shiva taught the ancient humans to cultivate harmony and bliss in the present moment. He taught our ancestors to 'be here now'. He taught them how to go beyond the confines of body and mind to the realm of consciousness, to the state of pure being.

Shiva's teachings, however, were not exclusively promoting yogic asceticism. He did not simply encourage people to retreat from society to meditate on the power of being in a Himalayan cave. He guided people towards a path of balance, a life for self-realization and the welfare of the universe. Even at the dawn of human history, Shiva had already understood the contemporary need to lead holistic, integral and transpersonal lives. For in tantric yoga, personal spirituality is based on achieving balance between body, mind and spirit, and social spirituality on seeing the interconnectedness and oneness of all beings.

Tantra's Ancient Future

Today, we are witnessing another tantric renaissance. Most books on tantra in the West, however, have been written by authors who either have a sexual or vedic-oriented focus. While the first category of books may be great introductions to a better sex life, they often create gross distortions and myths about this sacred wisdom tradition. In the second category of books, written by yogic and ayurvedic scholars and practitioners, there are indeed some fine introductory works. Still, these books, which promise to deliver the 'authentic' history, philosophy and practice of tantra, have equally been unable to shed light on several important aspects of tantra.

First, their authors are unaware of the illustrious 7,000-year-old history of tantra, the historical presence of its iconic founder, Shiva, and his monumental contributions to not only tantra and yoga, but also to dance, music and ayurvedic healing. Second, tantra as a living, dynamic tradition has undergone several major changes through the ages, many of which have not been properly recorded by these authors. These include the existence of legendary teachers such as Shiva and Krishna, and also lesser known teachers such as Hatha Yoga master Abhinavagupta and the sage Yudhisthira, who popularized the practice of pranayama, or breathing exercises, as early as 1500 BC. In recent times, Shiva's tantra has been revived by Anandamurti. Even though his teachings are not so well known outside India, he has, in true Eastern tradition, revitalized the old teachings and infused tantra with newly revealed wisdom in the form of fresh sutras, spiritual knowledge conceived through personal realization. This book will introduce many of these revelatory teachings.

Third, most books on tantra are scholarly in nature and thus often unable to bring alive the inner essence of this remarkably vibrant and love-awakening path. I have therefore made a point of seasoning each chapter in this book with inspirational stories from real life. It is my hope that this book will address these shortcomings and present a fresh, practical insider's guide to this extraordinary path of personal discovery and transformation. People today are genuinely searching for a spiritual path that is effective and experiential, at once meditative and body-centred, both down-to-earth and divinely inspired. In the chapters that follow, you will learn that tantra is, and has always been, such an integral and holistic path.

In the following pages, you will learn the basics of what tantra is all about. You will be introduced to the history, philosophy and cosmology of tantra. You will acquire new insights about chakras and mantras, and you will be introduced to tantric secrets about sex, ethics and healing. Finally, you will learn how to integrate all this knowledge into your daily life.

Seven Aspects of Tantra

There are seven fundamental aspects of tantra that will be explored in this book:

1. **Spiritual worldview:** One of the main reasons why we suffer is because of our materialistic or dualistic worldview. We see and experience life as a series of disconnected and separate events that bring either pleasure or pain. By cultivating a spiritual worldview, we can learn to see and experience the world as a continuum of events, and ultimately as non-dual oneness, as Brahma. We can learn to go beyond both pleasure and pain and find what we truly want – inner peace.

2. **Spiritual practice:** It is said that tantra is 95 per cent practice and 5 per cent theory. Without daily spiritual practice – yoga exercises, meditation, prayer, mindful living, etc., – we cannot expect to experience inner peace. Belief and faith in a higher power are a starting point, but not enough. Our spiritual worldview is internalized and becomes part of our personal nature through diligent practice. The specialty of tantric practice lies in its ability to embrace and transmute the power of opposites. Through various practices, desire is transmuted to go beyond desire; the mind is transmuted to achieve a non-dual state of no-mind; physical or symbolic

forms are transmuted to achieve a spiritual ecstasy beyond form.

3. **Spiritual lifestyle:** From tantra, we can learn many invaluable lessons about leading a more balanced, ecological and simple lifestyle. As philosopher Ken Wilber reminded us in an article, we cannot achieve sustainability without 'spiritual sustainability'.

4. **Spiritual cosmology and psychology:** The spiritual cosmology of tantra is non-dual at its core. That is, tantra avoids the common religious dualities of heaven vs earth, god vs goddess, as well as the scientific separation of matter and spirit. Tantra shows instead how these seemingly incompatible concepts can be integrated in a truly holistic cosmology. By integrating tantric cosmology and psychology – the various layers of the mind, kundalini, chakras, etc., – the reader will learn that tantra truly reflects the cosmic unity expressed in the alchemical saying: 'As above, so below'.

5. **Tantric history:** Largely shrouded in myth and secrecy for thousands of years, tantra and yoga are largely analogous paths of spirituality. Hence, their histories are often inextricably linked. New insights about these wisdom paths have recently been revealed by both science and authoritative tantric sources. Genetic research has, for example, confirmed important aspects of oral tantric history. And, as Alain Daniélou asserts in his book *A Brief History of India*, the tantric spirituality of Shiva spread far and wide in ancient times, may be even into Europe, where ancient yogic figures have recently been discovered.

6. **Tantric secrets of health and success:** There is also a close historical, philosophical and practical relationship between tantra, yoga and the ancient medical science of ayurveda. Ancient secrets about health from all three branches of wisdom will be explored, as well as Shiva's 'seven secrets of success'.

7. **Tantric stories:** Storytelling as a teaching tool is an integral part of all wisdom traditions, and tantra is no exception. Each chapter of this book contains several anecdotes – from my own life as well as from the lives of many famous yogic sages – to illuminate further the teachings discussed in each chapter. In the last chapter of the book, I have collected a handful of inspirational stories from my travels in India and Nepal, as well as from the lives of others on the path.

It is my hope, then, that this book will give the reader a few valuable glimpses into the resplendent path of tantra, this practical path of spirituality, which contains within its profound wisdom-teachings the universal essence of all perennial paths. This yogic tradition contains a treasure house of sublime practices from which all seekers of truth may find invaluable gifts to help quench their thirst for illumination. Indeed, the teachings of this ancient and empirical wisdom tradition seem as timely as ever.

Part I
The Spirit and History of Tantra

Chapter One

ALCHEMY OF LOVE:
THE TANTRIC PATH OF ECSTATIC UNION

My own journey through the world of tantra spans over three decades. It began in earnest during a nearly three-year long visit to India and Nepal in the 1980s. If you have been fortunate enough to have visited these countries as a tourist, you will know that the visit itself can be life-altering. But, for me, the exotic, geographical and cultural journey was just the beginning. The real journey started when I began learning about the inner secrets of tantra, one of humanity's oldest transformational paths.

In Kathmandu, Nepal, the Swayambhunath Temple is a sacred landmark. A large fresco painting of Buddha's meditative eyes can be seen for miles on top of the temple stupa. Built in the sixth century AD, this famous temple sits on top of a hill at the end of a steep pathway of more than 300 steps. When you finally get to the top, you will be greeted by Buddha statues, Tibetan Mani stones and hundreds of playful and perpetually hungry monkeys.

According to tantric oral history, this so-called 'monkey temple' is located on a favourite meditation spot of Shiva. It is said he used to meditate and teach in this area at the dawn of human civilization, nearly 4,500 years before Buddha attained enlightenment under the Bodhi tree.

It would soon be my fate to live in a tantric ashram just a few blocks from this awe-inspiring and legendary temple. Our small, rustic ashram was located in a rented house that belonged to an old and very happy woman. Her happiness, however, had not been long-lived. Only a few months before I got there, Mrs Chitrak's large property had been the embodiment of suffering.

Before our teacher, Acarya S., rented this house, it had been haunted by ghosts. Fire and noise would appear in the courtyard at night. Tiles and rocks would fall from the earth-coloured roof. Screaming and hollering ghostlike figures would frequent the empty rooms. The landlady, Mrs Chitrak, was unable to sleep and eat. When she met Acarya S., she was at her wits' end, ready to die a slow and sorrowful death. Acarya S., an adept tantric and well-versed in all things occult, knew exactly what was going on and what to do. He assured Mrs Chitrak that if she would rent one of her houses to him, everything would be all right. He was right. As soon as he moved in with a few students, he performed a cleansing ceremony consisting of several days of intense meditation and devotional kirtan singing. After that, the house was never again frequented by howling ghosts and flying bricks.

I asked Acarya S. for an explanation. Had there really been ghosts in the house? Or had all these crazy events simply been conjured up by an old insomniac's imagination? No, he assured me, there had truly been ghosts and noises in the house. He had experienced them himself.

'The house had been haunted by avidya tantrics,' he said. 'These black magicians sometimes drive vulnerable people out of their homes, either out of pure, wicked pleasure or for monetary gain. Vidya tantrics, those who practice spiritual yoga, do not need any special powers to drive out these avidya forces,' he assured me. 'All we need to do is to be brave and steadfast in our practices. Then the negative forces that they send out will return to them. They will suffer the consequences of their own karma.'

Wisdom and Ignorance: Vidya and Avidya Tantra

I had been introduced to the occult world of tantra in India a few weeks earlier at a large eco-village and ashram. An arid place on the border between Bihar and Bengal, it is famous among tantrics for its many tantra *pithas*, or places where yogis have achieved enlightenment. There I met an elderly yogi named Citgathananda. In his young age, the now greying monk used to spend nearly 20 hours each day in meditation. After a few years of such disciplined introspection, he invariably cultivated many kinds of occult powers. He could move objects at will. He could read people's minds. He could see into the future.

Citgathananda gradually developed a fondness for his ability to display occult powers in public. People would flock to him for advice and, due to his popularity he no longer had to worry about food, money or shelter.

In traditional tantra, the relationship between teacher and disciple is very close. An authentic tantric guru does not only teach; he or she also makes sure the disciple is living in accordance with those teachings. Thus Citgathananda's guru would regularly call on him for his semi-annual spiritual 'check-ups'. During one of these occasions, the guru simply told Citgathananda: 'From now on, your powers are in my pocket.'

'Spiritually, I was still a child with a distorted ego,' Citgathananda confided in me with a hearty laugh. 'My guru knew I was not ready to have these powers. So he snatched them away from me. And since that day, I have not been able to use my psychic powers. But I am actually glad. Now I experience more love, more bliss. Love is what spirituality is all about. In tantra we therefore say that occult powers are like ashes. Compared to my love for God, for all of creation, these powers are truly nothing but ashes.'

A few weeks after he told me that story, Citgathananda and I travelled together to Nepal. He was a wonderful companion, a very wise and generous spirit and with a keen sense of humour. After two days of dusty travel by train, we finally arrived at the Nepalese border where two large vultures greeted us on top of a sign that said: 'Welcome to Nepal'.

During the next few months of intense tantric training, I often imagined my ego being attacked by those two greedy vultures. When I was in a philosophical mood, I imagined them helping me strip my ego of its old conditioning, denude it of its old mindset, its overly rational, Western psychological make-up. But when I was in a more emotional state of mind, they transformed into the greedy parts of myself, those parts I had a hard time accepting. In fact, one of the most difficult things for me to get used to in the ashram was my attachment to 'good food'. No longer able to enjoy sweet yogurt, cold orange juice, chocolate and other delicious food items, my mind actually started to hallucinate them. This went on for the first couple months. During most of my meditations, my mind was busy imagining the vivid apparitions of cold Sunkist orange juice and dark Swiss chocolates.

In tantra, the powerful energy awakened by our desires can also become a source for transcending those very desires. This transmutation of desire is achieved in stages by gradually observing those cravings without rejecting them, without suppressing them. The same desirous energy spent in enjoying or trying to reject these hallucinations is instead channelled into a passionate wish to be skilled in yoga and meditation. Just like in tai chi, you gracefully turn 'the opposing force' into your own. So, through the silent recitation of mantras, the visualization of chakras, and the singing of Sanskrit chants, I gradually learnt to transform my disturbing mental energies into a constructive force of concentration and mental expansion. And, as these hallucinatory bubbles of the mind gradually subsided, I was able to experience the depth of true inner pleasure, the experience of spiritual bliss and ecstasy from the deep waters within. I realized that the pleasure of Sunkist orange juice was fleeting and superficial compared to the transcendent rapture of meditation. Finally, my culinary hallucinations eventually disappeared, and instead I became absorbed in the sacred world of ashram life. I even started to enjoy the simple food made of rice, lentils and vegetables.

***

A few months into my monastic training, I was walking on a meandering path through the jungles of southern Nepal with my teacher and fellow students. We had been invited to stay for a few days at the mountain home of a former Kumari. Now a fellow yogini, this former royal living goddess had turned her home into an ashram. Since it was a popular meeting place for spiritual seekers and wandering sadhus from all over Nepal, I was hopeful we would meet some genuine yogic saints there.

While we walked through the dense forest, Acarya S. shared with us some of the secrets in the life of a Kumari. Always a premenstrual girl chosen from the Buddhist Shakya caste, she leads a paradoxical life. Worshipped by Hindus and Buddhists alike, she lives in total isolation. She commands more power than anyone else, yet at the drop of a tooth, she must resign her heavenly throne and return to a life among us mortals. I had actually once drifted into a sea of Kumari devotees watching the legendary 'virgin goddess' peek through a small window at Durbar Square in Kathmandu. Thousands of worshippers walked by the small, unearthly face peeking through the wall; her hair in a topknot, a celestial third eye painted in her forehead, a serene, feminine smile from another world in another time.

While still contemplating the strange life of the Kumari, and also looking forward to meet one of these former goddesses face to face, I suddenly heard a terrifying scream. A dark, half-naked sadhu with long, matted hair had jumped in front of Acarya S. on the path. He shouted and waved with his ash-covered arms, one of which was cut off at the elbow. In his right hand, he held a long knife. His eyes gleamed with ferocious anger. I was afraid he was about to attack and kill our teacher. But he suddenly disappeared out of sight as suddenly as he had appeared.

Acarya S. turned around, looked at all of us terrified young, aspiring tantrics, and with a big smile and beaming eyes declared: 'He was an avidya tantric, and he has challenged me for a fight tonight at the graveyard.'

I was dumbfounded. I could hardly believe my ears. I was not even sure if I had seen what I thought I had seen. As if Acarya S. had read my mind, he said, 'Do not be afraid or confused. Avidya tantrics have no chance against the force of dharma. He will lose. He will surely lose.' Then, as if nothing had happened, he continued to wander down the damp and, suddenly, not-so-pleasant-looking jungle path.

The Kumari no longer looked like a virgin goddess. Instead, she was a sweet, educated and motherly woman of middle age with her long black hair tied in a traditional knot. When she heard about

Acarya S.'s planned battle with the black magician, she spoke in a slightly British accent, 'He will never change. Once a crazy tantric, always a crazy tantric. But don't worry, boys; he will survive. Trust me; this is not the first time he has met with such a challenge.'

We did worry, of course. In fact, we hardly slept that night. I tried to meditate, but most of the time, I looked down towards the river where a dozen or so sadhus had set up a primitive camp. I was amazed at their simple lifestyle. All they owned were a few cotton lungis, a begging bowl, which sometimes was made from a human skull, a knife, or a sword, and may be a pair of sandals.

Most of that night, I sat staring anxiously into the smouldering fires made by the sadhus, or into the empty darkness. What if Acarya S. was killed by that mad sadhu? I did not look forward to walking back through the jungle without our teacher. And what if some of the sadhus down there were avidya tantrics, as well? Finally, I did fall asleep.

At dawn, I was rudely awakened by a German student, Umesh. Excitedly, he pointed down towards the river. There, I saw Acarya S. walking nonchalantly towards our simple hermitage made of stone and thatched straw. He had the red, vertical marking of a Kapalika Tantric on his forehead. A real, polished and quite old skull was dangling from his right hand. When he came close, he beamed his characteristic youthful smile towards our sleepy faces and said, 'I won. I won. He finally ran away shouting and screaming.' Acarya S. then sat down and excitedly began to tell us about his adventure.

Once he had arrived at the appointed place, he used a short wooden stick to draw a circle of protection around himself. No matter what happened, whether attacked by snakes, rabid dogs or the terrifying visions of avidya tantrics, all Kapalikas had been instructed never to leave this sacred circle, he explained. No matter what. As soon as Acarya S. sat down inside the circle to start his meditation practice, the avidya tantric's demonic power play started. First, he was attacked by the ferocious barks of a pack of hungry hyenas. The mad pack of wild dogs was very close. He could feel the razor-sharp teeth snap at his head. He was terrified. He barely managed to keep his eyes closed and to concentrate on his mantra. Even though he knew these sounds were the fabricated hallucinations of the avidya tantric, they sounded and felt absolutely real. Then, suddenly, even though his eyes were still closed, the dark outline of a huge bull with large, hot flames hissing out of its nostrils, as if from a welder's torch, appeared in front of him. Only seconds later, he felt the cold skin of a large snake slither up his naked body.

These visions were much more intense than he had ever experienced, so he opened his eyes to see if they would all go away. It made no difference. He could actually see the profile of the large fire-spouting bull in the dark. He could still hear the jackals, and even though he could not see the snake, he could still feel it.

These terrifying visions and noises continued for almost an hour. When Acarya S. had almost given up hope of surviving the battle, he heard the voice of his guru in his inner ear: 'Do not give up. Continue to concentrate on your chakra, and recite the mantra.'

A few minutes later, Acarya S. heard screams coming from the forest nearby. 'I am burning. I am choking. I am dying. Stop sending your hellish powers towards me.' But Acarya S. could do nothing to help him. He had been too busy trying to stay alive himself. He was too absorbed in his concentration, too occupied in protecting himself against this madman's hellish onslaught of psychic powers. Besides, none of the powers that 'attacked' the avidya tantric were consciously his own. All he had tried to do was to create a positive, psychic shield to protect himself. And most of the time, he had barely been able to even do that.

Once again, he realized the mystical power of the science of tantric mantras. Once again, he realized how much he still had to learn. Most of all, he realized the sublime powers of the spiritual protection of his guru. For, once he had surrendered to the protection of the guru, he had received help. And, once again, he had experienced the law of karma: the vicious, hallucinatory forces sent out by the avidya tantric had gone back to haunt the black magician himself. For all he knew, the black magician might even have perished from the power of his own dark spells. All Acarya S. knew was that he was alive. He was alive, seemingly by the grace of his omniscient guru. And who was that actual guru? None other than God, or Brahma.

When Acarya S. finished his story, we were too awestruck to talk. We just sat quietly and listened to the sound of the river for a while. Some of the sadhus were already taking a bath, while others were still sleeping. Then Umesh, with his thick German accent, said, 'I wonder why the avidya tantric had only half an arm?'

'Because he has offered his own flesh to the flames in order to achieve psychic powers,' Acarya S. said. Then he began to explain the difference between avidya and vidya tantra.

'Since the beginning of time,' he began, 'human beings have wanted to explain and know the mystery of creation. They were in awe of the power and beauty of nature and they wanted to know the secrets behind it all. They discovered that there were both good and evil, constructive and destructive forces in nature; in life. These in essence are the forces of vidya and avidya. Later, the shamans and the yogis discovered that there are natural laws; that everything in nature follows a certain system (an order). In the body itself, they discovered energetic systems. These chakras, as they called them, were organized according to a certain system. In the heavens, they discovered that the celestial bodies were also organized in a certain system, according to a certain chakra. This cosmic system is called Brahma Chakra in tantra. And the nucleus of this system is the God or Brahma. In this Brahma Chakra, there are two forces working, the centrifugal force, or *avidyamaya*, and the centripetal force, or *vidyamaya*. Avidyamaya, or maya, is the force that moves away from the nucleus; it is the force of ignorance, of darkness, of evil, if you will. Maya is also known as the force that creates the illusion of separateness in our lives. But the vidyamaya force is the force that moves us towards the nucleus. It is the force of knowledge, of good and light. It is the force of unity.'

Acarya S. stopped for a while. He was obviously very tired. He asked for a glass of water. Spellbound, we watched him drink the whole glass in one gulp. We did not want him to stop, of course, so we eagerly waited for him to continue his informal, yet profound philosophical discourse on tantra. 'Both the avidya and vidya forces have two expressions each,' he continued. 'The avidya force contains a force or shakti that is repulsive and a force that conceals.

The repulsive force in nature drives us away from truth, from beauty, from God. The concealing force, on the other hand, hides it all away from us. It makes us ignorant and creates a separation between us and God. The vidya force also has two inherent forces or qualities, one that inspires spiritual awakening in us, and one that bestows happiness and bliss. You have all been awakened to the spiritual path. All of you have also experienced some inner bliss in your meditations, but you are also still under the influence of the avidya force, the force of repulsion and ignorance.'

'But I don't understand,' I interrupted him, 'how all this relates to the powers of the avidya tantric.'

'Because our lust for power, whether it is psychic power or material power, whether it is the lust for money or for knowledge, drives us away from the experience of God and that of spirituality,' he answered. 'Moreover, the more we attain of this power, the more we hunger for it. The more we are repulsed away from the spiritual, the more we are concealed in the illusion that it brings us happiness and contentment. It becomes an addiction. These avidya tantrics are addicted to their power, even though they have a lot of knowledge, a lot of wisdom. It is a very risky and dangerous path. On the path of vidya tantra, one may also attain occult or psychic powers, wealth and fame, but if one is sincere, one will not be attached or trapped by these forces of nature. So, you will have to decide, do you want to follow the path of ignorance or the path of wisdom, the path of avidya or the path of vidya? But ultimately – and this is key to understanding the essence of tantra – you will have to move beyond both avidya and vidya. In other words, a truly enlightened tantric is one who is beyond duality, beyond knowledge and ignorance. Tantrics are at one with the non-dual spirit. Thus, you will see that true tantric gurus sometimes use occult powers. They can do so because they are totally free, completely beyond their influence.'

Tantra: The Yoga of Sacredness

Thus began my colourful and captivating introduction to the native tantra of India and Nepal. Most people in the West still think of tantra as just a sexual practice. I learnt fairly early, however, that tantra, like life itself, can be interpreted and experienced in a myriad of ways. As tantric author Vimala McClure reminds us, tantra is not the yoga of sex. Rather, tantra is 'the yoga of everything.' Or, as I'd like to put it, 'tantra is the yoga of sacredness'.

Some contemporary spiritual teachers explain that the word tantra means technique. To them, the word connotes a transformative tool, a science, a way of life that brings joy and enlightenment. Others will tell you that the word tantra means to expand, as in expanding one's consciousness. Yet others will tell you that the it means weaving. Tantra to them signifies a kind of spiritual ecology expressed in concepts such as nature's web of life or the interconnectedness of all that is. Some religious scholars refer to it as a cultural tradition that emerged in the early Common Era within Hinduism, Buddhism and Jainism. All these interpretations are partly right. Yet to truly understand the inherent spirit of tantra, we must go to the root of the word and tradition itself.

If we break down this Sanskrit word into three syllables, we get *tan+trae+da*. The root verb *tan* means to expand, and the root verb *trae* means to liberate. So the etymological meaning of tantra is that path which leads to expansion and ultimately to liberation. It can also be explained as the practice that liberates us from dullness. The reason behind this explanation is that all Sanskrit letters have deep esoteric meaning, and the letter *da* is the 'seed sound' of dullness.

Tantra, then, has two implications: the path of liberation from dullness and the path of personal expansion and enlightenment. Moreover, a tantric is someone who practises tantra. And since tantra is a fundamental and universal spiritual science, tantric practitioners can be found, irrespective of religion, wherever there is spiritual practice, wherever there is an attempt to attain spiritual liberation. In other words, even though tantra as a specific path can be traced back to Shiva, in a more general sense tantra is found among mystics of all religions, especially within Hinduism, Buddhism, Sufism, Jainism, Zen and to some extent within mystical Judaism and Christianity. The history of tantra is much older than Hinduism and Buddhism, in fact, much older than any of the world's great religions.

Early forms of tantra emerged in the ancient shamanic cultures of Asia at the dawn of civilization more than ten thousand years ago. Deeply rooted in late matriarchal society, the life-affirming tantra was, according to the puranas and various teachers of tantra, systematized by Shiva and his wife, Parvati, in their agama and nigama teachings around 7,000 years ago. At that primordial dawn of human society – 4,500 years before Buddha and 5,000 years before Christ – tantra emerged as the world's most integral way of life. With its own spiritual practice, psychology, science, art and medical system tantra was, and still is, an integral path of personal transformation, a transpersonal way of being.

Yet the essence of tantra is not a belief system, nor is it a formal religion. Tantra is a spiritual practice, a science and a philosophy that expresses the perennial essence of our human quest for spiritual realization. Tantra represents our universal quest for truth within and beyond the world of science and religion. Tantra is also a lifestyle. Based on a spiritual world view and yogic practices, the tantric lifestyle helps invoke the sacred in everyday life. In fact, the essence of tantra – to quench our innate thirst for spiritual union – is at the heart of all yoga traditions. From Taoism to Hinduism, from Jainism to Buddhism, from medieval kundalini yoga to contemporary hatha yoga, from traditional raja yoga to ecstatic bhakti yoga, the essence of tantra flows as a seamless stream of transcendental knowledge. And, in a more general sense, tantra connotes the experiential and transformative mysticism at the heart of all the world's wisdom traditions. In that sense, both the Kali-worshipping Indian saint Ramakrishna and the God-intoxicated medieval Christian Saint Teresa of Ávila (AD 1515–82) were tantrics. In that sense, both transpersonal philosopher and meditator Ken Wilber and bestselling author and Buddhist teacher Pema Chodron are tantrics.

Tantra, which often is termed tantra yoga, cannot be divorced from the inner essence of its own spiritual heart, from the experience of bhakti, the expression of spiritual love. American poet Robert Bly aptly describes bhakti yoga as the path where 'the bee of the heart stays deep inside the flower, and cares for no other thing.'[4] This focus on passionate love is integral to tantra as it turns desire and attachment, the very antidotes of spiritual liberation, into an alchemical fuel for love and the emancipation of spirit by worshipping all as God. Thus the bee of the heart goes so deep into what it loves that it transforms into love itself. To become that love is the goal of the love-intoxicated path of tantra.

Tantric love is about creating spiritual oneness and union. As you will learn in more detail later in this book, tantra is about feeling connected to the spiritual essence of the universe. And what is this essence? It has many names: God, Spirit, Godhood, Tao, Allah, or simply the One. In tantra, this essence is called Brahma, or cosmic consciousness. And this Brahma is composed of Shiva and Shakti, the dual expressions of Brahma, just like light and heat are inseparably one with fire, yet also its dual expressions.

Shiva is Brahma as pure cosmic consciousness, and Shakti is Brahma as Cosmic Creative Energy, the force behind creation, the force that created you and me. Shiva and Shakti, like a wave and a particle in quantum physics, are never separate. They are always together, always the same. They are simply two different expressions of the same universal Brahma. Remembering these primal aspects of the world, we open up to see and experience oneness in duality everywhere. We open up to feelings of spiritual connectedness and love.

The primal, evolutionary force of Shakti – which is both real and symbolic – is that which inspires us towards illumination and wisdom. Yet the same force has the capacity to blind us, to drive us away from truth and self-realization. In other words, the duality of wisdom and ignorance, vidya and avidya shakti, exists at the very root of creation and life itself. Thus, no matter at which stage we are on the spiritual path, there is always the possibility of making mistakes. Hence, there is always a need for spiritual vigilance, always a need to transcend our own limitations and ignorance; a need to personify a deep, spiritual morality.

Our challenge is to go beyond the illusion of avidya shakti. When we take up that challenge, we are inspired to reach our natural state of spiritual being. And when we live and breathe from that state, we are supported by the spiritual power of vidya shakti. Then we will experience more and more synchronicity, harmony and vitality in our life. Still, after the spiritual light has awakened us, we must be vigilant. Tantra is thus a dynamic path and urges us to stay awake in the light of our spiritual being at all times.

The path of tantra is about experiencing spiritual bliss, to soak the human heart with divine spirit. Thus, it is often said that bhakti yoga, the path of ecstatic love, is the best and safest path. This yoga of love is beautifully exemplified in the life and poetry of, thirteenth century Persian poet, Rumi, who said, 'The taste of milk and honey is not it. Love instead that which gave deliciousness.' In other words, love that which is within and beyond all physical forms and expressions, that which is within and beyond food, sex, fame, and money. As the tantrics will say, when you cultivate love for that which gives you all that is delicious in life, namely Brahma, you will eventually experience love in everything. That is the spirit of tantra. That is the alchemy of tantric love.

This, then, is the path of vidya tantra – the path that leads us to experience the unity of Shiva and Shakti in our own hearts and minds, and, hence, to the realization of cosmic consciousness everywhere.

Tantra is Yoga, and Yoga is Tantra

If you are one of the millions of people today who practice yoga at home or in a studio, you are actually practicing a form of tantra. Because, just as the world of tantra is often viewed through a narrow lens today, so is the case with yoga. The physical yoga exercises that people of all faiths practice today are called asanas. Some enthusiastic practitioners of these exercises endure 105-degree sweats at a Bikram Yoga studio in smoggy downtown Los Angeles or New Delhi. Others start their day with a sun salutation exercise at a pristine yoga retreat in Hawaii. Yet others find it more convenient to practice at home watching their favourite yoga teacher on DVD. No matter which style, these asanas, which literally means 'comfortably held positions,' enhance physical well-being. But physical health was not the only reason tantric yogis developed these exercises.

There are two categories of these exercises: one is primarily for physical health and secondarily for spiritual growth, and one is primarily for concentration and spiritual growth. The well-known padmasana, or lotus position, belongs to this second category. Originally, asanas were prescribed to better prepare us for the spiritual aspects of yoga, namely the practice of long and deep meditation. With these insights in mind, we can now better understand why the tantric yogis termed the body a physical temple of the divine spirit.

The promises of health, relaxation, longevity and spiritual enlightenment have inspired many to take up the ancient practice of yoga today. Common to all modern yogis is the practice of some aspect or version of hatha yoga. Not all yoga students are aware, however, that their practices – whether it is asanas practised as Bikram Yoga, Iyengar, power yoga, Kripalu or Anusara yoga – have deep roots in the teachings of the medieval tantric sage Gorakshanath.

The achievements of this miracle worker and saint from the ninth century AD build on the tradition laid down in earlier eras by tantric yogis, including Matsyendranath, the founder of the Shiva-oriented Natha sect. The practice of hatha yoga culminated in the writing of the *Hatha Yoga Pradipika* text around AD 1400. Both the teachings of Gorakshanath and those in the *Hatha Yoga Pradipika* emphasize the importance of blending hatha yoga with raja yoga, which is just another way of saying that hatha yoga is best combined with tantra, since the raja yoga described by Patanjali in the yoga sutras, is basically the same as tantra. This so-called eightfold path was written down by Patanjali in the second century BC. However, most of these teachings are also tantra-based because many asanas and meditation techniques were already taught by the tantric sage Shiva thousands of years earlier.

Moreover, all of the path-breaking sages in the long history of yoga can be considered tantric, not always philosophically, but in their practice of asanas, the various meditation techniques, and in their scientific understanding of the subtle anatomy of chakras, kundalini, and the sonic science of using various mantras. In fact, all the various classical streams of yoga practice can be traced back to one common source: namely, Shiva's and Parvati's teachings on tantra.

Tantra: The Yoga of Union

What does the Sanskrit word yoga mean? There are various interpretations, the two most important are offered by Patanjali and by Shiva. Patanjali explains in his famed *Yoga Sutras* that yoga means the suspension of all mental tendencies or propensities. In other words, one attains inner peace when the mind is void of distractions and thoughts. This rather dry definition of yoga never quite took hold in Indian culture.

Shiva's popular tantric definition is more heart-centred and soulful. Yoga, said Shiva, is that process that creates unity between the individual soul and the cosmic soul.

Yoga is the inner state of well-being we feel when there is harmonious interaction between body, mind and spirit. As a lifestyle, yoga is a path of self-discovery. Through asanas and meditation, yoga promotes physical health, mental balance and spiritual peace. Spiritually, yoga means union, and according to tantra it means a state of enlightenment. As an art and a science, yoga aids us in developing a more healthy and balanced lifestyle.

The spiritual state of yoga, or union, is often expressed through spiritual love or bhakti yoga. In traditional temple sculptures, the unity of Shiva and Shakti, as well as our spiritual, non-dual union with the Divine, is symbolized by two lovers in a tight embrace. In the *Mayatantra*, one of the ancient texts based on Shiva's teachings, yoga is defined as 'the unity between the individual soul and the universal soul.' In another text, the *Kularnava Tantra*, the attainment of yogic union, is poetically described as 'water pouring into water'. Hence, tantra and yoga are like Shiva and Shakti, like two sides of one single sheet of paper. You cannot really have one without the other.

The Many Faces of Yoga

The ancient yogis were practical people. While yoga asanas are important for physical and mental well-being, people feel connected to spirit and the world in various ways. Some experience spirit's mysterious existence best when they think, teach or study. Some feel spirit most when they sing, dance or love. Yet others are awakened to spirit's presence through service or bravery. Hence there are three main ways to express spiritual union in yoga – through love, contemplation or action. In other words, through bhakti yoga, the yoga of devotional love, jnana yoga, the yoga of wisdom, and karma yoga, the yoga of service. No matter which expression feels most natural to us, the idea is to invoke the Divine with selfless devotion and dedication through self-expression.

The Many Faces of Tantra

The spirit of tantra implies a dynamic effort to overcome the dominance of avidyamaya, the forces of ignorance and lethargy that keep us away from doing the inner work needed to attain enlightenment. These dynamic, physical, mental and spiritual efforts can be carried out in largely three ways and are characteristic of the three main paths of tantra.

The Right-hand Path: Termed *dakshina marga tantra* in Sanskrit, this so-called right-hand path attempts to overcome avidyamaya, or ignorance and darkness, through the use of idols, devotional chanting and prayer to the gods and goddesses. It is imperative on this path of bhakti yoga to realize that the symbolic representations of the Divine are just gateways to the spirit realm. They are internal archetypes of the mind and spirit realm. Religious people with a pre-rational mentality often interpret their symbols and ideas literally. This is a potential limitation with such worship. It can lead to religious literalism and, even worse, to fundamentalism and dogmatism.

People on this path also tend to pray to receive boons from god, rather than to praise the divine with chants, music and poetry in order to feel oneness with god. So, in order to harness the spiritual potential of this path most effectively one must also understand these potential trappings. Yet even for those of a rational or even transrational (mystical) state of mind, such as the great sage Ramakrishna, there are subtle aspects of this popular path to consider. Ramakrishna, who was famous for his worship of Goddess Kali, or Shakti, and who worshipped her as a gateway to the realm of pure consciousness, achieved high states of spiritual enlightenment, but not the most sublime state of *nirvikalpa samadhi*, or complete yogic enlightenment.

It was only when the naked wanderer and tantric guru Totapuri initiated him in the practice of non-dual mantra meditation that Ramakrishna attained oneness with cosmic consciousness. He did so after Totapuri pressed a piece of glass into his forehead and told him to concentrate his mind in that point. Then, by piercing through the dualistic veil of Goddess Kali, Ramakrishna attained nirvikalpa samadhi. He remained in this mystical trance for three days continuously, a state that Totapuri himself had taken many years to attain. After that seminal experience, Ramakrishna was able to move in and out of this exalted world of non-dual bliss with effortless grace for the rest of his life.

The Left-hand Path: Termed *vama marga tantra* in Sanskrit, this path attempts to overcome the deceptions of avidyamaya by 'any means possible' but sometimes without a clear goal of attaining yoga, or spiritual union. This path is legendary for its highly advanced sexual practices and the explicit use of occult powers. Hence, it is also often considered a path of avidya tantra, or the kind of black magic that my teacher experienced. The main challenges on this path are the many temptations for misusing one's physical and psychic desires and powers.

Some tantric adepts on this path claim they have transcended all worldly attachments while making a show of doing whatever they wish – they drink heavily, they have excessive sex with multiple partners, they live in riches. While it may be possible such teachers are enlightened, it is nevertheless a risky path. Fraught with many contradictions and dangers – both for student and teacher – this path has many pitfalls and often lacks any clear ethical or cultural customs to be guided by.

In some schools of left-hand tantra, however, a disciple will follow strict codes of discipline and morality until he or she is allegedly enlightened and ready to lead the unconventional life of a crazy wisdom teacher. Because the left-handed path appeals to our contemporary excesses of sex, ego, fame and entertainment, it is often this path's gratuitous excess that is labelled tantra in the West. In reality, this path is quintessentially not representative of tantra, and its exaggerated practices are not required.

The Middle Path: Termed *madhya marga tantra* in Sanskrit, this so-called middle path is what is outlined in this book, and is the most common school of tantra yoga. It originated with Shiva and has been further advanced through the ages by various gurus and adepts, including one of the most revered sages of the past century, namely Anandamurti. It is generally considered the most mindful and dependable path. This middle path towards realizing the spiritual effulgence of Brahma removes avidyamaya's veil of ignorance through an integrated and balanced set of physical, mental and spiritual practices. Some also refer to this as the direct path since it employs mantras and visualization techniques to focus the mind to go beyond the mind and into a state of pure, flowing meditation.

Non-dual sages such as the revered Ramana Maharishi and also the popular contemporary sage Eckhart Tolle can be said to promote a direct path to realization. They advise us to enquire into our own deepest self, into our own state of pure being by bypassing the analytical mind and its false sense of egoic self. But to achieve this state of pure being is not as easy as it sounds. It is much easier to think that you have achieved pure being, to have an intellectual idea of what that means, than to actually be in a state of pure being. The tantric middle path circumvents this spiritual dilemma in a radical yet indirect way: by focusing the mind through meditation on the breath with a mantra.

While using the breath and a mantra to still and focus the mind's chatterbox, you gradually transcend the mind itself. To use the mind to transcend the mind, a seemingly contradictory practice, represents the real essence of tantric transformation. Breathing exercises, or pranayama, is another practice that aids in the process of accessing the deep waters of spiritual illumination, as pranayama makes it much easier to concentrate and thus still the mind. In addition, tantric meditation also employs chakra and yantra visualizations as well as devotional chanting and dancing. All these blissfully effective practices will be discussed in more detail throughout the book.

Dr Chris Kang is a tantric practitioner who holds a doctorate in religion and has written extensively on tantra and Buddhism. Once, during an e-mail exchange we had about tantra, he emphasized yet another equally crucial element in tantric meditation: to use the meaning of the mantra to direct the mind's attention towards its own nature. That is, we are not simply focusing or stilling the mind in one-pointed awareness, but also clarifying and sharpening our awareness so that it sees and knows directly the ultimate nature of the mind itself. This type of insight is possible because the mantra's meaning activates the mind's innate reflexivity and catapults the conceptual mind beyond itself and into its underlying, blissful luminosity. Hence, our awareness sees and knows itself by becoming itself in its natural state.

Mantra ideation facilitates this process. Pranayama, in combination with a mantra, is another practice that aids in the process of accessing the deep waters of spiritual illumination, since pranayama makes it much easier to concentrate and thus facilitates the mind accessing its own spiritual luminosity. In addition, tantric meditation also employs chakra and yantra visualizations as well as devotional chanting and dancing. All these blissfully effective practices will be discussed in more detail throughout the book.

In addition to these three paths, there are broadly five different schools of tantra that developed during the early Middle Ages, thousands of years after Shiva. These are the Shakta, Vaishnava, Shaiva, Ganapatya and Saura tantra schools. Moreover, when Jainism and Buddhism flourished in India, various branches of Buddhist and Jain tantra developed, which again sprouted many independent branches. The early Middle Ages also spawned such fabled paths as the left-handed Aghora tantra – today popularized in the West by the books of Robert Svobodha – as well as the well-known Buddhist Vajrayana tantra. By this time, many tantric schools had synthesized with the vedic tradition, and Shiva tantra lost some of its original form until it again was revived by Anandamurti in the last century.

In addition, there are four main aspects of tantra, which we will explore in the next chapter. These are mantra (words with spiritual power), diksha (initiation), yantra (geometric symbol), and guru (enlightened teacher).

Creating a Tantric Lifestyle

Tantric Philosophy: *Shiva Shaktiatmakam Brahma* – Brahma is the composite of Shiva and Shakti. *

Daily Contemplation: This Sanskrit sutra contains the basic concept of tantric philosophy, that Brahma, the supreme entity, is one but has two aspects, namely cosmic consciousness or Shiva, and cosmic energy or Shakti. In this physical world of duality, these two appear to be separate, but after attaining knowledge of non-dual Brahma, one sees them as one. There is no differentiation, only One without a second.

On a metaphysical level, the ultimate reality, Brahma, is expressed in the 'polarity' of Shiva and Shakti. Within our own conditional reality, this is expressed as the dualities of male and female, objective and subjective, masculine and feminine, without and within. Shiva and Shakti, as the perfect unity-principle, also symbolize integration; in Jungian terms, for example, the integration of animus and anima. In Taoism, which is a Chinese derivative of tantra, they are the esoteric twin pair yin and yang. Psychologically, this unity-principle represents our need to integrate our male and female

---

*All Sanskrit Sutras used in the section Creating a Tantric Lifestyle are from *Ananda Sutram* by Shrii Shrii Anandamurti, Ananda Marga Publications, Calcutta, 1990.

energies. Neurologically, they represent the integration of the right and left hemispheres of the brain. Ontologically, it is expressed when scholars seek to integrate spiritual and scientific knowledge. And spiritually, it is the way modern yogis embrace the roots of tantra by integrating spiritual exercises, such as meditation and chanting, and physical exercises, such as asanas, into their daily lives.

Daily Acts of Sacredness

One: As you can see, tantric metaphysics has far-reaching implications for how we can find balance and harmony in our daily lives. Contemplate this tantric unity principle of the cosmos. Envision how the tantric principles of wholeness embrace everything, even contradictions and unpleasant experiences. Use this vision to embrace aspects of life you are afraid of or reject or hide. Move beyond conflict and pain, and discover joy and peace in polarity.

Two: Everything in this world contains Shiva and Shakti. All things and beings are created by Shakti, and all things have in them the latent force of Shiva. Thus, all things are, in essence, Brahma. In this physical world of duality, things and people appear to be separate, but after attaining knowledge of non-dual Brahma, one sees that all are one.

Try to find as many situations as you can during the day when you can contemplate this union of Shiva and Shakti as Brahma. Try to feel that your food is Brahma before and during a meal. Try to feel that your friend is Brahma when talking to him or her. Try to see and feel Brahma in everything and everyone you encounter. The more you do this, the more you will become connected to the world around you in a deeply spiritual and sacred way.

Chapter Two

THE FOUR SACRED PILLARS:
MANTRA, INITIATION, YANTRA AND GURU

Once, while a young monk, I initiated another young man into tantric meditation. A black Rastafarian with a genuinely spiritual personality, he connected to the divine in a sudden and dramatic way. When he sat down in front of me as instructed, a thought suddenly crossed my mind: 'This young man has been a great yogi in his past life'. Without thinking more about it, I closed my eyes to meditate. As soon as I ended my meditation, I instructed him in the secret meditation process that culminated with my whispering a two-syllable mantra in his ear. As soon as he repeated the mantra, he fell backwards with a deep gasp. His blissful trance, or samadhi, lasted for nearly 20 minutes. The young man was as surprised as I was by this incident, and the natural explanation for him was that I was a great tantric guru with awesome occult powers. I tried to tell him that nothing could be farther from the truth. In fact, it was my guru's powers and those invested in the mantra, combined with his own special past-life karma, that had caused this sudden escapade into bliss, I explained. But to no avail. He kept insisting that I was an occult miracle worker, or siddha yogi, and that he would bring all his friends to see me. Indeed, the rest of that afternoon I was busy initiating his friends, but none of them had a similar experience.

The *kundalini*, or Shakti force, hibernating at the base of the spine, can be awakened by a single chant of a siddha mantra. Such a proven or effective mantra is a collection of sound waves that can produce a powerful resonance, or sympathetic vibration, in the mind. So when that young man received his mantra, the resonant vibration produced in his mind, due to his past lives' yogic karma, was so magnetic and forceful that it catapulted him into a state of unimaginable spiritual ecstasy. Similarly, some people have unexplainable spiritual experiences brought on by an accident, illness or inspiration that awakens kundalini and transforms their lives forever. Their past-life karma is the underlying cause, while the accident or tantric initiation is the apparent cause.

The Power of Mantra Initiation

The use of mantra is the very essence of the science of tantra. A mantra (man+tra = mind+liberate) means that sound which liberates the mind. During the daily practice of mantra meditation, which you will learn later in the book, your mind is guided back to its natural state of god-consciousness. How? By freeing your mind from being dominated by various thoughts and feelings. Not by dismantling the mind altogether, which is impossible, but rather by expanding the mind's focus away from its own impermanent murmur towards that which is permanent and peaceful, namely, the spiritual. Tantra is thus a practice of expanding the mind, from crude mind to subtle mind, from subtle mind to spiritual mind. And the final result of that process occurs when the individual mind itself merges in the cosmic mind. It is this union between the individual mind and the cosmic mind that we call yoga.

Through continued meditation practice, you will experience a shift of consciousness, a shift from ego-centred and mind-centred consciousness to spirit-centred consciousness, a shift from feelings of separation and fragmentation to feelings of connectedness and wholeness. In that process of gradual and sometimes sudden expansion is the beauty of tantra.

Authentic Sanskrit mantras are based on an elaborate esoteric science. They are invested with spiritual energy by a tantric guru and then transferred orally from a teacher, or guru, to the student. The archetypal sounds of each letter in the Sanskrit alphabet were formulated by tantric yogis. This discovery is perhaps one of the most important and least known innovations in the annals of human history. Just consider, for example, that 50 sounds, only audible to the inner ear, are located within the seven chakras or psychic centres in your psycho-physical body. These sounds correspond to the audible sounds of the natural universe inside and around you.

The Sanskrit alphabet has 50 letters, each one based on one of these acoustic roots. Each sound or letter serves as a direct sonic link between us and the universe, between our individual consciousness and cosmic consciousness. When chanting Sanskrit mantras, we literally vibrate from the inside out, gradually becoming more and more attuned to our body, mind and spirit. These mantras, when used properly, have tremendous power. Their enchanting and energetic capabilities have stricken many, including myself, with indescribable spiritual vibrations, insights and bliss. One should not underestimate the importance of knowing the right intonation and meaning of a mantra when embarking upon the transformative path of meditation.

Unfortunately, it is common that mantras found in books are misspelled, wrongly translated, or not translated at all. This makes them less likely to strike the right chord within our body-mind-universe and awaken us to personal growth, spiritual unfolding and enlightenment. In one of the books I read, written by one of the most popular self-help authors of our time, a tantric meditation mantra is introduced with syllables in the wrong order and as a result has no inner meaning. A bona fide mantra certainly has deep symbolic meaning, and if uttered improperly, or in the wrong sequence, will not bear the desired fruit. Therefore, it is best to learn tantric meditation from an authentic teacher who can convey the appropriate use of the potent spiritual elixir contained in the sacred siddha mantras.

I have experienced the mysterious power of mantra myself. Once in Nepal, I had been sick for weeks with blood dysentery and was so thin and weak that I could barely walk. One morning, after coming back from the primitive outhouse, which had basically been my home for the past few weeks due to near constant diarrhoea and stomach pains, I developed a severe fever and finally lost consciousness. All I can remember from that experience is that my mantra was 'hovering' outside my body, as if being recited by the breath of the universe itself. Even near death, I was connected to the sonic sound of the inner and outer universe. I was not fearful, and I realized the time of death had not come when the internal sound of the mantra was 'breathing me back' into my body. When I regained consciousness, a doctor was sitting beside my primitive bed made of blankets on the floor. He said, 'I am glad you came back. I was afraid we might lose you, since your fever was dangerously high.'

A few years later, I read in some old tantric scriptures that the mantra I had been meditating on for several years was described as 'the life force', and that it 'hovers to and fro outside the body'. That was exactly how I experienced it during my short stay in the realm between life and death.

When used as chants in kirtan music, or devotional songs praising the divine, mantras have great healing effects on the mind and soul. A *San Francisco Chronicle* music critic once called kirtan 'the new soul music'. Not surprisingly, neuroscience is finding that repetitive sounds are good not only for the soul but also for the brain. Our reticular activating system (RAS) is responsible for detecting new stimuli when we experience change and thus causes the brain to be alert. When stimulus is repetitive, as in chanting, the RAS is disengaged, which has a quieting effect on the brain. Brain wave activity is also affected, since alpha and theta activity is increased, which enhances awareness and relaxation. Heart rates are lowered, and stress is reduced.

The world's leading neuroscientist, N. Lyubimov, has found that chanting creates coherent activity in the brain, indicating left/ right brain activation. Chanting thus produces restful alertness and improved mental performance and greater creativity. If we add all the spiritual benefits – feelings of unity, devotion, love – then the age-old art of chanting mantras is surely one of humanity's most soulful and uplifting musical expressions.

Mantras are powerful tools of spirit. Some universal mantras can be learnt from books, such as the one you will learn in this book, but the safest and best way to learn mantra meditation is through initiation from an authentic teacher. If used mindfully, tantric mantras can keep us aligned with the eternal spirit that resides both within and beyond ourselves. One mantra, one breath at the time.

Sacred Geometry: The Symbolic Power of Yantras

My friend Bill is a tantric practitioner and a Reiki master. Once at a retreat, far from the nearest hospital, his Reiki skills were put to the test when a friend of his was bitten by a deadly rattle snake. During the long trip to the hospital, Bill sat in the back of the car applying healing Reiki energy on the poisonous wound of his friend's leg. When they arrived at the hospital hours later, they were surprised to learn that a serum injection was not needed. The doctor, who was as surprised as they were, explained that he would inject the serum anyway, since it was part of 'normal procedure'. Bill, of course, attributes the doctor's unusual statement and diagnosis to his application of Reiki.

There are many types of Reiki, but when Bill practises, he employs certain types of yantras, or mystical, geometric symbols. Along with mantras, the geometric yantras, often consisting of triangles, are powerful symbols employed in tantric rituals and meditation practices. The word yantra means a liberating instrument or device. A yantra is a microcosmic replica of the universe and its principal energies. If properly internalized, the yantra becomes a powerful meditation device, and it can aid the practitioner in ascending into a state of inner harmony and well-being, and occasionally into higher states of consciousness.

In tantra, there is nothing whatsoever that is not considered divine. Hence, all aspects of creation can be aids in realizing our inherent divinity and the divinity around us. For meditation, the vibrations of the universe are used in the form of sound mantras and the vibrations of the physical world are used as yantras. Yantra diagrams of apparently static lines and designed by an expert in this art and science will, when we meditate on them, create subtle vibrations in us like a finely tuned instrument. Shiva used a yantra called the *Bhairavi Chakra*, also known as the six-pointed Star of David. (In fact, some yogis I met in India claimed that this star was exported from India to Israel thousands of years before Christ and then became part of Jewish culture.) The triangle with the lower vertex means infinite knowledge, and that with the upper vertex means infinite energy or creative principle. Krishna used the same Bhairavi Chakra with a lotus in the middle. When this six-pointed yantra is properly designed, it can yield tremendous spiritual power. That is, the two triangles must be in complete symmetry, so that an equilateral smaller triangle is created at each of the six points, and an equal sided hexagon is formed in the middle. This design is crucial to the yantra's spiritual significance.

When one regularly gazes at a six-pointed star consisting of two such triangles, one can balance one's contemplative life with one's social life, one's inner knowledge with one's outward expression. This yantra is thus a perfect meditation device for spiritual activists and all those who need to balance their dynamic work in the world with inner peace to avoid a state of 'burn-out'. The appropriate application of yantras has powerful healing properties when used during a Reiki session, as we saw in Bill's case. Yantras are esoteric magnifying glasses that amplify cosmic energy to aid us in healing and the expansion of consciousness. These sacred, geometric yantras are symbols of great power and are best contemplated and employed with utmost respect and selfless sincerity.

The Guru Within

To many in the post-modern world, the guru is a relic from the past. In this cynical, narcissistic world, many spiritual seekers do not want to be beholden to anyone but themselves. Many thus question the need to have a spiritual teacher at all. To a tantric, however, the authentic guru is an essential spiritual guide. For the genuine spiritual master is one whose mind is the embodiment of spiritual effulgence, one whose personality is inexpressible, mysterious and powerful, one who has attained knowledge of past and future, one who lives and breathes in the here and now, one who can liberate anyone's mind at will, one who is always in a state of natural, intoxicated bliss.

Throughout human history, there have lived but a few illuminated beings, such god-like humans in flesh and blood, whose teachings resonate with the perennial wisdom of all sages of the past. Such supernatural beings hold the initiatory secrets to reveal spirit, bring down heaven on earth, and unravel the serenity of enlightenment for anyone. Such beings are the living testament of a spiritual lineage as old as civilization itself. When you first encounter such a being, his awesome mystery may elude you. That is exactly what happened to me when I met my guru. For that extraordinary man, dressed in white, appeared at first as normal as everyone else. His real personality eluded me, for that simple-looking man in white was nobody else but a reflection of my innermost, spiritual self. And so I gradually realized I could not completely perceive his grandeur with my senses. One cannot completely grasp a genuine guru's vastness with one's mind either. We can only see his vast personality through the vision of spirit. We can only feel his compassionate love in our own awakened heart. So, I gradually opened up to receive his radiant, all-knowing presence. And gradually, or may be it was suddenly, the mysterious being revealed parts of himself to me, just as my own soul reveals its own mysterious depths during meditation.

When Rumi met his own guru, the wandering dervish Shams–i-Tabrīzī, he immediately recognized who he was: 'What I had thought of before as God, I met today in a human being.' And through that meeting, Rumi's life transformed. He soon reached new vistas of spiritual wisdom and became one of the world's most prolific and beloved spiritual poets.

***

To be in the company of a great master is a unique experience, to say the least. So, let us venture off on a walk with my guru in his botanical garden, where, today, he is meeting with a group of scientists and researchers well-versed in the fragrant world of botany. For the guru is an avid collector of plants from all over the world's native forests, marshes and grasslands. The scientists are amazed at his encyclopaedic knowledge of plants. They marvel at his ability to explain their names, biological attributes, and medicinal qualities, whether in Latin, Bengali or English. They are awestruck by his ability to move from one subject to another, from one plant species to another, as fluid and elegant as a conductor of a symphony.

In between his scientific escapades into the history and science of plants, this unusual guru will amuse his audience of devotees by correcting or revealing some linguistic or poetic aspect of one of the 5,018 devotional songs he has composed in the past eight years. Some of these songs, spontaneously composed in the stillness of his oceanic soul, are today sung by hundreds of devotees. They have also gathered to be with him in this large, abundantly flowering garden on this hot and humid day.

Some of the singers are ecstatic. One devotee, a tall man, sways like a large date palm in a storm. Oblivious to anybody around him, he sings like a drunkard, completely out of tune. Suddenly, he falls backwards into the welcoming arms of the blissfully chanting crowd. As if they are of one mind and one body, they let him sink slowly to the sandy ground. There his inward gaze remains transfixed on some celestial realm beyond worldly description. Above him, the crowd of devotees continues to sway and sing. Shortly after that, the guru stops next to an orchid from Florida, the night-fragrant Epidendrum. While he gently holds the plant in his hand and talks to the scientists, he turns to his left and looks straight into the eyes of a man in the crowd who happens to be the one who has picked this delicate flower. This young man and his gift is recognized in a crowd of hundreds, even though the guru has never been told who brought this flower, even though the guru receives literally hundreds of plants from dozens of countries each day. The young man starts to sob, gentle tears of devotion, tears that none of these scientists will ever see nor understand.

A few minutes later, the guru stops for a few seconds in front of a woman whose mind and heart are in turmoil. She is wondering why she is here. She has been wondering why the guru has never given her any attention. But now he suddenly stands in front of her with a group of scientists behind him. Gently, he whispers to her, 'You have forgotten me, but I never forgot you.' She also starts to sob silently:

Tears of joy; tears of recognition. She now knows that the guru is truly a reflection of the deep within, and that he will always be there whenever she longs for him.

None of the scientists seem to have noticed that these spiritual interactions ever took place. They are too busy taking notes. Their hearts barren, they are too busy perceiving the world through their minds. Nor do they seem to notice that the guru continues to touch dozens of people's hearts, each in a very personal way, this day. They are too busy basking in the sun of scientific enlightenment, too busy to notice that he loves them as much as he loves his devotees.

Nor do any of the singing devotees notice that while the guru walks in his garden, he is also communicating with dozens of devotees around the world, devotees whom he visits, teaches and, sometimes, heals from various afflictions. He visits them in dreams, visions and meditations. For to the guru, the outside world is inside, easily accessible, easily charmed, easily transformed.

So, we all wonder: who is this loving, seemingly all-knowing guru? Is he man or God or both? He is both, of course. Nevertheless, to us, he remains an enigma. As he wrote on a small piece of paper when someone asked him to write his autobiography, 'I was a mystery, I am a mystery, and I will always be a mystery.' Yes, he remains an enigma, that is, until you realize the guru within; realize the enigmatic god within, who is none other than your deepest self.

I once heard the spiritual comedian Swami Beyondananda shout out into an audience, 'What is the meaning of the word guru?' He received a few muffled, unclear replies, but none that satisfied him. Then he blurted out: 'Gee, you are you.' Through that hilarious, koan-like answer, Beyondananda made us realize that the guru is the mystery of our own soul revealed from within. Because, when you become one with that mystery, you become the guru, you become one with Brahma. You truly become one with You. To be a catalyst in that subtle, transformational process is the indispensable role of the tantric guru.

***

In the presence of my guru, I witnessed a mind utterly beyond conventional thought and perception, a mind steeped in the gnosis of pure consciousness, and yet, a mind that was genuinely up-to-date and at one with the world, a mind that both transcended and transformed the world and those around him.

For the guru, as the word connotes in Sanskrit, is that being who, by dint of his or her enchanted spiritual genius, is able to help us 'dispel darkness' and 'remove ignorance' from our hearts and minds. In other words, a guru (gu+ru = dispeller of darkness) is the one who lifts the veil of existence and lets us see the true face of reality. The guru is the one who helps us move from the path of avidya to the path of vidya, from the path of ignorance to the path of knowledge. Indeed, as the word guru connotes, he is the remover of darkness and ignorance. He is our guide towards the light.

Since there is much scepticism, controversy and misunderstanding about gurus in the West today, it is important to understand in essence who the guru actually is. As I was taught in the ashram in Kathmandu, the quintessential guru is beyond physical form: *Brahmaeva Gururekah Naparah* – the guru is Brahma only, no one else. All great masters have clearly understood this. Jesus Christ explained this in his saying, 'I and my Father are One.' Lord Buddha explained this with the utterance, 'My thoughts are always in the Truth. For lo! My Self has become the Truth'. And Lord Krishna when he said, 'I am the goal of the wise man, and I am the way'.

Although great world teachers, such as Shiva, Krishna, Buddha, Jesus, and others, have been distinct historical personalities with a distinct physical body and an explicit set of esoteric teachings, their spiritual consciousness has been attuned to the one god of all, the one formless guru of us all. Thus, the manifestation of the physical, historical guru, no matter who he or she is, is an indispensable gateway to the divine. And they remain so, even after they are physically no longer with us, for it is their timeless being and their divine presence that we venerate and love.

Thus there is no absolute need to have a physical guru in your life. You may, for example, feel devotion for a great spiritual master who has already left his body. What matters is your love for that master and your ability to internalize the master's teachings and extraordinary state of consciousness. Similarly, when Rumi's guru, Shams-i-Tabrīzī, suddenly disappeared one day, Rumi went looking for him. After years of searching all over, one day in Damascus Rumi realized Shams was within him. There was no longer any need to search in the world for his guru. Rumi had himself become the embodiment of the guru and his teachings.

***

Still, if your goal is to find a living, realized guru, here are four important insights to keep in mind:

1. There are various kinds of gurus. Many so-called gurus who have arrived in the West are teachers and not authentic, self-realized gurus. And, unfortunately, some of these teachers do not deserve the unconditional veneration bestowed upon them.

2. If the teachings of a not-so-enlightened teacher belong to a genuine spiritual lineage, his or her teachings will still benefit you. As was evident with the man who attained a glimpse of enlightenment when he received a mantra from me, it is the authenticity of the teachings and the karma and sincerity of the student that matter, not simply the realization of the teacher. Hence, it is important to be devoted to the practice and the teachings while also being a discerning disciple.

3. While there have been many great sages and gurus throughout history, there have only been a few mahagurus or great gurus. A mahaguru is a human being whose consciousness remains a bridge between this world and the spiritual world. While many on the spiritual path have experiences of awakening and have transformed their normal perception into a glimpse of divine perception, there are few in whom this exalted intoxication is a constant way of being. Forever awake, the mahagurus are walking gods and goddesses whose consciousness is a door always flung open into infinite awareness. They know the world is merely the

divine play of cosmic consciousness. Knowing this allows them to move through the world of thoughts and things as freely as a bird through air.

4. In tantra, there is the concept of 'Taraka Brahma' – which literally means the bridge between the unmanifest and the manifest worlds. Taraka Brahma exists at the tangential point between these two worlds. In tantra, the mahaguru and Taraka Brahma are synonymous; they are the historical gateways to the divine. They have come to this world to show the way to liberation through the graceful portal of this tangential Brahma, this cosmic guru, or god-personality. Through them, this omnipotent cosmic guru is intimately close, the breath within our breath, and he showers us with grace. Hence, the tantric yogi has a passionate love relationship with both guru and god. The more we love both, the more god becomes a living bridge of love and grace in our life.

In tantra, an authentic mahaguru can, in part, be recognized through the embodiment of various occult *bhagas* or attributes. In my life, I experienced how my guru displayed many of these occult abilities, and as you continue reading this book, you will also learn more about such miraculous abilities. They are as follows:

Anima: The ability to become very little, to reduce the vibration of the mind in order to penetrate atomic and subatomic particles.

Mahima: The ability to become very great, greater than anything in the entire universe.

Laghima: The ability to become very light, to walk on water, to be omnipresent. This quality is achieved by controlling the psycho-spiritual properties of the navel and heart chakras.

Ishitva: The capacity to rule, the ability to understand all the entities of the universe, to direct and witness their actions. This power is achieved by controlling the qualities of the throat chakra.

Prakamya: The ability to take the form of anything. This power is achieved by controlling the lower portion of the chakra between the eyebrows.

Vashitva: The ability to bring things under control, to unify forces, to create new life, and to make the dead rise. This ability stems from controlling the upper portion of the chakra between the eyebrows.

Prapti: The ability to get or create whatever is desired – that is, whatever one thinks will be materialized.

Antaryamitva: The ability to see into the inner nature of any entity – a penetrating vision.

Virya: Power, command, influence, in order to guide humanity.

Yasha: Reputation, because a mahaguru is such a towering, non-compromising and revolutionary personality, he will both have many admirers as well as many detractors.

Shrii: Attraction, charm.

Jnana: Complete knowledge of the self.

Vairagya: Non-attachment. Great gurus remain in the world while not being of it. They are not affected by criticism or the allure of power, nor by worldly riches or fame.

***

Another important insight about great gurus is that they lead lives imbued with an impeccable spiritual ethics. While the Romans and the priests of ancient Palestine felt justified in attacking Jesus and his inspired followers for political reasons, they were unable to find any flaws in his personal morality. Likewise, after years of opposition against Shiva and his Dravidian followers, the invading vedic Aryans in India had to conclude that Shiva's spiritual personality and leadership qualities were beyond reproach. Hence, in light of the above, we can conclude that the vast majority of the so-called gurus who have visited the West since the 1960s do not qualify as mahagurus. Most of them are not even qualified to earn the title guru, because they are mostly teachers and seekers struggling with many of the same human desires, needs and faults as their students.

Hence, the many reports of unenlightened behaviour by so-called gurus who have misled their students through abuses of power, corruption or sex. Hence also, the many excuses and cover-ups to deny such immoral behaviour. Sometimes abusive, destructive and immoral behaviour has been written off as 'crazy wisdom'. That is, one is told the teacher is enlightened and just displaying strange behaviour to teach the student some important lesson in surrender or devotion. Or one is told the student lacks spiritual understanding, or is simply unable to see that the teacher is a mirror of the student's own limitation.

So we must make up our hearts and minds. Are we presented with the classic denial tactics used by cults where the victim is blamed for the group's or the teacher's transgressions? Or are we truly in the company of an enlightened being? Because so many students of Eastern spirituality have been faced with these complex questions, it is natural that many spiritual seekers today are sceptical of the guru–disciple relationship.

This dilemma can be resolved by, first of all, recognizing that irrespective of the teacher's qualities, the true guru is none other than the formless Brahma, the omnipresent god within and beyond us, the one and only true teacher of all. Second, it is best to connect with a trusted guru or lineage with a known history of one or a few recognized enlightened preceptors. And third, treat all teachers in the lineage, except your carefully chosen guru, as guides and not gurus. These teachers will often share many of the same personality flaws an average seeker on the same spiritual path is faced with. What is most important, after all, are the invaluable lessons you learn from practicing the authentic teachings of an authentic lineage. So, even if you have been misled by a less-than-perfect teacher, you need not leave the path.

The ideal spiritual teacher is a living example of the teachings he or she espouses. Some teachers, however, have great intellectual knowledge of spiritual philosophy and practice, yet their personal conduct is less than exemplary. One such teacher's controversial lifestyle was brought to the attention of the Dalai Lama by a group of Western Buddhist monks. What would be his advice, they wondered. The Dalai Lama's reply was profound and unmistakable: 'One's view may be as vast as the sky,' he said, 'but one's regard for cause and effect should be as finely sifted as barley flour.'

Each spiritual path approaches the guru as archetype in different ways, but, in essence, the spiritual goal of each path is the same – to reach the state of non-dual awareness. While the Zen Buddhist tradition sternly instructs us to kill the Buddha in order not to search for help from a superior being, the tantric tradition instructs us instead to embrace lovingly the Buddha figure as guru, as manifestation of our divine self. Through devotional visualization, the guru's form is embraced in the devotee's heart and mind. Thus visualized, the guru's mythic appearance will focus the mind to go beyond the mind and thus evoke the formless panorama of non-dual divinity. All forms are considered sacred, especially the form of the enlightened guru, who becomes a powerful gateway to spirit. In Andrew Harvey's book, A *Journey in Ladakh: Encounters with Buddhism*, such a meditation practice is beautifully described by a Tibetan tantric Buddhist master, thereby illustrating the similarities among the various tantric schools. Likewise, the image of Jesus has been invoked for centuries by Christian mystics who desire to drink from the deep well of the cosmic Christ.

Devotion to an authentic guru and lineage is an invaluable tool on the path of spirituality. But this devotion must be carefully evaluated by our own rational and ethical standards. In other words, it is as important to be a qualified student as it is to have a qualified guru.

In summary, tantric meditation practices, whether employed by Buddhists, Hindus or Christians, use the visualization of various forms and symbols – including the nucleus of a chakra, the form of the master or a yantra – as focal points of concentration to achieve ecstatic states of spirit beyond form. This seemingly paradoxical practice is also used with great effect during mantra meditation, when a mental sound is used as a stepping stone to enter the celestial garden of spirit beyond the mental realm.

Creating a Tantric Lifestyle

Tantric Philosophy: *Anandam Brahma Ityahuh* – This infinite bliss is called Brahma.

Daily Contemplation: Everything is Brahma. All that we can experience with our senses – see, hear, feel, taste or smell – is, on a deeper level, nothing but Brahma, or cosmic consciousness. Even physicists have now realized that the physical world is not solid at all, but that everything is both a particle and a wave simultaneously. Indeed, even some scientists have realized everything is Cosmic Consciousness. We are nothing but non-dual cosmic awareness at all times. But we forget.

So, shift your worldview. Shift your outlook. Begin today by seeing the world as Brahma. Begin today by embracing the world as God. Enjoy the many synchronistic shifts that will start to happen!

Daily Acts of Sacredness

One of the most common and easiest ways to experience yogic union is by meditating on the breath. Through the breath, we are connected to our own soul and to god. When we are at peace, we breathe deeply and slowly. When experienced yogis are in deep trance, their breath may entirely stop for long periods of time.

It is no accident then that deep, soulful and attentive breathing, often with the use of a mantra, is an integral aspect of many important tantric practices. In the words of the poet Kabir, God is 'the breath inside the breath'.

One: Start meditating deeply and peacefully on your breath for five to ten minutes or more each morning and night. Let your mind gently flow with the in-breath and the out-breath. Let your thoughts pass by like clouds in the sky. Simply meditate on your breath, and you will gradually find peace from within. The most important thing is that you make this simple practice into a daily habit. Even if you have little time, still take a few minutes off to meditate on your breath: Twice a day, every day. Feel Brahma as the breath within the breath.

Two: Before you eat, close your eyes and visualize all the food you are about to eat as a gift from Brahma. Then visualize that this food is pure cosmic consciousness and that you, the consumer of the food, is also pure cosmic consciousness. This practice is called *Madhuvidya* – honey knowledge. It will transform all your food into pure, spiritual deliciousness. Enjoy!

Note: Feel free to substitute the metaphysical concept Brahma with any concept of your choice, whether it is god, goddess, spirit, the divine, or any other name.

Chapter Three

DAWN OF ENLIGHTENMENT: A BRIEF TANTRIC HISTORY

India's great civilization was born about 11,000 years ago, during or shortly after Neolithic farming settlements were established in the Fertile Crescent in the Middle East. Indeed, it is becoming increasingly evident that India is, in so many ways, also the cradle of human civilization, not just geographically and culturally, but also spiritually. For South Asia, which includes India, Pakistan and Afghanistan, was one of the first areas on the planet where people settled to farm and create urbanized city complexes on a considerable scale. In Mehrgarh, an area in today's Pakistan, wheat, barley and eggplant were cultivated, sheep and cattle were domesticated and people lived in cities as early as nine thousand years ago (7000 BC).

India is also the birthplace of the world's first great religions, Buddhism and Jainism. Most importantly, long before the birth of Buddha (500 BC), India had already developed the sophisticated sciences of yoga, meditation, ayurvedic medicine, and one of the world's most sophisticated and sacred languages – Sanskrit.

While there is general agreement among scholars regarding the antiquity of India's civilization, there is less agreement about how and when it developed its sophisticated culture and sacred traditions. There are currently three main theories on ancient Indian history:

1. Most Western and Indian academics hold the view that India was invaded by Vedic Aryan settlers around 1900 BC. These Aryans worshipped the sun god, Surya, and brought with them their Rig Vedic religion based on sacrifices and rituals offered to 'placate and please the Gods, and to force them to fulfill wishes and demands.' These patriarchal and martial Aryans soon conquered northern India and destroyed the

great Indus Valley Civilization, where yoga was already practised by tantric (Shaiva) ascetics. They massacred populations and reduced the surviving Dravidian shudras to slavery (dasyu) without regard for rank or learning. This conflict has been described in the famous epics Mahabharata and the Ramayana. Over time, India became a blended civilization – part Aryan Vedic, part Dravidian Shaiva, with a liberal admixture of Jain and Buddhist traditions – and this blended culture is what we today know as Hindu civilization.

2. Western yoga scholars, including Georg Feuerstein and David Frawley, as well as some Indian writers, especially within the Hindutva movement, subscribe to the theory that there was never an Aryan invasion around 1900 BC and that yoga comes solely from the vedic tradition. I call this the 'one-river theory'. Rather than being destroyed by nomadic warriors, the Indus Valley Civilization, they claim, was destroyed and abandoned due to climatic changes. According to these writers, the Aryans are indigenous to India and represent everything that is noble about Indian culture. In their book *In Search of the Cradle of Civilization*, Georg Feuerstein, Subhash Kak and David Frawley outline 17 points for why the invasion never took place. In one of these points, however, they reflect on the possibility that the Aryan settlers arrived in India at a much earlier date. (This is exactly what I am proposing in this book.)

3. This last option brings us to the theory that the history of yoga represents a blend of the tantric and vedic traditions of India. I call this the 'two-river theory'. According to Puranic history, some tantric scholars, as well as genetic science, the Vedic Aryans arrived in India at an early age, most likely as early as 5000 BC. Therefore the blending of the vedic and tantric cultures of India had already matured by the time the Indus Valley Civilization was destroyed and depopulated around 2000 BC. Not long after, around 1500 BC, India produced the world's first coherent philosophy and cosmology,

namely sage Kapila's tantric-inspired Samkhya philosophy, which today is popularly known as the philosophy of ayurveda, India's ancient medical science. About 700 years after Kapila, some of the greatest spiritual literature the world has ever witnessed, namely the oral teachings in the epic Mahabharata, the Vedantic Upanishads, the spiritual teachings of the Bhagavad Gita, and the historical mythology of the Ramayana, were written down for the first time. And around 200 BC, sage Patanjali wrote his yoga sutras and codified the oral teachings of the tantric yogis for the first time in the form of asthanga, or raja yoga.

While these three versions of Indian history may seem entirely at odds, there are important overlapping agreements, and the theories do in many ways complement each other. The first theory has dated the Aryan invasion rather late (1900 BC) and does not reflect the genetic research of Dr Spencer Wells, who claims the invasion started much earlier – about 5000 BC. As suggested as a possibility by Feuerstein and Frawley – proponents of theory number two – this invasion thus took place when the Rig Vedic Aryans arrived via the Russian steppes and the deserts of Iran about 3,000 years before the Indus Valley eventually was abandoned. Looking for better pastures for their cattle, and for other riches, these skilled warrior nomads arrived in successive raids and migrations over a period of several millennia. They arrived in an already inhabited land, and its peoples – the Dravidians, Mongolians and Austrics – had already developed a sophisticated, urban culture, and the art and science of tantric yoga was already in practice among them. In other words, by the time the Indus Valley was finally abandoned around 1900 BC, the indigenous Indians and the invading Aryans had already experienced 3,000 years of conflict and gradual integration. Hence these two peoples, representing two different civilizations, cultures and outlooks – one priestly and one yogic – gradually formed what we know today as the Indian, or Hindu civilization.

The Two-River Theory

In his award-winning book, *A Brief History of India*, Alain Daniélou outlines in broad, colourful strokes an ancient history of India that contrasts with the one presented to most Western yoga students, who are often told tantra and yoga comes from the vedas. Daniélou reminds us, however, that yoga originated with the ancient sage Shiva and that these practices were 'wholly unknown' to the early vedas and their authors, the invading Aryans.

Daniélou is not alone in this assertion. According to multiple sources – including ancient scriptures such as the Puranas, the Agamas, the tantric literature of South India, the various tantras of the Middle Ages, and the writings of N. N. Bhattacharya, A. L. Basham, Thomas McEvilley, Anandamurti, and others – it was the Shiva tantrics who taught the early Indians yogic spirituality, the arts and sciences. Moreover, these Shiva teachings – which according to Anandamurti originated with the historical Shiva some 7,000 years ago – remained the dominant culture and spiritual teachings in India, even though its adherents were often violently attacked by the early Vedic Aryans. The tantric teachings of Shiva continued to be the religion of the people, Daniélou asserts, and what we today have come to appreciate as Indian spiritual culture and religion was more influenced by tantra than the vedas. This assertion, which will be emphasized in this book, is contrary to what most modern yogis are taught about the history of their practice.

Daniélou also emphasizes the importance of Shiva tantra in shaping yoga philosophy, culture and practice. 'It should be remembered', he writes, 'that in Hinduism, Yoga is a discipline created by Shiva ...' From early on, the culture and spiritual practices that originated with Shiva's tantra also spread outside India, even as far as Europe. Writes Daniélou: 'Although – due to scarcity of documentation – the importance of this great fundamental religion in the formation of later religions has been largely under-estimated, it was almost universal.' [5]

If Shiva's teachings are 7,000 years old, why were tantric wisdom and rites only written down as late as AD 500, thus making most scholars and lay people believe this is when the history of tantra began? Because tantric teachings were, and still are to a great extent, oral teachings preserved in short sutras and slokas and transmitted to the students by a competent teacher. Almost all of the great spiritual texts of India were also based on ancient oral teachings and history, such as the Agamas, the Upanishads, the Brahmanas, and the tantras, and they were transcribed right before or during the so-called Tantric Renaissance of the Middle Ages (circa AD 400 to 1500). As many scholars have pointed out, tantric teachings were assimilated into vedic and Brahmanic teachings and writings at an early age; thus one will find tantric influences in the earliest writings in India, starting around 700 BC with the compilation of the vedas. All of the yogic references to breathing exercises and yoga in general in the Atharva Veda can, according to Anandamurti, be traced back to the tantra of Shiva thousands of years earlier. So, by the time of the 'Tantric Renaissance', when tantric yogis further developed hatha yoga, tantra had already blended with and influenced Hinduism and Buddhism to a great extent.

Vikings and Tantrics

Long before I knew anything about tantra and ancient Indian history, I met a traveller and writer from Norway, my native country. He had just returned from an adventurous trip to Afghanistan, Nepal and India. Inspired by American spiritual seekers, most notably well-known psychologist and author Ram Dass and popular beat poet Allen Ginsberg, he was one of the first Europeans to visit these countries by travelling over land through Turkey, Iran and Iraq. His name was Eivind Reinertsen, and he told remarkable tales from his many trips to the East. He published a landmark book called *Journey without Arrival (Reise Uten Ankomst)* about these travels, and a few years later became an award-winning poet.

I met Reinertsen during a visit to some student friends living in an alternative community in Oslo. My friends had recently learnt transcendental meditation, so our conversation that night focused mainly on their newfound practice. Our topic quickly changed, however, when Reinertsen suddenly made a startling claim. He said there had been a secret society of tantric yogis on the west coast of Norway during the Viking era (circa AD 800–1200).

The Vikings were not exactly renowned for their peaceful and introspective ways, so the story seemed a bit far-fetched, but his story did pique my interest in yoga. Shortly thereafter, I began reading about the mysterious world of tantra – its philosophy, history and especially its yogic practices. Although I have never been able to verify Reinersten's rather fantastic historical possibility, there are interesting clues scattered about in Viking history that makes Reinertsen's claim seem at least remotely probable.

Some time after I met Reinertsen, I was reminded of his fantastic stories by a photo I discovered of a bronze sculptured yogi sitting in lotus position on a 'bucket' found on the *Oseberg*, Norway's most famous and best preserved ship from the Viking era. In the summer of 2005, I visited the Viking museum in Oslo to see this remarkable bucket with my own eyes. This so-called 'Buddha bucket' is a wooden pail made of strips of yew held together with brass bands. The 'ears' to which the handle is attached depicts two yogic brass figures sitting in lotus position with closed eyes. Prominently displayed on the chests of these two meditating yogis are four swastikas or 'hakekors,' as the Vikings called these sacred symbols. The swastika, a symbol of spiritual victory in tantra, has been in existence in India since the time of Shiva, but is also known as a sacred symbol among the Vikings, the Greeks as well as the Egyptians. In fact, the swastika is a symbol of Shiva and Shakti and is often prominently displayed on houses and temples all over Asia. Unfortunately, the Nazis misused this deeply spiritual symbol for their evil purposes.

What could be the origin of this 'meditating Viking'? Such practices could have originated from the contact Europeans had with Asian people during the migration times. On the other hand, the technique could have been known among Celtic and Germanic people, passed down since the time of Shiva. It is also possible, but less likely, that these meditation practices developed independently by Nordic shamans. Shamanic elements are well-known in the North Germanic religions as well as in most native cultures all over the world. We also know that the term 'útisetia' (literally 'sitting outside'), from ancient Norse literature, indicates a 'trance technique' that could indeed refer to yogic meditation. We know for certain that the practice of sitting in the lotus position is not common among shamanic cultures. Hence, it is very likely the Buddha bucket illustrates a Viking practicing yogic meditation. Even the figure itself is most likely to have been made locally, since a similar figure with the same metallurgical composition has been found at Myklebostad in Norway.

Not long after I encountered the Buddha bucket figure, I learnt about the Gundestrup Cauldron (400–100 BC), a silver bowl found in a peat bog in Denmark. This famous artefact appears to depict the image of Pashupati or Shiva. The image of the alleged Shiva on the Gundestrup Cauldron is strikingly similar to the many seals attributed to Shiva found in the Indus Valley during archaeological digs by Sir John Marshall between 1922 and 1931. Commonly known as a place where tantra was widely practised, this great culture, located at the archaeological site of Harappa and Mohenjo-daro (4000–2000 BC), is as old and as sophisticated as the ancient civilization of Mesopotamia. At the time, these and the other rice-growing areas of Asia boasted a concentration of approximately one-quarter of the world's population.

In the famous seals found at Harappa and Mohenjo-daro, Shiva sits in a yogic posture allowing the back to remain comfortably erect and thus to make it easier to concentrate during meditation. His feet are formed into an advanced tantric practice that forms a lock under the genital area and thus helps direct psychic energy up through the spine. On the Gundestrup Cauldron, however, the Shiva figure sits in a different posture, in the 'easy pose', also commonly used for meditation practice.

During my monastic training in India in the 1980s, I became intimately familiar with Pashupati – the lord of the beasts. It happened while I spent time alone as a sadhu, meditating and begging for my food near Pashupatinath, a Shiva temple located in the small town of Deopatan, to the east of Kathmandu. This ancient temple is a major destination for Hindu pilgrims from all over India and Nepal. It is situated to the south of a gorge carved out by the Bagmati River. Pashupatinath, often crowded by both pious pilgrims and wild monkeys, resides by the river, above the sacred funeral ghats where the dead are cremated daily on top of large piles of burning wood.

Snaking along the Pashupatinath temple walls, the Bagmati is considered as sacred as the Ganges itself. For Hindus, to bathe at Pashupatinath on particular phases of the moon is to ensure a place in Shiva's paradise, Kailash. For tantric yogis, however, all rivers and places are sacred, and Shiva's paradise is to be realized within each yogi's own heart, not in some distant place in the afterlife or at a sacred site.

Like the Indus Valley seal, the Nepali temple is dedicated to Pashupati. Pashu means 'beast', or animal, so the esoteric meaning of Pashupati in tantra is 'the controller of animal instincts'. In other words, in order to become free, we must redirect and become free from our instinctual tendencies, our psychological bondages. According to yoga, there are eight bondages, or *asthapashas*, which includes fear, shyness, doubt, pride of heritage, pride of culture, vanity, and backbiting, as well as the six enemies or *sadripus*, which includes lust, rage, greed, attachment to objects, pride, and envy. Lord Pashupati is thus a symbol of someone who has overcome these inner beasts, and tantric yoga is a spiritual path whose ultimate goal is to overcome, or not be controlled by, these 'wild beasts' of the mind.

Embracing the Wild Beasts of the Mind

That first day at Pashupatinath, I was walking by the river in the evening, careful not to step on meditating or sleeping yogis. I noticed a group of half-naked bodies sitting in a circle around a towering figure with long, matted hair and beard. He was seated, like Shiva himself, in the lotus position. A few of his words, drifting in the smoke-filled breeze, caught my attention. 'Astapasha and sadripu …' Then he recited them, first the eight bondages – '*bhaya, ghr'na, lajja, shamka, kula, shiila, mana, yugupsa*'. Then the six enemies, '*kama, krodha, lobha, moha, mada, matsarya.*' The ancient Sanskrit flowed out of him like poetry. And even though I did not understand the Hindi commentary that followed, I sat down to join the small circle of yogis around the glowing embers from the dying fire. After some time, the yogi on the tiger skin became silent. His eyes of piercing kindness looked into mine for a moment. Then, oblivious to the chatter and commotion among the pilgrims along the river, he closed his eyes and began to meditate.

A few days later, I walked down a street near the temple towards the fireplace where I prepared my one meal for the day. My cotton shoulder bag contained two potatoes, a handful of rice, a few coins, some matches and one red chili. The meagre collection from my begging round that morning was not unusual. Most shopkeepers thought it rather unlikely a Westerner could be a wandering sadhu, at least not a real holy man. Thinking I was a fraud, they often refused to give me anything. They were partly right, of course. As part of my monastic training, I was a wandering beggar, but only for a while, not for life.

An old woman, a real beggar, suddenly stopped me on the street and held out her hand. I was not allowed to speak during my begging period, so I gestured with my hands that I did not have anything to give her. My answer did not satisfy her. She became very angry, waved with her hands and pointed at my tan yet unmistakably white skin. Obviously, she was unable to tell that I also was a beggar, even if only temporarily. To her, I was simply a 'rich Westerner'. So, I gave her my last few coins, which I usually used to buy matches and cooking oil with. Not satisfied, she threw them on the ground and spat on them. Disappointed, I asked her to open her own bag, and I emptied my own bag of goods into hers. Potatoes, rice, chili, matches, coins – all my money and my one and only meal for the day – it all disappeared into the old beggar's dilapidated bag. That, I thought, was a truly benevolent act. I had given up all my food for that day to an old woman, a beggar for life. I was proud of myself for accomplishing such a great act of unselfish service, despite my rather poverty-stricken condition.

After the old woman looked into her bag, she became more furious. She was truly insulted. How could I, a rich Westerner, give her so little? She stamped her bare feet; she spat; she held up the two potatoes. Then she threw both of them on the ground and walked away.

My inner beasts, especially the fetters of pride and rage, were cruelly awakened that day. When I finally succumbed to my day of hunger and meditation, and my anger subsided, I was humbled, truly humbled. I had yet to learn the art of true selflessness, to give the gift of love and compassion without expecting anything in return. But since tantra teaches us that our problems are our best friends, I eventually learnt to look at that old, angry beggar as a great friend and teacher.

Tantra and Ayurveda

A few years before my journey to India and Nepal, I received my initiation in tantra meditation at a retreat in a pine forest in Sweden by a tantric monk in saffron robes who had recently arrived from India. In accordance with ancient tradition, the charismatic monk whispered a mantra into my right ear and told me it was never to be uttered aloud, except back to him. He prescribed a specific technique for withdrawing my mind from its external preoccupations, guiding it away from attachment to the body, and meditating on and become one with the mantra's deep meaning. I was to recite the mantra silently, in harmony with my breath, while concentrating on a particular chakra. This first of the six lessons I was to learn in tantric meditation seemed a bit complicated at first, but I soon got the hang of it. Indeed, I experienced some very powerful visions and spiritual insights at that very first retreat. I had found my spiritual home, and ever since that gathering, I have practiced tantric meditation daily.

Later on that auspicious day, I heard several stories about Shiva, not the well-known Hindu deity, but the historical Shiva, a living person who, like the Buddha, was an enlightened yogi. According to the oral history of the tantric tradition, it was he who systematized tantra yoga and who also enhanced 'Vaidik Shastra', the ancient system of yogic or tantric medicine, which is basically the same as what we today know as ayurveda. In the book *In Search of the Medicine*

Buddha: A Himalayan Journey, David Crow quotes a contemporary ayurvedic alchemist, practicing this ancient art and science in Nepal today, who says, 'Lord Shiva was the first Ayurvedic physician.' [6] It is common knowledge among ayurvedic doctors in Nepal and India that there is a historical and spiritual interrelationship between tantra and ayurveda. Furthermore, when I was in India, I was taught that Shiva was the preceptor of the first group of ayurvedacharyas, or the teachers of ayurveda.

When I studied ayurveda at the California College of Ayurveda, a school that maintains that ayurveda is a vedic science only, I learnt that Lord Dhanvantari was 'the God of Ayurveda and of healing'. Lord Dhanvantari is said to have been a high-caste king of Benares, which during Shiva's time was called Kashi, and who taught an ayurvedic form of surgery. From a tantric perspective, it makes sense that Dhanvantari taught surgery because that was part of the science of tantric ayurveda. Dhanvantari could not have been a follower of the vedas, however, since vedic dogmas prohibited high-caste Brahmins to touch people of a lower caste, and thus prohibited them from performing surgery. As it is said in the oral tradition of tantra, it is more likely to conclude that Dhanvantari was a tantric and also Shiva's first and main apprentice in ayurveda. In other words, as Anandamurti claims, Dhanvantari was most likely the world's first ayurvedic teacher.

Contemporary ayurvedic writers, including Deepak Chopra, David Frawley and Vasant Lad, have, in their books, revealed some of the sublime wisdom found in ayurvedic medical texts, including the famed *Charaka Samhita.* Yet these popular writers have overlooked the fact that ayurveda's ancient roots also trail back to tantric teachings passed down through the ages since Shiva's time. 'Indian medical science as revealed in the *Charaka Samhita* and *Sushruta Samhita* is basically tantric', writes N. N. Bhattacharya in his acclaimed book *History of the Tantric Religion.* [7]

Tantric and Ayurvedic Medical Science in Ancient India

According to ayurveda, disease occurs when the balance of the body is lost due to an increase or decrease of the body's three humours – *vata, pitta* and *kapha*. Medicine is applied to restore balance. If the amount of vata or pitta decreases, medicine is applied to increase it; if the amount of vata or pitta increases, medicine is applied to decrease it. This, in simple terms, is the ayurvedic system of medicine.

Rudimentary forms of ayurveda were possibly brought to India by the Aryan people as early as 8,000 years ago. About 7,000 years ago, Shiva further developed the tantric system of medicine that incorporated and refined ayurveda. This new, advanced system of medicine also included surgery. For thousands of years, the Indian medical system was a mixture of these two schools of medicine – tantric and vedic. Thus, in the ayurvedic teachings popularized today, it is difficult to distinguish which feature is tantric and which is vedic.

At the time of the Mahabharata, around 1500 BC, surgery, ayurveda, vaidik shastra, and even a rudimentary form of homeopathy existed in India. During that time, Lord Krishna developed another branch of medicine called 'Visha Chikitsa' or toxicology. Due to certain vedic religious dogmas, however, the tantric science of surgery was largely, discontinued because it was forbidden to touch dead bodies.

From the ancient tantric seers, we have learnt there were eight main branches of medicine, which form the basis of the eight main divisions of ayurveda:

1. *Salya tantra*: Healing of wounds in the lower limbs through surgery.
2. *Salakya tantra*: Healing of wounds in the upper limbs through surgery.
3. *Kaya chikitsa tantra*: Healing of internal and external diseases.
4. *Bhuta vidya tantra*: Healing of mental diseases.
5. *Kaumarabhritia tantra*: Healing of children's diseases.
6. *Agada tantra*: The science of toxicology.
7. *Vajikarana tantra*: The science of sexual balance and vigour.
8. *Rasayana tantra*: The science of rejuvenation.

In ayurvedic books today, we learn that the medical source for this ancient science is a book called the *Charaka Samhita*. This book, however, is actually a revised version of an earlier work called *Agnivesa Tantra*, written by the tantric sage Agnivesa. These ancient tantric yogis were also skilled in the art of alchemy and, much like today's homeopaths, used many altered toxic substances, including mercury, for healing and transformation. In tantra, the body is seen as the microcosm of the universe. Longevity and health are thus achieved through spiritual union with cosmic consciousness and in living in harmony with the complex, yet orderly, natural forces in the cosmos within and beyond us.

Did Shiva Travel to Europe?

In 1979, I had another pivotal experience in my understanding of tantric history. It occurred during my meeting with my spiritual guru, Anandamurti. An enigmatic person who allegedly could wake people from the dead, read people's present and past lives like they were books, Anandamurti was hailed as 'one of the greatest philosophers of modern India' by former Indian president, Giani Zail Singh. Already well-known in India with a fast-growing group of devoted followers, he had embarked upon a whirlwind tour to nine countries on four continents.

After a few days of listening to this electrifying and mysterious man's lectures and watching people fall into yogic trance or samadhi, around him, I found myself walking beside him with a group of people along a mountain road in the beautiful Fiesch valley in Switzerland. Once in a while, my guru would stop, point towards a flower I had never seen or towards an unusual shrub and explain in detail the plants' local and Latin names, their medicinal properties and the kind of soil they best thrived in. At other times, he would pick up a rock and give a lengthy description of its various mineral properties, or point at a picturesque farm far away and explain in great detail what kind of fruit crops the farmer cultivated and what other types of crops would be good to grow in that area. His encyclopaedic knowledge of the flora and fauna was simply breathtaking, especially since he had never before been to that part of the world.

On one of these walks, Anandamurti suddenly stopped and looked out across the snow-covered Swiss Alps and exclaimed that Shiva travelled from India to this valley about 7,000 years ago on a yak.

During his European trip in 1979, Anandamurti made some predictions about the future. While standing beside the infamous Berlin Wall, which at that time still divided West Germany from East Germany, Western democracy from Eastern Communism, he said, 'This wall symbolizes the brutal suppression by Communism against human liberties. It is a kind of artificial madness. In the near future, you will see this wall crumble piece by piece, stone by stone. East and West Germany will be united as one.' As predicted, this historical unification occurred 10 years later, in 1989. Two years earlier, in 1987, Anandamurti made another prediction about the future by saying that Communism would soon 'fall like a house of cards'. Indeed, it did – in 1989, in country after country, Communism disappeared in Eastern Europe.

I have often wondered, is it not conceivable that this mystic seer and sage, who could read people, rocks and plants as if they were books, who could look into the future as if it happened before him – that he could also, with equal accuracy, look into and explain the past?

When a tantric yogi, through psycho-spiritual practice, makes his mind as expansive as the cosmic mind, he can receive information directly from that source. This is sometimes referred to as the 'Akashic Records', a cosmic storehouse of information and knowledge, easily accessible to psychics and clairvoyant yogis. In other words, by mentally accessing this subtle field of consciousness, it is thus possible for a great yogic master to reveal the secrets of both the past and the future.

So, if Shiva, the father of tantra indeed left his Himalayan abode to travel all the way to Europe, one might assume that some of the tantric teachings also took root in the rocky soil of the Swiss Alps and from there ventured beyond. In accordance with my Norwegian author friend, as well as Dr John Mumford, a scholar and yogic adept who has written about the ancient interconnection between pagan and yogic history, tantra, at least in mythological form, could thus have spread towards the Celts in Germany, France and the British Isles and even farther north towards the Bronze Age farmers and Vikings of Scandinavia.

Tracing Tantra from its Roots

India is an enormous country with a long and culturally rich history. In the past, it has included Pakistan, Bangladesh, Afghanistan, Burma and Sri Lanka. Perhaps the most ancient civilization on the planet, India has an uncanny ability both to move beyond and embrace its past. And, more often than not, this multifaceted country mirrors the vastness, depth and history of humanity itself.

Indian civilization may not only be the planet's oldest continuous civilization, but also the one with the richest and most enduring spiritual legacy. As Anandamurti has explained, basic forms of tantra existed even prior to Shiva's time, leaving a trail back to early shamanic cultures. In fact, he once directed some of my yogi friends to a cave in Northeastern India where they discovered depictions of the esoteric yogic chakra system painted in graphic detail on the cave walls. These cave paintings, it is estimated, are nearly 9,000 years old.

Many writers on yoga today claim that tantra had its early roots in the scriptures of the vedas (circa 1500 BC). It is more probable, however, that the vedic and the tantric traditions are two parallel streams of Indian history. The vedic stream originated with the Rig Veda, the oldest and one of the four books of vedic scriptures. Yoga scholar Georg Feuerstein writes that many Hindus 'distinguish between Vedic and Tantric – vaidika and tantrika – currents of Hindu spirituality.' [8] Anandamurti would agree with this assertion. He makes a clear distinction between tantra and veda. Tantric teachings represent, according to him, a predominantly yogic path, whereas the vedas are more philosophical, mythological and ritualistic in orientation. Although the tantric oral tradition is more than 7,000 years old, the tantric books, or tantras, were not written before around 500 CE.

Anandamurti's contribution to this historical and philosophical quandary is to trace many of the original tantric teachings scattered throughout the vedas, the puranas, the agamas, and the Upanishads. By applying his exceptional spiritual vision and scholarly erudition, he has highlighted the timely validity and renewed significance of these ancient teachings.

In India, I was taught that the earliest systematic tantric teachings are formulated in the *Agama* and *Nigama Tantras*. These esoteric teachings are allegedly based on conversations between Shiva and his wife Parvati. The *Nigama* teachings constitute the philosophical teachings of tantra, or the deeply inquisitive questions that Parvati posed to Shiva. The *Agama* teachings make up the practical aspects, or the answers that Shiva gave.

The more I delved into Anandamurti's teachings, the more I realized how tantra had influenced the vedas. I found that the Atharva Veda, for example, is marked by a distinct tantric influence. The *Nrsimha Tapaniiya Shruti*, in particular, clearly demonstrates tantric rather than vedic influences. The Upanishads, which were written after the four vedas, also include many references to tantric concepts, including the subtle life-force energies, or *vayus*, and the psychic energy vortexes today commonly known as chakras. Most importantly, the deep philosophy of the Upanishads flourished in a culture steeped in tantric practice. 'The Tantric esprit', writes Feuerstein, 'continues to evolve through the period of the Brahmanas and Upanishads (2000 BC), as well as the intellectually and spiritually fertile era of the Mahabharata, until it reached its typical form in the Tantras of the early common era'. [9] In the ensuing centuries, tantra experienced a booming renaissance, and its philosophy and practices had a remarkable influence on Tibetan Buddhism, Hinduism, as well as the lesser known Jainism.

Dispelling Some Myths about Yoga and Tantra

The more I learnt about the tantras and the vedas, the more I also learnt about the several misconceptions about tantra among yoga scholars and practitioners today. One of the most common misunderstandings people have is that the vedas – as taught by the Rishis and the Brahmin priests – are the original source of yogic philosophy and practice. This misunderstanding, I discovered, has in part arisen because many important tantric texts were not written down before the early Common Era. Like the vedas, the oral teachings of tantra were transmitted from guru to disciple for thousands of years before being written down. But the main source of this misunderstanding arises from the vedic Brahmins themselves. Although many of them practised tantra, due to their own prejudices they attempted to demonstrate the vedic origin of tantra and yoga. Therefore, writes N. N. Bhattacharya, 'They often twisted Vedic passages to suit their own purpose'.[10]

One may find an example of such misrepresentation in the *Rudrayamala Tantra*, where it is said: 'The science which comes from the mouth of Lord Shiva, goes to the ears of Parvati, and is approved by Lord Krishna, is called Agama.' As Anandamurti has pointed out, however, it is illogical that Krishna of the Mahabharata era (1500 BC) would approve something that Shiva said 3,500 years earlier. This aphorism, Anandamurti asserts, 'was cleverly included in the *Rudrayamala Tantra* by the protagonists of the vedas.'

Arthur Avalon (aka. Sir John Woodroffe), the famous British writer on tantra, spent half his life searching for secretly-guarded tantric texts in India. In his path-breaking book on the chakras and the kundalini, *The Serpent Power: The Secrets of Tantric and Shaktic Yoga*, published in 1918, he also traced the origins of tantra back to the vedas. Avalon, as well as many other eminent Western writers on tantra and yoga today, vehemently proclaims the vedic origins of tantra. They do not explain, however, why tantric spirituality in India has long been considered *veda-bhaya,* an inferior path that belongs outside the vedas. While we may excuse these Western writers for their ignorance, history speaks for itself: for several millennia, the followers of tantra faced ridicule and suppression, its practices have been misunderstood, and its origin as the source of yoga either ignored or forgotten.

Despite these misgivings, Avalon is unparalleled in his comprehensive understanding of tantra. More importantly, for those on the spiritual path, Avalon reminds us that tantric spirituality 'has the supreme merit of accomplishing within a short time what other methods can hardly accomplish within a life'. Even *Yoga Journal* – undoubtedly the most popular magazine on yoga in the world today – perpetuates the myth that the history of yoga and tantra started in the vedic period. One of this magazine's regular contributors, Linda Sparrowe, writes that the history of yoga started in the vedic period (1500 BC), continued to grow in the preclassical period (800–500 BC), was systematized by Patanjali in the Classical Period (200 BC), and has continued to develop into our times. She writes: 'Tantra emerged early in the post-classical period, around the fourth century AD, but didn't reach its full flowering until 500 to 600 years later.' She concludes that, for most students of yoga today, tantra 'represents a rather radical departure for yoga philosophy.' In the same esteemed journal, Maria Carrico writes that the vedas, India's ancient religious texts, gave birth to both the literature and the technique of yoga.

Veda and Tantra: The Two Spiritual Rivers of India

When studying Tantra in India, I found such bias to be quite common among vedic scholars. Many of the tantric teachers and scholars I met, however, explained that tantra developed in the pre-vedic period (when it was popular among the Dravidians and the Mongolians and to a lesser extent among the Austrics). It was during this time, Shiva's authority as tantric yogi, spiritual preceptor, medical scientist and musician emerged.

It is impossible for us to fully measure the comprehensive nature of Shiva's influence today, but it appears that Shiva was not only the 'King of the Yogis' but also the leader of many tribal groups. Thus, as popularly accepted in India, none other than this tantric yogi, deserves the term 'father of yoga' as well as 'father of Indian civilization'.

That said, I also discovered that there are many philosophical similarities between vedic and tantric teachings. This similarity you will especially discover in many Sanskrit verses from the vedas and the tantras. In the vedas, it is said:

Yato va' ima'ni bhu'tani
Ja'yante yena ja'ta'ni jiivanti.
Yatprayantyabhisam'vishanti
Tadvijijina'sasva tadbrahma.

All created beings emerge, are maintained and finally dissolve in the flow of Cosmic ideation. Make an attempt to know that Supreme Entity, the veritable Brahma.

In tantra, a similar idea has been expressed:

Yato vishvam' samudbhu'tam' yenaja'tainca tis't'hati.
Yasmin sarva'n'i liiyante jinayam' tadbrahmalaks'aen'aeh.

The entity in whom the creation, preservation and destruction of the universe takes place is Brahma.

Both the vedic and tantric teachings are in philosophical agreement that Brahma, the cosmic consciousness, is the all-pervading source of all creation. Moreover, both paths believe that the goal of life is to realize this infinite source. So, what has been the most obvious difference between vedic and tantric teachings? Its practices. While tantrics meditate and practice yoga asanas, the vedic Brahmin priests chant hymns and offer ablutions to the sacrificial fires. Since the dawn of tantra, many vedic Aryans practised tantra, however, and thus over time, these two distinct streams of Indian culture have fed and nourished each other.

In one of his many discourses, Anandamurti said that it has been tantra, and to a lesser extent the vedas, that has been the sacred thread holding the colourful fabric of Indian society together. Indians have always been deeply spiritual, and tantra has been part and parcel of their daily lives since the early dawn of civilization. While in India, I saw firsthand how tantric culture is expressed through the devotion people have for such popular deities as Kali, Durga and Shiva. An especially popular practice is the age-old worship of the Shiva *lingam* and the *yoni,* ancient male and female fertility figures.

The lingam and yoni were originally worshipped by the early fertility cults. But over time, these sacred stones were infused with tantric esoteric meaning. The male lingam represents Shiva, and the female yoni represents Shakti, of the tantric cosmology. In other words, the lingam is the masculine Shiva, and the yoni is the feminine Shakti principles of creation. Merged together in union, they are the two faces of Brahma – the sublime fusion of duality that dissolves in cosmic non-duality.

But what is the main reason that so many believe tantra came from the vedas? First, the *Tantra Shastras* – the tantric writings of the early Common Era – were, to some extent, influenced by vedic philosophy. Second, the vedas were also influenced by the tantras, because many, if not most of the vedic sages and philosophers, including the famous vedantic yogi and philosopher Shankaracharya (AD 788–822), were tantric adepts. Why? Because it was tantra, not the vedic teachings, that contained the more practical and sophisticated wisdom and techniques needed to attain spiritual enlightenment. It is namely within the tantric heritage that one will find the time-tested tools to become an accomplished yogi or yogini, including the esoteric sciences of kundalini awakening, yogic breathing, yoga exercises, and mantra meditation.

In summary, tantra influenced the vedas and the vedas influenced tantra. However, it is the tantric path that is most responsible for the teachings we today commonly know and practice as yoga and meditation. If you already are a yoga practitioner, you may have learnt that it was the famous sage Patanjali who codified yoga philosophy in his famous *Yoga Sutras* (200 BC). This complex treatise, from which most ancient and modern yoga philosophy has been derived, was not solely based on the vedas, however. These ancient sutras were also formulated from the ancient teachings of tantra. In fact, one can trace most forms of yogic philosophy and practice back to Shiva and Parvati. How? Patanjali was influenced by Kapila's Samkhya philosophy, which also evolved from tantra, and many aspects of this philosophy and, most notably his eightfold path of ashtanga yoga, also evolved from tantric yoga. Indeed, Anandamurti maintains that of the eight practices of Patanjali's asthanga yoga, at least six had been systematized by Shiva almost 5,000 years earlier.

For Swami and writer S. Abhayananda, it appears that the Dravidian civilization was based on a 'full-blown Shiva-Shakti mythology' and that we can trace the tantric and yogic tradition back to pre-Aryan India. [11] As my guru repeatedly stated, all authentic yoga practice is based on tantra.

Shiva, according to Alain Daniélou, 'is the Central figure of pre-Aryan Dravidian religion in India and in all its branches in the Near East and around the Mediterranean, as far as pre-Celtic Europe.' [12] Daniélou further claims that Shiva tantra at one point was 'almost universal' and has maintained its original form in India until today. The widespread veneration of Shiva in prehistoric times – from the banks of the Ganges to the shores of Europe – may explain the legends and sculptures of Viking yogis, puts in perspective Shiva's seal found in a Bronze Age peat bog in Denmark, makes it possible that Shiva travelled all the way to the Alps, and might be the source for why the Greeks speak of India as the sacred homeland of Dionysus.

Creating a Tantric Lifestyle

Tantric Philosophy: *Sukhanuraktih Parama Jaevritti* – The deep yearning for happiness is the primary propensity of all living beings.

Daily Contemplation: Contrary to some spiritual paths, which view overcoming suffering as the main purpose of life, tantra has a refreshingly life-affirming attitude. Deeply lodged in the first chakra, we have two main propensities for pleasure: kama (physical pleasure) and moksha (spiritual pleasure). In other words, we are hardwired for happiness and bliss. Happiness is our goal and our birthright. It is important, however, to distinguish between these two types of pleasures. Physical pleasure gives us momentary happiness but can also lead us towards addictions to money, food, drink and sex. Spiritual bliss, on the other hand, gives us lasting happiness and has no physical or mental side-effects. Pleasure is simply the congenial environment necessary for life, and life's goal is infinite bliss. So when you engage in physical pleasures, think of these acts as your spiritual practice.

Daily Acts of Sacredness

One: When you wake up in the morning visualize that your whole day will be filled with lasting spiritual happiness. Whatever you are doing, touching, seeing and hearing, it brings you happiness.

Two: When you go to bed at night visualize that all your dreams are blissful and spiritual; no matter if a dream is fearful or sad, the dream's ultimate, deeper message is freedom from unhappiness.

Chapter Four

TWO RIVERS:
A BRIEF TANTRIC AND VEDIC HISTORY

Most contemporary yoga scholars maintain that tantra as a spiritual path has virtually disappeared from India. They maintain that tantra is practised only in Tibet in the form of tantric Buddhism. To make matters worse, many Indians think of tantra as black magic and that it only exists on the periphery of Indian culture, among magicians and obscure sects of naked sadhus. But nothing could be farther from the truth. The teachings of Shiva flows like a subterranean river throughout most of Indian culture.

Since Shiva's time, tantra has been widespread in India and other parts of the world in broadly two ways – as a culture and devotional practice for the common people, and as a sophisticated yogic path. Although the vast majority of Indians do not practice the more esoteric aspects of tantra yoga, tantra is alive and well in India today as a way of life, as a religious myth and a devotional source of inspiration. 'The Hindu religion, as it is practised today', writes Daniélou, 'is tantric in character, based almost exclusively on the Agama(s) .... If we wish to understand Indian thought, we must return to its sources ... the Shaiva religion, the cosmological theory called Samkhya, the practices of Yoga, as well as the bases of what we consider to be Hindu philosophy, are part.'

Tantra for the Masses: A Brief History

While only a small percentage of Indians are engaged in tantric meditation practice, tantric bhakti yoga as spiritual practices and ways of life is very popular and has the same ancient roots, namely the teachings of Shiva and Krishna. Krishna lived in India around

1500 BC and advanced the popular movement of bhakti yoga, the yoga of devotion. Krishna also introduced the concepts of karma yoga, the yoga of action, and jnana yoga, the yoga of knowledge, and he emphasized, in typical tantric style, the importance of maintaining balance between these three paths of spirituality. And from these two great personalities, Shiva and Krishna, the tantric esprit has transformed and inspired Indian society over thousands of years.

Tantra is thus widely recognized and practiced not only in India but throughout the world. Even in the most commercialized and body-centred yoga studios in Hollywood, various derivative forms of tantra yoga are practiced, since hatha yoga was originally developed by Shiva tantrics. Bhakti yoga – from idol worship to devotional bhajans and kirtans – is also an expression of tantra. This form of ecstatic, trance-induced worship is widely practised in India today. In the West, especially in the US, kirtan and bhajan concerts have also become popular among practitioners of yoga and meditation, thanks, in part, to kirtan singers like Jai Uttal and Krishna Das.

In India, many worshippers pray to the physical form of a deity rather than directly to the spirit beyond form. While this kind of idol worship is considered a style of meditation or sadhana in tantra, it is acknowledged as a rudimentary style. The practical and liberal path of tantra simply recognizes that not all people have the inclination or time to engage in sophisticated meditation techniques or practice advanced yoga postures.

One of my favourite Indian saints, Ramakrishna Paramahansa, was also one of the most prominent and beloved tantric gurus in India in the 19th century. Famous for his worship of the image of Goddess Kali, an expression of Shakti, Ramakrishna worshipped this divine creative principle both day and night. His spiritual fixation or devotion to Goddess Kali was so strong that he was often seen talking to her as if she was a real person. From Ramakrishna, we thus learn one of the most important lessons of tantra: The objective world of duality and form is, for the saints, nothing but non-dual divinity, nothing but pure consciousness. Ramakrishna's devotion teaches us that the image of the goddess, or any image of the beloved, is the form that can open our hearts to the formless bliss of yogic union with the divine. For in tantra, through the fixation of mind on a deity, mantra, yantra, or the image of the guru, we can, if we have the proper technique, transcend form altogether and ecstatically reach mystical union with spirit. We will then realize the deep, inner essence of tantra – that all forms are a continuum of cosmic consciousness.

Praising the divine through devotional songs and chants is commonly practised by millions of people in India. Bhakti yoga, the yoga of the heart, is considered one of the most refined forms of tantra. Once, I experienced this simple yoga of joyous rapture while walking down a quiet street in Kathmandu at night. After strolling down the narrow dirt road, I ended up at an open square with a small pavilion in the middle. Upon the circular platform, a group of about a dozen men sat around singing devotional bhajans to the accompaniment of a drum and a harmonium. There was nobody else around. Obviously, they did not sing to entertain, earn money or seek fame, they simply sang because of their love for god. Although I did not understand much of what they sang that night, I walked away deeply touched by their effortless hymns of ecstatic devotion.

No one group of people embodies the spirit of tantric bhakti yoga more than the Baul singers of Bengal. These wandering minstrels, whom I sometimes encountered on my travels in Bengal, have always lived beyond the narrow confines of religion. Their philosophy and tradition of devotional chanting grew out of the culture surrounding the Jain tantrics of the Middle Ages. Their culture was also greatly influenced by the bhakti yoga in the Vaishnava tantra movement of Chaitanya Mahaprabhu, who lived around AD 1100. Clad in colourful, flowing robes, strumming the one-stringed ektar, the Bauls have long been an integral part of Bengal's lush cultural landscape, wandering from village to village singing of a universal God. Their message of spiritual love has also crossed the borders of India, since many of the songs composed by popular American kirtan performer Jai Uttal are inspired by the enchanted Baul singers. Unfortunately, the Bauls, like many tantrics in the past, are often perceived as heretics and still sometimes experience persecution from fundamentalist Muslims and Hindus.

Tantra: An Indian Way of Life

In India, among poor and rich, in cities and in remote villages, I often encountered a simple celebration of life. This celebration of the pure joy of the present moment can in large part be attributed to the tantric embrace of life in all its brutal and beautiful glory. Indeed, Shiva's Sanskrit aphorism, *Varttamanesu Vartteta*, simply encourages us to live in the present. Shiva urges us to embrace life as it is, right now, in this very moment. Because, by living in the present, just like the Bauls of Bengal, our mind becomes intuitively receptive, fresh and open for spiritual revelation, synchronicity and rapture.

Once, at a sacred Shiva festival in Nepal, I experienced yet more expressions of tantric bhakti yoga in the form of the common people's devotion and adoration for Shiva. Each month of February, during the Shivaratri festival, hundreds of thousands of devoted pilgrims arrive at Pashupatinath Temple from all over India and Nepal to honour the greatness of Lord Shiva. Preceding the pilgrims, and often the centre of attention at the festival, half-naked sadhus arrive with matted hair and their skin covered in ashes. Some sadhus can be seen demonstrating intricate yoga positions or sitting silently, lost in deep meditation. Others sit in the lotus position, explaining minute details of yogic philosophy. Long queues of devout Shiva worshippers snake up the temple steps, over the bridge and up the steps on the other bank. Devotees bathe in the shallow river and walk up the steps to enter the sacred temple, offerings in their hands.

There I was in the middle of it all, a European dressed like an Indian yogi. I had come from far away to experience the ancient depths of tantra for myself. I had come to dedicate my life to meditation, yoga exercises, vegetarian food, fasting, the singing of devotional songs, and the study of Sanskrit aphorisms. Although a foreigner – a Viking among the indigenous followers of Shiva – I truly felt at home there. I truly felt that the love for Shiva and the practice of tantra are alive and well in India. Shiva is undoubtedly one of the most popular deities in the Hindu pantheon. So, to claim that the Shiva devotees and ascetic yogis at Pashupatinath are not tantric, as well as millions of others like them all over India, is to overlook the simple fact that India, in its cultural essence, is fused with the spirit and practice of tantra. Historian Alain Daniélou maintains that Hinduism owes much more to its pre-vedic tantric tradition than it does to the vedic tradition. [13] Noted Indologist N. N. Bhattacharya also observes that 'Tantrism as a heterogeneous set of ideas and practices characterized the religious fabric of India – ancient, medieval, and even modern'. [14] And in the words of Anandamurti: 'Not only in India, but in quite a large part of the world, in every sphere of life, the laws and injunctions of Shiva alone prevailed for a long time. Even today the civilization of modern India is intrinsically tantric. On the outside only is there a vedic stamp'.

Furthermore, there is, in essence, no significant difference between tantric Hinduism and tantric Buddhism. As Anandamurti reminds us, 'Tantra is one and only one. It is based on one sentiment, on one idea.' And that one idea, that one spiritual destination, is achieved through tantric practice, until one day our mind dissolves in cosmic consciousness, or Brahma. For the tantric Hindu, this means to reach the lofty abode of *Parama Purusha*, and for the tantric Buddhist, to be elevated to the state of *Shriman Mahasukha*. These are simply two different names for the same inward peaks of spiritual enlightenment. [15]

The Aryan Controversy

In order to understand the ancient history of tantra, one needs to understand the complex relationship between tantra and the vedas. Indeed, one needs to learn about the often contentious relationship between the vedic Aryans and the tantric Dravidians of ancient India. So, let us venture on an exciting journey together, back in time to the beginning of humanity's ancient myths and spiritual teachings.

During my first journey throughout India, I discovered a country with great ethnic diversity. In southern India, I met Austric peoples whose facial features and complexion were similar to Africans or the Australian aborigines. In the south, east and west, I also met the generally tall and dark-brown complexioned Dravidians. In the north of India, and in Nepal, I met people whose facial features revealed various ethnic backgrounds. Some appeared Caucasian, some had light, yellowish skin and were Tibetan or Mongolian, and others had Dravidian features. It appeared as if I had arrived in an ethnic melting pot, a place where all the peoples of the world had congregated.

India is composed of largely four main ethnic groups – the Mongolians, Dravidians, Austrics and Aryans. But where did these people originally come from? Most scholars thought for many years that Indian history started when ruthless, blue-eyed Aryans conquered the indigenous population in successive raids from 1500 to 1200 BC. Advocated by German-born Sanskrit scholar Max Müller, this theory made universal and bold claims. 'The Aryan nations have become the rulers of history,' he once wrote. [16] In other words, Indian civilization was great only because of its white-skinned, Aryan origin. In Europe itself, the ideals of Aryan supremacy was, of course, promoted to its ultimate extreme by Adolf Hitler and his Nazi Party. Later in his career, though, Max Müller retracted this idea. The Aryans, he more accurately ventured, indicated a group of people speaking Indo-European languages.

So what does the word Aryan actually mean? To the vedic people in early India, the Sanskrit word *arya* meant 'noble' or 'cultured'. In the ancient vedic texts, the place between the Himalayas and the Vindhya Mountains were called *arya-varta,* or 'the abode of the noble people'. A third meaning is 'the people from Iran'. Aryan is also used by scholars as an ethnic or racial label for the Caucasian peoples.

Since Max Müller advanced his invasion theory; there have been several alternative theories about the origin of the Aryan people in India. Many scholars now agree there was a succession of Aryan migration into India, but they disagree about whether these ancients were warlike invaders or peaceful immigrants.

The idea that a group of noble, vedic Aryans invaded a primitive Indian culture around 1500 BC was, according to many scholars, overthrown in 1920 when the Indus Valley Civilization was discovered. This discovery proved that the achievements of ancient India could no longer be credited to the descendants of the Aryan invaders alone. Why? Because the aboriginal Dravidians of the Indus Valley had planned cities and a standardized system of weights and bricks for at least two thousand years before the alleged invasion. Indeed, their civilization was more advanced than the nomadic tribes that supposedly conquered them.

But the controversy does not stop here. Were the people of the Indus Valley vedic, or were they tantric? I had always taken for granted that they were tantric, because that is what I learnt in India. A popular, alternative idea about Indian history today suggests the Aryan invasion theory is at worst based on a racist myth and at best on faulty scientific evidence. This idea has been promoted by some of the world's most prominent scholars on yoga, tantra and ayurveda. According to them, the Aryan invasion never took place.. For these scholars, the only alternative appears to be that the Aryans must have been indigenous to India. The Aryans are, according to them, the 'noble' and 'cultured' people of Indian civilization, those who invented yoga, advanced spiritual philosophy, built the Indus Valley Civilization and developed ayurvedic medicine. But is this truly what happened?

The Aryans could also have come from outside India and settled in the Himalayas and northern India. According to Anandamurti, the pastoral Caucasian nomads came at various times to India through Iran from Central Asia. For yoga scholars David Frawley and Georg Feuerstein, however, there appears to be only one possibility: the Aryans have always been indigenous to India, and they are the people from the highest, noblest castes of society, most notably the Brahmins. For these authors, the Aryans represent all that is noble and great about Indian civilization, namely the vedic cultural heritage. But is it true that the Aryans were simply noble and spiritual people?

The Real Story about the Vedic Aryans

If you have read the vedas, you will have discovered that they contain some of the most sublime philosophical truths humanity has ever conceived. Yet, you will also have noticed that the same vedas, like all religious scriptures, also contain many religious dogmas, including animal sacrificial rites to conciliate the gods. Moreover, is it not also a fact that the culture that advanced these texts also instituted a caste system in which millions of people to this day are treated as virtual slaves? In addition, surgery was forbidden by early ayurvedic doctors due to possible 'contamination' by lower castes. Women, according to many vedic injunctions were considered too low to study and teach the scriptures. Indeed, it was only a few years ago that a famous religious authority, the Shankaracharya of Sumerpeeth Kanchi, declared that women should not recite the vedas. Such religious practices would be detrimental to their health and prevent them from having healthy babies, he claimed. [17] Tantric teachings, on the other hand, have always been against the caste system and have generally held women in high regard. Indeed, it is inconceivable that an authority on tantra would ever warn women from studying the scriptures.

But where did the Aryans come from? The revisionist historians who claim that the Aryan invasion never occurred, at least not around 1500 BC, leave the possibility open that people from outside the Indian subcontinent might have arrived thousands of years earlier. As you will learn, this is what appears to have taken place. Among most scientists, the idea of one single, violent invasion by barbarian Aryan hordes has been replaced by immigration and acculturation over a long period of time. Recent genetic and other scientific evidence supports this historical scenario. All the various peoples of India – the Austrics, the Dravidian, the Mongolians and the Aryans – came, at some point, from somewhere else.

Genetic and Linguistic Science and Ancient Indian History

On a rainy evening in 2003, I sat glued to the television screen watching the PBS programme, *Journey of Man,* by Dr Spencer Wells. The main reason I was so captivated by this programme was that Dr Wells offered scientific evidence for what Anandamurti and others had claimed – that the Aryan vedic people migrated to India from the steppes of Eastern Russia and the Middle East.

Indeed, the genetic discoveries by Dr Wells confirm the many stories I had heard from scholars and storytellers in India. His extensive research shows that India experienced four large migratory settlements over a period of nearly 55,000 years. By sampling DNA of people in a village close to Madurai in Tamil Nadu, he spotted a genetic mutation that had been passed on to aboriginal people in Australia – thus offering the first biological proof that African ancestors of the Australian natives passed through India on the way to their new home. His research also proved beyond a shadow of doubt that the people who later moved into India in the north were of Aryan stock.

A few days after I had seen this captivating PBS programme, I continued my research and located an interview with Dr Wells in the online Rediff magazine. There he states emphatically that there is genetic evidence that 'the Aryans came from outside India'. The Rig Vedic Aryan peoples, he claims, emerged on the southern steppes of Russia and Ukraine about 5,000–10,000 years ago. He emphasized that 'The Aryans came from outside India. We actually have genetic evidence for that. Very clear genetic evidence from a marker that arose on the southern steppes of Russia and the Ukraine around 5,000 to 10,000 years ago. And it subsequently spread to the east and south through Central Asia reaching India. It is on the higher frequency in the Indo-European speakers, the people who claim they are descendants of the Aryans, the Hindi speakers, the Bengalis, the other groups. Then it is at a lower frequency in the Dravidians. But there is clear evidence that there was a heavy migration from the steppes down towards India.' [18] This shows that he does not agree with scholars David Frawley and Georg Feuerstein, who claim the vedic Aryans were the 'original inhabitants' of India. To Dr Wells, there is clear genetic evidence that 'the Aryans came later, after the Dravidians'. [19] In other words, Wells's genetic research clearly supported my spiritual teacher's assertions, as well as those of tantric scholars such as Alain Daniélou and Lalan Prasad Singh.

A year later, I came across the research work of a team led by Michael Bamshad of the University of Utah in Salt Lake City. They compared the DNA of 265 Indian men of different castes with DNA from nearly 750 African, European, Asian and other Indian men. First, they analysed mitochondrial DNA, which people inherit only from their mothers. When the researchers looked at specific sets of genes that tend to be inherited as a unit, they found that about 20 to 30 per cent of the Indian sets resembled those in Europeans. The percentage was highest in upper-caste males, which is natural since the early Aryan settlers were by and large upper-caste Brahmins and Kshatriyas.

The genes that entered India when Aryan settlers emigrated from Central Asia and the Middle East are still there. And, according to these scientists from the University of Utah and from Andhra University in India, they still remain entrenched at the top of the caste system. The invaders apparently subdued the local men, married many of their women and created the rigid caste system that exists even today. Their descendants are still the elite within Hindu society. Indeed, I had finally found scientific support for the stories I had heard from my tantric guru in India. [20]

Later, I learnt from the work of geneticist Lynn Jorde of the University of Utah that 'a group of males' was largely responsible for the Aryan invasion. If women had accompanied the invaders, the evidence should be seen in the mitochondrial genes, but it is not evident. The research team found clear evidence that women could be upwardly mobile, in terms of caste, if they married higher-caste men. In contrast, men generally did not move higher, because women rarely married men from lower castes. Since the caste system is still in vogue today, the same practice prevails. Thus, as you can see, genetic science corresponds with the tantric view that the Indo-Europeans, or true Aryans, indeed came from the outside and conquered the northern parts of the Indian subcontinent. The people they subdued – the Mongolians, Dravidians and the Austrics – descended from the original inhabitants who had arrived thousands of years earlier from Africa, the Middle East and other parts of Asia.

Finally, I pieced together information about the speakers of the various languages of India based, in part, on studies conducted by the People of India project of the Anthropological Survey of India.

This project assigned the entire Indian population to 4,635 ethnic communities and put together detailed information from over 25,000 individual informants from all over India. It was found that there are four major language families in India – Austric, Dravidian, Indo-European and Sino-Tibetan. These languages also correspond to the four main racial groups in India: the Austrics, Dravidians, Aryans and the Mongolians respectively. [21] According to this study, it appears the Indo-European Aryans brought the vedic language to India from Central Asia, a fact that has also been substantiated by the historical sequences and details outlined in Anandamurti's many farseeing discourses on the history of India.

Fig. 1. Brief overview of the main ethnic and linguistic groups that peopled ancient India.

Linguistic Group	Ethnicity	Arrival in India	Religion
Austric	Austric (Auistraloid)	60,000 BC from Africa	Animism
Dravadian	Dravadian	10–8000 BC from Near East	Proto-Tantra
Sino-Tibetan	Mongolian	10–8000 BC from Far East	Proto-Tantra
Indo-European	Caucasian	6–4,000 BC from Central Asia	Rig-Veda

The Vedic Aryans and the Tantric Dravidians: A Clash and Fusion of Civilizations

Sometimes when we study and practice Indian spirituality, vedic and tantric teachings will flow through us quite seamlessly, like a sacred river of spiritual wisdom. At other times, we will find the teachings to be distinctly different. Anandamurti often emphasized that the early parts of the vedas, the Rig Veda, were composed outside of India. This took place both long before and during the time of Shiva, at a time when these fair-skinned Aryan composers migrated into India.

Is there any proof of this? Authors like N. N. Bhattacharya and Alain Daniélou have remarked on the lack of references to agriculture in the Rig Veda. They think the main reason for this was that the early Aryans were pastoralists. In contrast, the tantric Dravidians were rice-growing farmers. Moreover, you will not find any descriptions of the Indus Valley Civilization in the Rig Veda. Nor will you find any references to the sophisticated grid pattern of streets. Nor will you find any mention of the careful engineering of the drainage systems, granaries, warehouses and areas of intensive craft production, and neither to the various seals found there.

Some vedic scholars and writers on yoga, however, argue that the Indus Valley Civilization was purely a vedic civilization. Popular writers like David Frawley, Georg Feuerstein and Deepak Chopra promote this view. This so-called cradle of human civilization, they affirm, had few or no traces of tantra. But is this a correct assertion? Sir John Marshall, Bhattacharya, Daniélou, and other scholars point out that many of the various artefacts found in these ancient ruins are, in fact, yogic or tantric in nature. These include proto-tantric fertility symbols such a lingams and yonis, or figurines of goddesses. The alleged yogi Shiva, in the form of the Pashupati seal, is one of the most common figures found in these ruins. Here archaeologists have also discovered a marble statue of a yogi with eyes fixed on the tip of his nose and draped in cloth designed with bilva leaves. These leaf designs are significant as they have been used in the worship of Shiva, the king of yoga, for thousands of years. This marble statue displays a type of yogic gaze that I am quite familiar with. This trance-inducing gaze is actually an essential element in one of the tantric meditation lessons I received several years ago.

These archaeological finds, according to many scholars, all point in one direction – that tantra was widely practiced in the Indus Valley Civilization. This does not mean, however, that all members of this society were meditating yogis. Much like in today's India, we can assume that only a minority of the people were practicing tantric meditation and yoga. Like today, most people were worshippers of tantric gods and goddesses, but not always practitioners of its advanced spiritual sciences. Archaeological digs have also unearthed fire pits used for vedic rituals in these old ruins. Therefore, I think it is reasonable to conclude that the Aryan and Dravidian peoples and cultures coexisted in northern India for several millennia. Indeed, by the time of the Indus Valley Civilization, they probably lived together much like people from various castes, cultural and spiritual traditions coexist in India today.

This coexistence was not always peaceful. While the Rig Veda contains hymns of sublime spiritual knowledge, including a few references to yoga, many of its stories are focused on the nature-worshiping rites of pastoral warrior clans. Some also tell colourful tales about the conquest of the 'dark-skinned devils', namely the Dravidians of India. The Aryan priests made it painstakingly clear that non-Aryans (Anarya) were not allowed to pollute their culture and blood. In India you will find vestiges of this racist superiority even today. In personal ads in the newspapers, you will quite often find men and women looking for a marriage partner with 'wheatish complexion'.

So, what about all the symbolic references in the vedas? Do all of them contain subtle messages of transcendental meaning? And do they therefore prove that the vedas are the source of all Indian spirituality, including tantra? When the Rig Vedic people spoke of the sun god, Azura, for example, did they describe a deep state of meditation as some contemporary vedic writers today want us to believe? Did they describe the 'spiritual sun within'? Since this was the age of magic and mythic power gods, it is more likely that the early vedic people thought the sun had magical powers. Hence, they worshipped this bright, life-giving entity in the sky directly. They literally believed the sun was a god. In other words, to the Aryans, the sun was not a symbol of a transrational state of meditation. Their devotion to Azura simply represented a pre-rational belief in the magical powers of that extraterrestrial and life-giving planet.

Indeed, most people at that time (12000–6000 BC) believed in a variety of nature's magical powers and spoke quite literally about those beliefs. Similarly, when the early Aryans called the dark-skinned people *devils*, they also meant it rather literally. They were not speaking of some symbolic struggle between good and evil. Their verses were often fearfully direct, and many symbolic references are often incorrectly attributed to higher, transcendental truths, or were added later in the written versions. My guru, Anandamurti, pointed out that many of the gods and goddesses described in various Indian religious scriptures were, in fact, representations of actual historical leaders. Krishna of Hindu mythology is a prime example, for he was, according to Anandamurti, a non-Aryan tantric yogi and a king who united Bharata (India) around 1500 BC in a mighty war described in the classic epic Mahabharata.

Likewise, many of the mythological demigods of the vedas, such as Indra, Agni and Varuna, were actual warrior leaders. Indeed, it was warrior leaders such as these who after a few thousand years of gradual migrations and conquests finally conquered most of northern India. 'It was not difficult for the healthy, martial, almost invincible Aryans to conquer northern India', writes Anandamurti. 'The victorious Aryans treated the vanquished non-Aryans as slaves, trampling them underfoot to the bottom of their trivarna (three-caste) society – their society of Brahmins (priests), Kshatriyas (soldiers) and Vaishyas (merchants). There the non-Aryans became the fourth class, or Shudra Varna, while society became a caturvarna (four-caste) society.' While the Aryans maintained political control in northern India, the Dravidian influence in the social and cultural sphere gradually increased. According to Anandamurti, 'From the non-Aryans the Aryans acquired a well-knit social system, subtle insight, and spiritual philosophy and tantra sadhana.' [22]

Thus, we can safely conclude that the so-called Indus Valley Civilization eventually became a composite culture influenced by both tantric and vedic traditions. A similar merger between two civilizations took place in Europe when the Romans conquered Greece.

Harappa, Kashi and Mehrgarh: Ancient Cities of Tantra

While researching the complex history of India, I received help from many sources, from friends and books, from dreams and e-mails. One day after I had a wonderful dream about Shiva, an e-mail from a friend, who got to know that I was writing a book on tantra, alerted me to the connection between ancient tantric peoples and the Tamil language of today. The Tamil language of south India is considered one of the world's oldest living languages with its own script. An ancient Dravidian language, Tamil is more than 6,000 years old. In fact, an ancient form of Tamil, or Dravidian, is still spoken by the Brahui people today in the central Baluchistan region of Pakistan and Afghanistan.

When the first vedic Aryans migrated to India through the Khyber and the Bolan passes, and mingled with the local population of the north, the north Indian proto-Dravidian languages changed to a great extent. However, in the area where the Brahui people still live, the old Dravidian language has remained virtually unchanged for millennia. The language of the Brahuis of Baluchistan has many linguistic similarities to the Dravidian languages still spoken by the Tamils in south India today. Scholars have noted similarities in the numerals, personal pronouns, syntax and other linguistic features between Brahui and Tamil.

It is not only linguistics, however, that makes Baluchistan such an interesting historical area. This region, at the foot of the Bolan Pass, is also the site of Mehrgarh. Estimated to be more than 8,000 years old, it is regarded as the largest town of early antiquity. Covering an area of over 500 acres, Mehrgarh's population may have reached to nearly 20,000. In comparison, the population of Egypt at the time was about 30,000. Living in brick houses, skilled in pottery making and the cultivation of rice, these ancient shamanic and proto-tantric Dravidians were likely to be the first Indians encountered by the invading Aryans more than seven thousand years ago. Urban culture was thus already in existence in India at the time of Shiva. Indeed, Mehrgarh had existed for almost two thousand years when Shiva was born. There is thus evidence of a continuous urban culture from Mehrgarh around 7000 BC to the Harappan and Mohenjo-daro civilizations in the Indus Valley around 4000 BC. The current consensus is that the primary language represented by the Harappan script is related to modern Dravidian. The archaeologist Sir John Marshall was the first person to suggest a linguistic link between the Harappans and Dravidians.

As mentioned elsewhere, the complex and ancient Indus Valley Civilization, which stretched from Afghanistan to the River Ganges, was largely a tantra-oriented culture. In fact, the word '*hara*' refers to the destroyer lord or Shiva, and '*appa*' means father in the Dravidian language. The city of Harappa in the Indus Valley can thus be considered a place dedicated to Shiva, who by many today is considered the father of Indian civilization.

Since tantra existed in India before Shiva, it is possible that the old tantric civilization in India had its early roots in Mehrgarh, was systematized and refined during the time of Shiva and continued to flourish for thousands of years in the Indus Valley Civilizations of Harappa and Mohenjo-daro. While Mehrgarh is the oldest archaeological city in the world, Kashi or Benares (now called Varanasi) is the world's oldest living city. In Indian mythology, Kashi is considered the 'original ground' where Lord Shiva and Parvati stood at the beginning of time. Benares is the point in which the first *jyotirlinga*, the fiery pillar of light by which Shiva manifested his supremacy over other gods, broke through the earth's crust and flared towards the heavens. More significant than the cremation ghats, and even the holy River Ganges, the Shivalinga in the golden temple remains, to millions of Shiva devotees, the devotional focus of Kashi.

Once again, Indian mythology leads us to a deeper understanding of history; the historical Shiva did, according to traditional sources, spend many years in Kashi, especially during the cool winter months, when Kashi – the 'holiest' city in all of India today – was his favourite resting abode. Shiva's and tantra's immeasurable contribution to humanity urges us to correct the common misconception that tantra and yoga are relatively recent expressions of Indian spirituality. Indeed, the classical yoga period did not actually start with the famed

Yoga Sutras of the sage Patanjali, but rather with Shiva, almost 5,000 years earlier. Most fundamental aspects of yoga – including many of the yoga exercises, breathing and meditation techniques used today – originated with the teachings of this great sage. What we today know as hatha yoga was consequently developed by tantric sages over thousands of years, most notably by the writings of the Natha tantrics in such texts as the *Hatha Yoga Pradipika* (AD 1400), the *Shiva Samhita* (AD 1500) and the *Gheranda Samhita* (AD 1700). These books were all dedicated to Shiva (also called Adinatha) and are based on the earlier oral tradition of tantra.

Fig. 2. Brief history of Tantra: Most dates are approximate.

9000–5000 BC: Proto-tantra
Rudimentary forms of shamanistic tantra practised by Dravidians and Mongolians. Proto-tantric city complex established at Mehrgarh around 6000 BC.

5000 BC: Tantra systematized by Shiva
Agama and Nigama, the philosophical and practical teachings, are given by Shiva and his wife Parvati. Shiva introduces concept of Dharma – the path of spirituality and righteousness. He also introduces tantra yoga, including practices such as asanas, pranayama, dharana, pratyahara, and dhyan, as well as two versions of the Panchamakaras (Five Ms), one for the common people and one for yogis. Shiva also refines and systematizes ayurvedic and tantric medicine, also termed Vaidik Shastra and Siddha medicine. Moreover, Shiva formulates the marriage system, the musical octave and mudraic dances (with his wife Parvati). Tantra spreads to other parts of Asia, Europe and the Middle East.

5000–2000 BC: Tantra-oriented civilizations in India
Tantric civilization established in Kota, Rajasthan, more than seven thousand years ago. Shiva establishes a city in Kashi (Benares), on the banks of the River Ganges. The

Dravidians establish tantra-oriented civilization in the Indus Valley region. People worship the mother goddess and also the father god (Pashupati). Tantric yogis understand these expressions as Shakti and Shiva, the dual nature of Brahma.

2000 BC: Transformation of the original Shiva Tantra

Shiva Tantra (also termed the Shaivite tradition) transforms into two branches, the Gaodiya and the Kashmiri Schools. The Gaodiya School was popular in East India (Bengal) and only marginally influenced by the vedas.

1500 BC: Krishna and Kapila

Krishna formulates three branches of yoga – action (karma), devotion (bhakti) and knowledge (jnana). His teachings greatly influence the later school of Vaishnava tantra. Yudhistira, a disciple of Krishna, popularizes the tantric practice of pranayama or breathing exercises. Tantric and yogic teachings spread all over the Far East. Maharishi Kapila formulates *Samkhya*, also termed Kapilasia Tantra, the world's first philosophy. Based on tantra, the Samkhya philosophy is dualistic, but share many similarities to the non-dualistic tantric philosophy outlined in this book. Samkhya also forms the basis of ayurvedic philosophy, as well as forming many of the basic principles of most aspects of the Six Classical Schools of Indian Philosophy, namely the Yoga Sutras, Samkhya, Vedanta, Nyaya, Vaishesika, and Purva Mimamsa.

200 BC: Patanjali

Inspired by the tantric Samkhya philosophy, Patanjali systematizes important aspects of tantra into the eightfold path of asthanga yoga. The idea that Brahma comprises both Shiva and Shakti was now widely accepted and consummated in the Ardha-Nareshvara, an idol depicting half a man (Shiva) and half a woman (Shakti).

AD 100: Tirumular

Shiva tantra adept from South India, a proponent of bhakti yoga and author of the famed *Tirumantiram*, which is considered to be one of the greatest yogic canons of all time.

AD 400–1200: Tantra Shastras

Most of the important tantric texts were written in this period, and thus to many scholars this was the 'Tantric era' of Indian spirituality, but in reality this literature was based on the oral tradition which started in 5000 BC and lasted for thousands of years. Such texts include the *Kularnava Tantra* and the *Mahanirvana Tantra*.

AD 600: Age of Buddhist, Hindu and Jain Tantra begins

Tantra shastras are written and influence various schools of Buddhism, Hinduism and Jainism. Shiva tantra evolves into five branches, or *Pancha Tantra*: 1. Shaiva Tantra, 2. Vaishnava Tantra, 3. Shakta Tantra, 4. Ganapatya Tantra, 5. Saura Tantra. Famous Buddhist tantric yogis from this period and onward include Naropa, Milarepa, Saraha, Prahevajra, Je Tsongkhapa and Wangchuk Dorje.

AD 800: Yoga Vashista

Sage Valmiki, the great tantric yogi, returns from China where he learnt the subtle practice of tantra meditation, which shows that tantra came to China at an early age. His esoteric teachings on tantric meditation and philosophy are compiled in the book, *Yoga Vashista*.

AD 900: Abhinavagupta

This tantric Renaissance man revives Kashmir Shaivism, lays the foundation for Indian aesthetics, and writes an encyclopaedia on non-dualist tantra.

AD 1000: Kularnava Tantra

This seventeen-chapter work contains over 2,000 verses and is considered one of the most important tantric texts.

AD 1000–1200: The Nathas Develop Hatha Yoga

The founder of this movement, Matsyendranath, was a Shiva tantric whose main disciple, Gorakshanath, systematized and further advanced the practices of hatha yoga.

AD 1100: Mahanirvana Tantra

Considered by some as the most important of the Hindu tantric scriptures, this fourteen-chapter text defines yoga in accordance with Shiva's teachings as the union of individual self (*jivatman*) with the cosmic self (*paramatman*).

AD 1271–1296: Jnaneshvar

A genius Renaissance man and tantric adept, Jnaneshvar composed the *Gitagovinda* at the age of 19, an epic poem reenacting the Bhagavad Gita. Merging the Vaishnava movement with Kashmir Shiva tantra, Jnaneshvar created a popular Bhakti movement in north India. The nineteenth-century sage Ramana Maharishi called him the 'king of saints'.

AD 1500: Chaitanya Mahaprabhu

A tantric adept, Chaitanya Mahaprabhu is undoubtedly the most well-known and celebrated bhakti yogis of India.

AD 1500–2000: Tantra Influences Many Spiritual Teachers and Paths

Some well-known spiritual teachers and leaders influenced by tantra include Kabir, Guru Nanak, Ramakrishna Paramahansa, Swami Vivekananda, Swami Shivananda, Swami Satyananda Sarasvati, Nityananda Avadhuta,

Subhash Chandra Bose, Swami Lakshman Joo, Swami Rama Tirtha and Ramana Maharshi. Tantric philosophy and practices greatly influence several schools of Buddhism and, in general, all the movements within the Hindu yoga tradition. Contemporary Buddhist tantric teachers include His Holiness the 14th Dalai Lama, Lama Yeshe, Tulku Rgyen Rinpoche, and Jamyang Khyentse Chökyi Lodrö.

AD 1914: John Woodroffe
The seminal book *Principles of Tantra* is first published. Woodroffe's second classic on tantra, *The Serpent Power*, was published in 1918.

AD 1921–90: Shrii Anandamurti, Swami Satyananda and other teachers.
Anandamurti synthesizes the main features of Shiva's original teachings, incorporates ashtanga yoga and hatha yoga, unites the essence of the five schools of tantra, and develops a comprehensive system of tantra yoga for the current era based on a new collection of tantric sutras in the book *Ananda Sutram*. Swami Satyananda establishes the Bihar School of Yoga, writes many books on tantric practice and philosophy.

Creating a Tantric Lifestyle

Tantric Philosophy: *Brhadesana Pranidanam Ca Dharma* – To desire after the Great is the Dharma (fundamental characteristic) of humanity.

Daily Contemplation: Human dharma is not the Christian dharma, the Hindu dharma or the Buddhist dharma. Human dharma is the same sacred journey for all humans irrespective of religion. All humans desire to seek oneness with God, Brahma or Spirit. The names of god are many, the paths may be many, but the goal is the same, and this goal is the one and only human dharma.

Daily Acts of Sacredness

Visualize that you are like a drop merging in the ocean of Brahma; that there is no separation between you and Brahma – that infinite cosmic ocean of bliss. Breathe in and feel that you are that bliss; breathe out and feel that you are that bliss.

One: Find a quiet place in the morning. Sit cross-legged with your spine straight. Feel that you are surrounded by an infinite ocean of bliss. When you breathe in, you breathe in that bliss. When you breathe out, you breathe out that bliss. Practice for 5–10 minutes.

Two: Practice the same meditation in the evening.

Part II

Tantric Philosophy, Cosmology
and Psychology

Chapter Five

MYSTERY OF SPIRIT:
TANTRA AS PERENNIAL WISDOM

A few years after I received tantric initiation, I realized what yogic union or spiritual bliss is all about. This took place during a visit to a friend in a small village outside Copenhagen, where I was living at the time. He had been attending one of my yoga classes in the city. Now he wanted to spend a few days alone with me to learn more about the tantric path and our guru. His second wish was to introduce me to his girlfriend. He hoped that she would also be inspired to take up meditation and yoga.

The narrow streets in his peaceful and charming village were lined with white houses with thatched roofs. His house was no exception, and behind the two-storey building was a well-maintained and colourful flower garden with half a dozen apple trees and one large cherry tree – all in full bloom. His idyllic garden had the perfect ambience for long hours of meditation and quiet, spiritual conversation.

We spent most of that afternoon and evening meditating under the cherry tree and talking sitting on a bench in the garden. After sunset, when the mosquitoes became too intolerable, we went inside and had a light vegetarian meal. Afterwards, I told my friend instructional and inspirational stories about tantra and our guru.

A Mystical Dream

Late that night, I went to bed in a spiritually intoxicated state – partly due to the devotion the stories had evoked and partly due to the many hours of meditation in the garden. During sleep, I did not really sleep in the ordinary sense. I was awake in my own lucid dream and was transported to a small room in India where I prostrated at the feet of my guru, who sat on a small, white cot. As I witnessed all this, I remained conscious I was dreaming and simply let myself be a witness to what took place.

In tantra, it is of great spiritual importance to touch the guru's feet, and I did so quite eagerly. As soon as both my hands touched his left foot, barely visible under layers of a white, cotton dhoti, my whole body was filled with an effulgent light of golden and fiery bliss. Soon, my whole being was aflame with ecstasy. Simultaneously, I heard a male and female voice that seemed to come from the outer reaches of the cosmos itself. In a united and clearly audible whisper – as if coming from the other-worldly lips of Shiva and Shakti themselves – I was told: 'We love you. We love you. We love you.'

Seeing visions and hearing voices are common 'diversions' when accessing higher states of consciousness. So after hearing those words, I did not get attached to them, nor did I attempt to interpret their meaning. Instead, I simply surrendered to the feeling of ecstasy, and soon my guru and I dissolved in a single continuum of cosmic consciousness. That is, I lost awareness of the outer world and merged in the all-pervading vastness of spiritual bliss.

When I finally returned from the cosmic state in my lucid dream, I could still feel the same ecstasy as when I touched my guru's feet in the vision world. The dream and the wakeful state were one seamless reality. I sat up in my regular meditation position. I looked around and saw that the room was real, and I realized I had just come out of a state of deep, spiritual awareness, a state of yogic union or samadhi. Since I wanted to experience more of that exalted state, I began to meditate, and soon I was again lost in the effulgence of bliss. Several hours later, the loud alarm clock went off and broke my trance.

After a shower, at about 6 in the morning, I went out into the garden and sat down under the cherry tree to meditate again. As soon as I started the process of meditation, the blissful ecstasy returned. I do not know how long it all lasted, but when I finally opened my eyes, I saw in an instant, that the branch with white cherry flowers hanging down in front of me was transparent. It looked as if form and formless space was one continuous flow. The vision only lasted a short while, but it has been my perennial inspiration ever since.

During the next several days, I experienced a state of nearly continuous bliss and telepathic clairvoyance. The bliss was very enjoyable, and the telepathic experiences made me see and feel the world and people in new and unexpected ways. Sometimes what I 'saw' or 'heard' was not so pleasant.

Swami Vivekananda recalled a similar touch from his own guru, Sri Ramakrishna. The first Indian yogi to visit America, Vivekananda gained worldwide fame at the 1893 World's Parliament of Religions in Chicago, and eventually became the most well-known disciple of Ramakrishna. Once, while having a discussion with a friend about whether it was true that all material things are god, Ramakrishna walked up to them, enquired affectionately about what they were talking about and then touched the young Vivekananda while he himself went into yogic trance. 'At the marvelous touch of the Master,' Vivekananda recalls, 'my mind underwent a complete revolution. I was aghast to realize that there really was nothing whatever in the entire universe but God. I remained silent, wondering how long this state of mind would continue. It didn't pass off all day. I got back home, and I felt just the same there; everything I saw was God.' [23]

Tantra as Perennial Spiritual Practice

That morning near Copenhagen, I experienced what mystics from all the worlds wisdom traditions have talked about for thousands of years: that reality is multi-layered – physical, mental and spiritual. The same sages have also taught that if you want to experience the celestial realms of the spiritual – the most subtle and incomprehensible of all states of reality – spiritual practice is of fundamental importance. It is not enough to read spiritual books, believe in God or Allah, or to listen to great lectures on various metaphysical subjects. Instead, the mystic sages of the past have demonstrated the importance of practice, of meditating, of closing our eyelids and awaken the spiritual eye of contemplation from within. We are urged to practice what they have preached.

Each of the three realms of reality is experienced on their own terms – by our senses, our mind and our spirit. In other words, while a scientist may extend his senses by employing a telescope to study celestial bodies, a mathematician will employ the rational mind to study the Pythagorean theorem, and a tantric mystic will use contemplative or meditative practice to experience the realm of spirituality. Each realm of reality can be experienced and verified, but in order to do so, different injunctions are used. To understand the spiritual realm, we employ the injunctions of spiritual science, not those of physical or mental science. Hence, in order to see and experience spirituality, we employ the spiritual injunction and practice meditation.

This simple yet profound insight is vital to the understanding of tantra as well as any other authentic wisdom tradition. If you want to know *that*, if you want to know the 'great mystery', if you want to merge in the cosmic bliss of Brahma, you must follow the injunction, take up that practice which is capable of transforming your mind to experience the transcendental reality of spirit, of cosmic consciousness. And once experienced, that which was once a great mystery is no longer a secret – it is no longer a fanciful dream or a belief; it is a reality, an authentic realization, a spiritual awakening.

The Perennial State of Reality

In any given twenty-four hour period of our lives, we journey through this so-called 'great chain of being', from gross body to crude mind to subtle mind to spiritual mind – we think and feel, we dream, and we enter deep dreamless sleep. But when we are in a meditative state, we experience all these three states of human reality while remaining conscious. Therefore, the state of spiritual bliss is also often referred to as a state of superconsciousness.

This mystical realization is at the heart of what German philosopher Gottfried Wilhelm von Leibniz termed *philosophia perennis* or perennial philosophy. English writer Aldous Huxley made this term famous in a book with that very title. The perennial philosophy affirms that we have devolved from a single source and that the process of spiritual development is completed and perfected when we return to that one source. In tantra, that one source is termed Brahma and we attempt our return to that source through sadhana, the practice of tantra meditation and yoga.

A few fundamental aspects of the perennial philosophy and tantra are:

- Brahma is both immanent and transcendent. That is, Brahma or consciousness exists both within and beyond the material world.

- Creation exists as a hierarchy of levels – as matter, mind, consciousness, as the five levels of mind, and so on. The higher levels transcend and include the lower levels.

- Creation also exists as a holarchy on each level. Each level of evolution is both a part and a whole. An atom is a whole in itself, but part of a larger atomic structure within a cell; a human cell is a whole, but part of an organ, and so on. All of creation's parts and wholes are embraced by the ultimate Omega Point, the all-pervasive Brahma.

- There is both devolution and evolution. Creation starts from Brahma, devolves through space to create the five fundamental factors – ether, air, fire, water and earth – to create matter. From matter life is created. Matter contains consciousness, since consciousness created the five elements and is therefore the fundamental basis of matter. Through the evolution of life, plants and animals are created, then humans and finally enlightened humans who eventually reunites with Brahma. This is the cycle of creation, of devolution and evolution.

- The human mind is composed of various levels of consciousness. When we reach the highest state of consciousness through meditation, we reunite with Brahma. This process of conscious evolution is the very goal of life.

So, according to the perennial philosophy of tantra, our purpose in life is to become more conscious, more aware. During the day, when we are awake, all the layers of mind – from crude to causal – are active. But we are generally only aware of our most basic levels of mind, because these are the states we normally use. Preoccupied with thinking and remembering, we often remain oblivious to the subtler layers of our mind – our spiritual nature. Similarly, in a state of dreamless sleep, although we are in touch with our deepest spiritual mind, we are not consciously aware of it.

Through the practice of tantra meditation, we can consciously access deeper states of our being. In profound states of meditation, we can even enter the causal mind, while still remaining conscious. In that super-conscious state, we experience a deep sense of peace, bliss and oneness. We are beyond ego, one with our true, inner self, one with Brahma or God.

Thus, in accordance with tantra, each human is composed of six layers of being. The first is the human body, the physical level. In addition, there are five states of mind, which contain the conscious, subconscious and unconscious levels of mind as well as the two causal levels of mind, or the purely spiritual states of mind.

Metaphorically speaking, the five states of the human mind are layered just like a banana flower. In tantra these five layers of mind are called *koshas*. Above these psychic and spiritual layers, above the koshas, there is the individual soul, the *jiivatman*, and above the jiivatman there is the *paramatman*, the cosmic soul. When the individual soul merges in the cosmic soul, one becomes one with God, one attains the spiritual state which I glimpsed under the cherry tree, which Vivekananda experienced for several days, and which the enlightened Buddhas and yogis experience as a permanent state of being. In that state of enlightenment one becomes god-like or goddess-like.

Similarly, in Buddhism, there are the eight *vijanas*, the eight levels of awareness. In Kabbalah one speaks of the *Ten Sefirots* and mystic Christians speak of matter, body, mind, soul and spirit. Although the various traditions describe these layers of reality somewhat differently, the point is that reality is multi-layered. Moreover, spirit or cosmic consciousness is inherently present at all stages. Thus the tantrics do not shun the physical realm as some religious mystics do, they embrace it. For in tantra the body is seen as a divine temple, the perfect abode from within which all humans can attain spiritual realization.

The seven chakras, or esoteric wheels of energy, located along the spine, are the controlling stations of our mental and spiritual expressions, our propensities. The first five chakras correspond to the five koshas, while the two highest chakras are above mind and refer to the state of the yogic soul. Chakras are thus yet another way in which tantra maps our multi-layered human experience in the spirit of perennial philosophy.

An important aspect of these layers of mind or realities is that the higher level transcends and includes the lower level. In other words, an enlightened being, whose mind is at ease in sublime states of spiritual awareness, can still see and feel the body, can still think rational thoughts, speak and smile. One is still human but, like Shiva or the Buddha, one has become a god or goddess in human form. Another way of describing this is that the two causal minds contain and are broader than the unconscious, subconscious and conscious levels of mind.

Each jivatman, each human soul, is thus composed of all these five layers of mind, and the aim of tantra yoga meditation is to unite the individual soul with the cosmic soul. This ecstatic union is called yoga. And this yogic trance or spiritual fusion of a person into the One, is the ultimate goal of tantric practice.

The Perennial State of Being

The morning of my ecstatic lucid dream and meditation, my friend introduced me to his fiancée, who lived a few houses down the street. She was a natural beauty, a tall blonde with long hair and a finely drawn face. Immediately upon receiving her pleasant welcome, I realized their relationship was not to last. I knew it as surely as I physically perceived my friend standing proudly beside me.

That whole day, I had been somewhat distracted by my sudden intuitive insights, and in the afternoon my intuitional vision was confirmed. While we had been out for a walk, his fiancée had slipped a letter under his door. She was in love with someone else. Tears streamed down my friend's face when he read the short letter. He held the letter with one hand and the returned engagement ring he had given her a few months earlier, in the other. He sobbed quietly and read the short letter again and again.

Metaphorically speaking, life is like a movie, and by that afternoon, my friend snapped out of being a character in his own movie. He realized it was unlikely his former girlfriend would ever have joined him on the spiritual path. He realized his strong interest in tantra yoga was the primary reason she left him. More importantly, he recognized he no longer needed to be attached to the hurt character she had dumped for someone else in the movie of his previous life.

To cultivate a tantric vision is to watch the movie of life without getting too attached to the characters on life's screen. We may watch and enjoy and be aware that all of life is a movie, and that deep within us there is a still, soulful and enlightened witness to that movie. The more we associate with that inner witness, that deep sense of awareness, the less we suffer. It does not mean that our problems disappear, but the more we grow spiritually, the less we cling to them, and the more we are able to tap into our own 'perennial state of being'.

This perennial state of being is, at its purest and highest, the direct realization of yogis, sages, mystics and saints. This realization, this way of being, is not a figment of someone's imagination, a delusion, a fantasy. This state of spiritual realization is not the prerogative of one spiritual path or one religion. It is available to all, and it is as real and pure and as palpable as water from a mountain spring.

St Teresa of Ávila described the universal nature of the mystic path by dividing it into four stages: In the first stage, there is a restless struggle to experience peace, devotion and concentration during meditation and prayer. Many people find this stage to be difficult and frustrating and thus give up spiritual practice altogether. In the second phase, one is often able to draw water from the deep well of spiritual bliss. But even then, one is unable to fully grasp or attain these deeper states for prolonged periods of time. In the third state, one feels nearly always close to God, to the non-dual union with the divine. In the fourth stage, the soul enjoys the ecstatic bliss of god-realization, of complete surrender to the grace of divine revelation, at all times.

That fourth state is what all of us on the spiritual path seek and, when finally attained, embrace and become. For most of us, this state appears in glimpses, deep in meditation, in dreams, or in spontaneous raptures and insights. The more frequent these insights occur, however, the more spiritual water we are able to draw from this perennial wellspring of inspiration, and the more fulfilling our lives become. The more we experience these blissful and detached states of mind, the more we seek inspiration and wisdom from the truly enlightened ones – from those who embody spirituality as a permanent state of divinity, the enduring state of oneness with all. [24]

Through the immense scope of these levels of mind, or spectrum of consciousness, the human mind is finally enveloped in pure spirit and is able to realize oneness with the divine. Although each tradition explains these layers somewhat differently, it is a natural and universal process of gradual unfolding and eventual awakening. As British stage director John Caird said so beautifully in his book *An Introduction to the Philosophy of Religion*, we 'appropriate that infinite inheritance of which we are already in possession'. But, perhaps none could have expressed this simple yet advanced process better than the poet and artist William Blake: 'If the doors of perception were cleansed, man would see things as they really are – infinite.'

Anandamurti notes that the yogis who experience this cosmic state of mind have cleansed their perception by converting the mind into a mirror, every level of mind, every kosha, has become 'transparent and crystalline ...' He furthermore states that 'through the medium of kosha-wise [meditation] ... the fuller [the spiritual practitioner's] entire entity will become with divine radiance, with divine bliss'. [25] The universal aspect of this process is illustrated by the writings of many mystics and saints from various traditions. In the words of the Christian mystic St John of the Cross: 'A soul makes room for God by wiping away all the smudges and smears of creatures, by uniting its will perfectly to God's ... When this is done the soul will be illumined by and transformed in God. And God will so communicate his supernatural being to the soul that it will appear to be God himself and will possess what God himself possesses.'

The Western Christian medieval mystic, Jakob Böhme, explained his own spiritual awakening in terms that are similar to the tantric kundalini experience: 'For the Holy Ghost ... rises up like a lightening flash .... The Holy Spirit rises up, in the seven unfolding fountain spirits, into the brain, like the dawning of the day ...' In the East, the tantric sage Ramakrishna attests to the universal experience of kundalini arousal. 'A man's spiritual consciousness is not awakened unless his kundalini is aroused'. And since the time the 'thousand-petal lotus in the head blossomed,' Ramakrishna explained, 'I have been in this state.' [26]

Clearly, the tantric and Christian mystics echo each other's description of the contemplative climb through the higher koshas *and* chakras. Both traditions also agree that spiritual awakening culminates in the ultimate union between the individual and the cosmic soul. For some sages, such as Ramakrishna, the state of enlightenment becomes a more or less permanent state of being.

Tantra and Perennial Philosophy

The profound philosophical and practical beauty of tantra is its embrace of the duality of existence. In tantric philosophy, Shiva and Shakti, are united in the non-dual Brahma. For the tantric yogi this is actualized by the realization that all of reality is nothing but Brahma, nothing but god. The leaf on the cherry tree, in other words, is both matter and spirit, both physical form and formless consciousness. All of existence is one. But when our consciousness remains in the lower koshas, we are not able to experience it.

One of the fundamental aspects of the perennial philosophy is that cosmic consciousness exists both as permanent and other-worldly essence as well as immanent and physical presence. This paradoxical truth means that god is not only the cause of creation but that god also is, in the most real sense, the very substance of creation. God is both in the earth and in heaven.

God is you, the reader, and this book, as well. Indeed, god's spirit is the ever-present and most subtle essence of each manifest form, whether animate or inanimate, whether in the relative appearance of a stone, a plant, an animal, a human, the sky, or the stars. Thus, there is nothing whatsoever which is not soaked in spirit, which is not filled to the brim with the subtle elixir of cosmic consciousness. Why? Because, cosmic consciousness is simply all there is. Cosmic consciousness is the highest goal and the very base of being. The whole of creation is the one turning itself into many while always essentially remaining the one.

The tantric worldview is thus truly holistic. For tantra, the material and the spiritual are but two different expressions of the same source, the cosmic consciousness, or Brahma. In tantra there are none of the trappings of dualism so common in various religions, whose dogmas often have exclusively focused on the celebration of either earth or of heaven. In these religions the focus has often been on praying and sacrificing for the mercy of the goddess or the stern dictates of the god. Both of these worldviews have caused humanity unspeakable suffering as human sacrifices have been made and wars fought to increase the fertility of the Goddess of Earth or to appease the wrath of God in Heaven. But throughout the ages, mystics of all major religions have avoided to be snared by the dualism of their faiths, of their respective religions' descending or ascending worldviews. Instead, they have sought to find integration and ultimate peace in the non-dual state of mystic union where god and goddess, Shiva and Shakti, merge as one truth. In other words, for tantra, god and goddess are one. For tantrics, every mundane act is seen as an expression of godhood, every act becomes an act of service to the divine. This sublimely all-embracing approach to life is the essence of tantra.

The Perennial Spirit of Mysticism

The tantric teachings in the various wisdom traditions all point towards the same revolutionary yet simple fact – we need a practice, a vehicle to bring us to the spiritual state of being beyond form, to the spiritual vista beyond the manifest world of the many. For, there is a fundamental difference between the belief systems and faiths of religion and the practice of spirituality. While religious doctrines inspire us to think and believe, the spiritual path of tantra teaches us what to do and ultimately what to become. On the spiritual path of tantra there is some philosophy and there are guiding precepts, but tantra is mostly based on experiences and insights, not on belief systems or dogmatic doctrines. Tantra, like all perennial wisdom paths, is therefore not a religious belief system, it is a spiritual art and science, a practical path of self-transformation and god-realization.

Therefore, writes Anandamurti, every spiritual practice 'that aims at the attainment of the Supreme, irrespective of its religious affiliation, is definitely tantra; for tantra is not a religion, tantra is simply the science of sadhana – it is a principle'. [27] While tantra has its own specific history and practices, the path of spirituality in general – whether it is the systematic and personal effort to attain yogic samadhi, Zen Buddhist kenzo, or Christian mystic union with God – has in essence the same goal. That goal is to realize the link between the finite and the infinite reality, and the practice to realize that goal is also commonly referred to as the path of mysticism.

This does not mean, however, that religious doctrines are necessarily tantric. One must distinguish between the religious, contemplative mysticism of someone like St Teresa of Ávila, which is transrational and revolutionary, and the religious doctrines of the church, which can sometimes be quite irrational and conservative.

Therefore, all the mystical paths can be considered tantric in spirit. Furthermore, the world's contemplative traditions, whether tantric, Taoist, Christian, Sufi, or Buddhist in orientation, reflect the inner essence of the perennial philosophy.

In Lex Hixon's classic book *Coming Home: The Experience of Enlightenment in Sacred Traditions*, a book about the experience of enlightenment in various wisdom traditions, the sage Plotinus (205–270 CE) is described as having realized that the 'One is not a philosophical category but a spiritual reality.' Plotinus had also realized, writes Hixon, that this state is 'the intrinsic nature of all beings and all planes of Being'. [28] These realizations, that spirituality is an experience and not a belief system, and that this experience is available to all, is the very essence of tantra and all perennial traditions and philosophies.

Tantric Wisdom and the Great Chain of Being

My experiences that pivotal night, morning and day exemplify the insight of tantra as well as other, genuine mystical paths: Reality, as Huston Smith says, is a 'Great Chain of Being'. In successive and all-embracing stages, this great chain of being reveals life in both its transcendent and immanent beauty, reveals the whole of reality as both spirit and matter; both Brahma and the world; both the infinite and the finite; both cosmic consciousness and ordinary consciousness. The great yogis and mystics of the present and the past are soaked in this transparent, superconscious awareness, not just in short glimpses, but day in and day out.

In perennial philosophy the great chain of being is expressed both on the microcosmic and macrocosmic level. In tantra, the microcosmic chain of being is manifested by the various koshas or levels of mind while the macrocosmic chain of being in tantra is called the 'Brahmachakra', the cycle of creation.

During a morning lecture at that pivotal retreat I attended in Sweden years ago, the Indian monk drew a large circle on a blackboard. He explained that this circle symbolized macrocosmic reality from the point where Brahma, with the aid of Shiva and Shakti, creates the three elemental forces of the universe – the *gunas* – the three levels of cosmic mind, the five elements of ether, air, fire, water and earth, and thus matter. From matter, life is created from plants to animals to humans. Then he taught us how each human being is composed of a small chain of being, the koshas, and that through the practice of tantra meditation one can unite one's individual soul with the cosmic consciousness and thus complete the journey through the Brahmachakra, the cosmic journey from one to the world of many, and from the world of many back to the one.

In this cycle of creation, all the levels of reality are infused with spirit, with cosmic consciousness, with Brahma. There is no place along this circle of creation where Brahma does not exist. Cosmic consciousness is the one and only essence of all the levels. Only the forms are varied, because cosmic consciousness is both the ground and depth of all animate beings and inanimate things through all of creation. Thus, from a spiritual point of view, when we speak of the body or the material realm, we include consciousness, because according to tantric philosophy, the world is also consciousness. Even inanimate rocks and crystals are made up of this subtle essence. Indeed, matter is nothing but 'bottles of energy' and energy is nothing but cosmic consciousness.

But why don't we always experience the world this way? Why don't we see the world as I saw that cherry blossom that morning in my friend's garden? Because we see the relative world around us mostly through the sensory perception of the eye of flesh and the rational logic of the eye of mind, not through the meditative state of the eye of spirit. If we did, the whole world would be permeated by cosmic consciousness all the time. We would always experience the ecstatic state of non-dualism, the essential nature of pure consciousness, which is nothing but God, Brahma or Tao. It was indeed that exalted state which I was graced by in my dream, and later glimpsed in its immanent expression as a cherry branch of pure formless form, as spirit in matter, as Brahma in the world.

As was my experience in meditation that night and morning, the great chain of being for us as individuals is realized as an increase in feelings of unity and higher awareness, from an identity with the body to an identity of the mind to the feeling of unity with spirit, and finally a literal embrace of all manifestation as spirit, as God.

The Personal and Social Implications of Tantric Spirituality

The great, God-intoxicated tantric sage Ramakrishna, whom Lex Hixon aptly called 'an Einstein of the planetary civilization of the near future', [29] describes tantric non-dualism as follows:

'Supreme Reality alone exists as [Shiva], the Pure Consciousness within and beyond all finite forms of consciousness, and as Shakti, the primordial, evolutionary Divine Energy. They are not two ...

when contemplating the wetness of water one inevitably thinks of the water itself. Precisely the same is true of the Absolute and the relative, which are indifferentiable in essence. The absolute is inevitably expressed by the relative, and the relative is inevitably contained by the Absolute.' [30]

Spirituality, as opposed to religious dogma or belief, is the great unifying link in the great chain of being. Because the highest expression of spirituality is anchored in pure, non-dual consciousness, and is indifferentiable, it also embraces and appreciates differentiation, the various states of manifest reality. That is, spiritual realization does not preclude an awareness of the intellectual or rational realm; rather it simply puts it in its right, relative perspective.

Ramakrishna once illustrated how such an 'integrated differentiation' is expressed on a personal level. One of his dear friends, Krishnakishore, was a radical Vedantist (a follower of Vedanta, the path of non-dualism), constantly on fire with the most intense spiritual insights. 'I am the principle of empty space, within which and by which all phenomena transparently manifest,' he once told Ramakrishna. This great yogi was not a sage in a Himalayan cave; he was a devout family man engaged in all the social responsibilities of daily life. Ramakrishna thus informs us that Krishnakishore was a rare human being, a man comfortably attuned to the mundane and spiritual worlds of reality – the infinite and the finite, the cosmic and the worldly. [31]

Let us imagine, for a moment, that Krishnakishore's 'state of mind' has become the attitude of thousands, inspiring a new global worldview. May be we then can begin to perceive the extensive social ramifications of the inner, spiritual quest and envision the contours of a new, spirit-centered civilization. What we will begin to realize, I think, is that a spiritual society does not have to regress into an isolated commune of navel-gazing cave-dwellers, nor does it have to neglect the objective and material world. Rather, society can blossom into a well-balanced community of people where material development, human rights, environmental protection, and spiritual values are incorporated. In short, a society that can both differentiate as well as integrate the various levels of existence – from the most mundane to the most sublime. This circular, or holistic understanding, which, when embraced fully, will foster a universal worldview that is more whole and sublime than even the total sum of its many parts. This, then, is the circular worldview and spiritual insight of tantra, and of all genuine mystical traditions.

The Dalai Lama says unequivocally that 'our very purpose in life is to seek happiness.'[32] But what is true happiness? Where can it be found? According to Buddhism and all the other wisdom traditions, the ultimate state of happiness is 'a state of mind or being'. And this ultimate state of being can first and foremost be realized through spiritual means – through love, compassion, selfless service and ultimately through spiritual enlightenment.

If spiritual emancipation indeed is the decisive state of fulfilment and the transcendent glory of human life, then the goal of society should be to foster an environment in which this spiritual happiness can be achieved. This simple, unmistakable notion is one of the primary imperatives of this book.

Tantra and Various Schools of Indian Philosophy

The non-dual state of Brahma, as experienced in deep meditation by sages of all perennial wisdom traditions, is essentially the same. Yet when these sages try to explain this transrational state of mind, they invariably give that one invisible reality different names. More importantly, they also formulate various schools of philosophy that differ to some degree or other. Certain aspects of perennial wisdom are emphasized by some schools, while neglected or modified by others. When interpreted by less enlightened followers, further changes take place.

Therefore, the conceptual interpretation of the non-conceptual state of spirituality is, in many ways, as important as the experience itself. Because it is this verbal and written elucidation that formulates the philosophies and worldviews on which many of our ethical and social behaviours are based. In other words, how the enlightened masters choose to explain their experiences effects the way we feel, think and relate to the world around us.

The spiritual goal of Buddhism and tantra is the same – enlightenment. But while Buddhism emphasizes that the reason to seek enlightenment is to end suffering, tantra's emphasis is that the purpose of our spiritual search is to experience divine bliss or happiness. While both advaita vedanta and tantra believe that non-dual Brahma is absolute truth, advaita vedanta point out that the world is an illusion, while tantra emphasizes that the world is real and thus relative truth.

If we compare, for example, the poised description of Shiva and Shakti in tantra to the notable Samkyha philosphy – propounded by Maharishi Kapila some 3,500 years ago, and also a tantric inspired philosophy – we will notice that Kapila put more emphasis on Shakti. He argued that Shakti is not only more important than Shiva, but that she is an independent force altogether. It should be mentioned here that both in tantra and Samkhya, Shiva is often termed *purusha* (cognitive principle) and Shakti is termed *prakrti* (operative principle). In Samkhya, however, the main emphasis is on the role of Shakti, as Shiva is seen as inherently dormant.

In advaita vedanta, on the other hand, which was advanced by the brilliant scholar and tantric mystic Shankaracharya in the eighth-century, the world of creation is simply the deceptive camouflage or illusion of maya. To the doctrine of vedanta, there is only Brahma. As Georg Feuerstein maintains, to the vedantic 'the world is a phantom produced by the unenlightened mind. When the root ignorance is removed, the world reveals itself in its true nature, which is none other than the universal singular [Brahma].' Feuerstein continues: 'What is implied in this concept is, among other things, the idea that the transition from the One to the Many is not genuine emanation but only an apparent evolution (vivarta).' [33]

Although the great Shankaracharya was a tantric practitioner, and thus a person with detailed perennial knowledge of the various levels of mind, his philosophy differed from tantra in that he preached the idealist doctrine that '*Brahma satyam, jagat mithya*', which means Brahma is truth, this world is false. This idealist doctrine is thus based on Absolute truth only, that Brahma alone is real. Shankaracharya's understanding was that due to false perception or *adhyasa*, we experience this illusory world as real, as if seeing a snake instead of a rope. For him ideas alone were the real truth, hence his followers denied the world in order to seek Brahma. This doctrine – which, due to Shankaracharya's fame as a brilliant logician and spiritual master, eventually defeated the Buddhist influence in India – has been prominent in Hindu thought for the past 1,200 years or so. (Unfortunately, Shankaracharya did not speak out against the caste system, thus India has continued to suffer from this social plague until today.)

In contrast, the materialist doctrine of the Cārvāka philosophy, which is a kind of religious dogma itself, claimed that 'God is false and this world alone is real' or *Brahma mithya, jagat satya*'. The Indian Cārvāka philosophy, which precedes its twin-soul, Marxism by more than two millennia, was basically the world's first materialist or 'flatland' philosophy. According to this doctrine, mind evolves from matter while tantra believes that cosmic consciousness creates matter and then mind evolves from the material realm.

Neither Cārvāka nor Marxism consider the existence of individual soul (jivatman) or supreme consciousness (Paramatman) to be real, because to a materialist only the perception of the eye of flesh and the eye of mind are real.

Seen through the eye of spirit or the perennial philosophy, on the other hand, it is materialism which is limited, even superstitious and irrational. Seen in this light, writes Ken Wilber, Marxism can be considered 'the first truly great modern religion – that is, a religion that tried to make scientific materialism, gross-realm naturalism, and flatland holism into an emancipatory God.' [34] Consequently, the worldviews that are solely based on the study of the material dance of atoms and molecules, the interactive relations of natural organisms, or simply the breathtaking beauty of nature, cannot be considered perennial philosophies. For, on the ladder of perennial being – from matter to mind to spirit – these concepts will forever remain on the lowest rung.

On the other hand, the social implications of a perennial philosophy in which the relative world we live in is seen as a mere illusion has also negative consequences. Thus, the great insight of tantra is its emphasis on maintaining a dynamic balance between the relative or dualistic reality of the objective world and the absolute or non-dual reality of the spiritual world. For tantra there is a dynamic and real interrelationship between spirit and matter, between that world and this world.

Non-dualism: The Tantric Embrace

Tantra explicitly proclaims that this world is neither just ordinary matter nor an illusion. This physical world, as perceived through our sensory organs, is considered the relative truth. It is relative truth because it always undergoes the change of birth, growth and death. Nothing, not even geological structures, are immune to the ravages of time in this relative world. Therefore, only Brahma – the supreme consciousness which eternally resides within and beyond all forms – is infinite and absolute.

The eternal and omnipresent Brahma thus exists in two states simultaneously: one state which can only be perceived by the eye of spirit; the other can be perceived both by the eye of flesh and the eye of mind. The first state is an absolutely transcendent state, which we can only experience in deep meditation. This otherworldly state is not 'qualified' or affected in any way by the operative principle (Shakti). In tantric terminology this state is called *Nirguna Brahma*, the state of 'non-qualified consciousness'. The second state is termed *Saguna Brahma*, a state of 'qualified consciousness'. This second state, then, is the world we daily engage in with our bodies and minds – the world of mind and matter.

What we term matter, then, is nothing but a condensed state of Brahma. It is not crude matter as such, the cherry branch is not just plain wood and sap, it is wood and sap in the form of metamorphosed cosmic consciousness.

Although both Nirguna and Saguna Brahma appear to be fundamentally different, both states are intrinsically made of the same substance, namely Brahma.

The above ideas have been beautifully summarized in this ancient, simple yet unmistakable, aphorism: 'There is nothing that is not Divine ... to know all as illusion is ignorance, to know all as God is knowledge.' Such is the true essence and beauty of the non-dual tantric awareness. Such is the unsurpassed spiritual nature of perennial philosophy.

In a language more prosaic but no less profound, Anandamurti describes how the non-dual approach of tantra implies an adherence to a principle he terms 'subjective approach (spiritual) through objective adjustment (social)'. It is crucial, he writes, to observe this kind of 'yoga in all three spheres of life'. [35] Anandamurti also termed this vision 'non-dualistic dualistic non-dualism', emphasizing that there is both an ultimate, non-dual reality (Brahma) and a relative and dualistic reality (the physical and mental realms). When an enlightened human being achieves oneness with non-dual Brahma, the three levels of the cycle of evolution – non-dualism, dualism and again returning to non-dualism – has been completed.

This tantric insight, that it is of crucial importance to balance spiritual wisdom with the mundane reality of the world, is an essential truism to follow in today's materialistic and imbalanced world. For, tantra does not encourage escape from an illusory world nor refuge in material enjoyments only. Rather, tantra's emphasis is to create a harmonious relationship between the spiritual and material world.

Sustainable Body, Sustainable Spirit

Tantra seeks to avoid the trappings of past non-dualist teachers, those who inspired an avoidance of social, economic and political development by proclaiming that the world was an illusion, or maya. Through spiritual vision and perennial wisdom, tantrics aspire to maintain balance between body, mind and spirit – between the physical, mental and spiritual spheres of existence. For the physical world is nothing but a psychic projection or expression of the Creator. The whole world and all our actions are, in essence, the thought-waves within the psychic mind of the Creator. Nothing remains outside this cosmic mind. And, if we act in accordance with this understanding, we may better be able to maintain harmony between heaven and earth – between animals, plants and people, between spiritual, social and economic development. For, we cannot develop a truly sustainable society without sustainable spirituality.

This then is the essential goal of tantra: to perceive the all-embracing, transcendental union of the physical, mental and spiritual worlds. In social terms this means that the integration of spirit and society will arise when both are actualized as coexisting parts of reality. The main goal of society is thus to foster an environment in which the state of non-dual, dualistic, non-dualism can be realized and expressed. Such a society would strive to achieve a harmonious union between the three worlds of existence, an integrated balance of body, mind and spirit: A society that lives and breathes in harmony with the universal flow of our planet's perennial wisdom.

The Eternal Embrace

The central claim of the perennial philosophy is that Brahma or God exists as an all-pervading consciousness in and beyond all animate and inanimate things, and that all humans, through a combination of physical, mental and transcendental practices can climb up the hierarchy of existence and become one with this all-pervading consciousness. Apart from this central claim, there are, as we have seen above, subtle but important differences in how the various wisdom traditions describe the distinct spiritual and ontological aspects of the great chain of being. Some emphasize the ascending path towards god, whereas others, such as tantra, seek to strike a balance between the ascending and descending path – between the wisdom of the absolute (spirit) and knowledge of the relative (body and mind).

What is absolute knowledge and how can it be perceived? Anandamurti explains that absolute knowledge is called *apta vakya* in Sanskrit. Since this kind of knowledge is received directly from the cosmic mind, this purely spiritual knowledge is true and beneficial for all people in all ages and in all countries. Relative knowledge, on the other hand, is called *prapta vakya* and is received either through sensory perception, inference, or through an authoritative source. This knowledge may or may not be correct or in harmony with absolute knowledge, and it is relative because it is subject to change. What physicists know about subatomic particles today may be obsolete tomorrow. What empirical science knows about certain chemical effects on humans today may be archaic tomorrow. How electricity is used today may radically change in the near future, and so on.

The vedas explain the state of the absolute this way: 'The supreme self lies hidden within each and every object. It is impossible for the crude organs to see or understand this deeply hidden entity'. One can only perceive the eternal nature of supreme consciousness if one's mind is cleansed through meditation and becomes a mirror in which the supreme effulgence of consciousness can be reflected. This spiritual perception is beyond the comprehension of the senses and of the rational mind. To realize the all-encompassing subtle principle of Brahma, to see with the eye of spirit – we must therefore employ contemplative introspection in accordance with techniques taught by the spiritual masters of absolute knowledge. Similarly, to perceive an electron – the eye of flesh, in the form of optic nerves, is too limited – the aid of an electron microscope is needed. Furthermore, the electricity flowing through our electrical cords cannot be seen but only inferred with the eye of mind. Each level of reality or truth, whether relative or absolute, is perceived with different means and through a distinct process.

For clarity and distinction, let us term the perennial wisdom absolute wisdom and the other relative knowledge. Striking a balance between them allows for a broader scope of knowing, feeling and processing that goes far beyond the limited scope of rationality that so far has been employed by the Western enlightenment. Within this framework, the priorities undergo a radical shift. They move from the relative towards the absolute. Thus the source of absolute wisdom – the spiritual reality – informs and governs all other arenas of human life. This new perspective generates a synthetic or transrational outlook, or what we may call a 'spiritual vision'. This spiritual vision, if it is truly holistic, will include both the absolute and the relative aspects of reality. This cosmic union of Shiva and

Shakti is the eternal embrace of existence, all at once and at all times. Forever united as the infinite and singular Brahma.

Self and Society

According to the perennial wisdom of the tantric worldview, the individual does not seek to avoid or escape the relative world – neither from the individual body/mind, nor from the collective body/mind of society. Rather, the relative – the personal and social body – seen as the place where harmony with absolute spirit is sought continuously. The tantric goal is thus to ensure that there is as little conflict between the relative and the absolute worlds as possible. For a tantric, to neglect both the well-being of self and society is to live in delusion.

From a human point-of-view, as seen from within the relative body/mind of reality, the world is not illusory. It is indeed real. The problems within it are also real. Solutions are thus sought through practical means, not explained away by fatalism or sought to be cured through wishful myths. Illness or poverty is no longer timidly accepted as a curse from god or simply a result of bad karma. Cancer is real. Hunger is real. Distressing conditions such as these must be altered through both personal and social change. Moreover, physical fitness and mental health are not seen as narcissistic attachments, as a fit body and balanced mind makes it easier to both transcend and enjoy the relative world. Pollution becomes real and its harmful presence in the environment may be countered through a combination of lifestyle change and social activism. In the spirit of tantra, the problems of others, of society, are our own. This realization empowers us to help implement social change. Tantra thus affirms that both individuals and society must work together and serve together to overcome the physical, mental and spiritual obstacles that arise on the path of evolution towards spiritual emancipation.

All of us are part of evolution's ongoing and unending variations as they arise as both new possibilities and new obstacles. Since Brahma is an infinite and eternal ocean of which individuals and society are but many waves, spiritual people do not live outside of society but reside deeply and actively within it. And while living, we form relations with everything around us. We are responsible for sustaining the whole by serving the parts.

This relationship of service to others is our sacred link with our environment – with nature, people and god. Through our service to the world, we preserve our spiritual connection to the whole, to the perennial flow of the great chain of being. More importantly, acting from a state of loving kindness, we still remain happy. In the midst of trying circumstances, we remain true to our goal in life, which, as the Dalai Lama said, is to seek happiness.

The Perennial Path of Body, Mind and Spirit

According to tantra and perennial philosophy, microcosm is a reflection of macrocosm. All individual atoms, cells, plants, animals and human beings are a reflection of the greater cosmos.

The human body refers to the physical body of blood, bones, muscles, nerves, senses, etc., and all their interrelated functions. This physical body is the vessel in which the mind and spirit rests and functions. Some religious doctrines refer to the body as sinful and wretched, but the perennial wisdom of tantra views it as sacred, a temple where mind can dwell and transcend into spirit. The body is the abode of the soul, or the atman. Here 'the drop' of the individual soul can become one with 'the ocean' of cosmic soul, or Paramatman. A healthy and vibrant physical body is therefore of utmost importance on the perennial path of spirituality.

In tantra, the body is viewed as the 'seat' in which an individual can realize a spiritual bond with the mystery of life. The origin of this concept is a direct outcome of tantra's interconnected worldview in which the whole spectrum of reality – from body, mind to spirit – are seen as an integral realm in which everything is undeniably real. And if the larger body world of creation is real, the individual physical body is of course also real, indeed it is divine. It is divine because the body is the manifestation of the divine Shakti, the cosmic operative principle responsible for creating the world perceived and enjoyed by the eye of flesh. The human body is a precious gift and a result of the spirit's evolutionary journey to complete the cycle of creation. In the human body, spirit, in the form of Shakti, has created a structure that is refined, complex, and strong enough to experience the full expression of Spirit's effulgence.

In the *Kularnava Tantra*, it is said that the human body is difficult to obtain and should be seen as a 'ladder' to climb towards spiritual enlightenment. And, since this body is not infinite and eternal, because it suffers from disease and the frailties of old age, it is recommended to begin the spiritual path as early as possible. When old age or sickness arrives, the mind is thus better prepared to transcend the limitations of the body.

Our Perennial Thirst for Happiness

The human thirst for wisdom and knowledge is infinite. The great Mughal Emperor Aurangzeb, studied many philosophical and religious scriptures, but on his deathbed he had to admit: 'I have learnt so much, and still I do not have the answers to my questions: "Where did I come from? Where am I going? Why have I lived on this earth?"' The answers to these questions are found in the perennial philosophies. Or, more correctly, the answers are realized when the spiritual aspirant reaches the goal of the perennial path.

While the perennial wisdom teaches us that there is a perfect state of supreme consciousness, which is both the cause and essence of creation, the perennial practice of yoga and tantric meditation is about becoming illumined by and becoming one with that universal radiance. This, indeed, is the core concept of all the wisdom paths: to become the blessed one, to realize our awakened self, the Buddha, the Shiva, of our own being. The goal of the perennial practice is to embody the perennial wisdom as naturally as we dwell in our own physical beings, as naturally as an infant's smile, as naturally as a soft breeze pregnant with the fragrance of roses. As the sufis say, the goal of life is to become *al-insān al-kāmil*, the universal human. This inner state of the universal human being, whose mind has become exalted by the spiritual state of non-dualism, is beautifully expressed in these two lines by Rumi:

'The drop becomes the ocean
But the ocean also becomes the drop.' [36]

When the drop becomes the ocean, the individual human mind has received the spiritual life's final award, the golden crown of universal humanness. And when the ocean becomes the drop, the individual has reached the ultimate spiritual state of enlightened permanence. There is no longer any separation between the mind and Brahma, yet one is still an individual, still going about life as if nothing has changed. The Buddha-mind still has to feed the body! Hence, one is simultaneously both the drop of humanness and the ocean of enlightenment. Such is the attainment of yoga, or union. One has reached infinite bliss. And by that achievement, all questions have been answered. All inner thirst has been quenched.

Indeed, the goal of the perennial path of tantra is to quench our limitless thirst for happiness. By quenching our spiritual thirst, we can truly find the spiritual blessedness which the Dalai Lama says is the very purpose of our life.

Creating a Tantric Lifestyle

Tantric Philosophy: *Tasmadharma Sadakarya* – Let all your actions be guided by Dharma.

Daily Contemplation: Think of God or Brahma every time you act. Feel that everything you touch, eat and see is Brahma. Feel that everyone you speak to is Brahma. Ideate on Brahma and you will gradually become Brahma.

Daily Acts of Sacredness: Start by thinking that all the food you eat is Brahma.

One: Live in this world like the lotus flower, which grows in muck and filth but whose flowers are always white.

***Two*:** Continue by thinking and feeling that every time you speak to someone, you are actually speaking to Brahma. Continue to find more and more opportunities to feel Brahma everywhere.

Chapter Six

Dance of Macrocosm:
The Cosmology of Tantra

I was standing with my grandfather on the porch on a cold December night, when I was six. We were looking up at the bright stars. 'The universe is so big,' he said. 'In fact, it is so huge that some think it has no end.' I felt very small, but with the help of my grandfather's carefully chosen words, something magical happened. He helped me realize that these celestial bodies were more than just 'decorative lights' in an enormous, black, heavenly ceiling. The darkness, I suddenly realized, was the space of the universe, and the stars and the earth – including my grandfather and myself – were floating in that seemingly endless space.

That day, when my grandfather's long, thin index finger parted the dark surface above me, was the beginning of my realization that humans, as the saying goes, cannot live by bread alone. I gradually realized that we humans are inherently spiritual. Therefore, we ask the deep questions: What is the purpose of life? Who are we? Where do we come from? These are life's perennial questions, and finding an answer to them is part of being human.

A few of those answers I found in the Biblical stories my grandfather taught me as a child. But when I became a teenager, the Bible was – to paraphrase mythologist Joseph Campbell – no longer able to provide me with a cosmology to live by. I wanted a worldview that satisfied both my intellectual curiosity and my sense of awe and wonder. Like the famous German poet, Johann Wolfgang von Goethe, I had understood that those who cannot draw on thousands of years from the well of perennial wisdom indeed are living from hand to mouth. But I did not know where to look for answers beyond the secular vision of my parents and the religious beliefs of my grandparents. Indeed, I did not know that it was possible to reconcile rationality with mysticism at all. Not until I encountered the wisdom teachings of India.

Hence, my dual thirst for both truth and meaning was not quenched until I plunged into the non-dual waters of tantra. And, curiously, it was a simple circle drawn by the Indian monk on a blackboard at my first spiritual retreat that did it. The circle, he said, was called Brahmachakra – literally the cycle of Brahma – and, as I learnt, it provides, in all its logic, mystery and splendour, a detailed metaphor for how the universe was created.

It is not accidental that the tantric universe is symbolized by a circle. For, as philosopher Jan Smuts reminds us, all of nature is an interlacing network of wholes – wholes within wholes, and the largest whole is the infinite universe itself. Smuts also reminds us that this cosmic whole is not a static place; it is infinitely dynamic and creative. Moreover, this infinitely creative universe unfolds in time as a process creating evermore expansive, inclusive and organized wholes. This cosmic process as it evolves in time is what scientists call evolution. Thus the tantric circle, the tantric whole called Brahmachakra, is nothing but a symbol of the circle of cosmic and natural evolution. Yes, nothing but a symbol. It is important to remember that this map you are about to learn is simply a map, not the territory of the cosmos or cosmic consciousness itself. Similarly, it is also important to remember that maps are important. We need them to remind us where we are, and to show us where we are going.

Myth, Mysticism and Science

As mentioned earlier, the vedic worldview was to a great extent mythic and religious. The early vedic people believed it was important to appease the wrath of the mythic gods though animal sacrifices and fire rituals. The vedic people also believed in the irrational caste system – that people were unequal, that some were slaves and others were masters.

The tantric worldview of Shiva, on the other hand, represented perhaps the first rational or dharmic worldview in human history.

Shiva's tantra did not support the caste system, nor did it believe that life would improve if a horse or a goat was sacrificed. Instead, Shiva tantra was based on self-realization and mysticism, on the practice of realizing Brahma from within through the practice of meditation and yoga.

Throughout history there have often been great differences between the mythic worldview of religion and science. But since mysticism and science are both experiential and evidential – these two worldviews are much more complementary than science and religion, since religion is mainly based on belief rather than experience. While the tantric concept of Shakti as intelligent creator of the universe has not been verified by reductionist science, there are many scientists today who also claim that intelligent design is an integral part of evolution. While most scientists believe that mind was created from matter, tantra concurs, while adding that matter in turn was created by the cosmic intelligence of Shakti. Thus the mystical worldview of tantra complements rather than opposes our rational or scientific understanding of life and the universe.

The Universe as Design

For materialist scientists the universe has been created by chance. Yes, by accident! With their powerful telescopes, traditional scientists have been able to go back to the beginning of the known universe, back to the Big Bang twelve billion years ago, but when they explain how the Big Bang happened, how life was created, how you and I exist, they are literally at a loss. All they can come up with is that the universe was created by chance.

Some scientists, however, including Sir Fred Hoyle and F. B. Salisbury, have shown that one cannot even produce a single enzyme by chance in twelve billion years. In other words, they claim, something other than chance and random events are behind the creation of the universe we live in.

Tantric yogis have observed that the universe is created by a conscious intelligence. This cosmic intelligence is infinitely resourceful and infinitely creative. Thus, according to the yogis, the universe has always existed and will always continue to exist. It is indeed infinite.

The language of tantric cosmology is philosophical and metaphysical, and its methodology is 'intuitional science'. The tantric cosmology has been developed by omniscient sages for thousands of years and contains some of the most basic answers to our perennial questions. While many of the practices of tantra have remained the same since Shiva's time, its philosophy and cosmology has undergone some changes, and, I believe, the most sophisticated tantric cosmology is today expressed in the Brahmachakra, or what we could call the cosmic cycle of creation, as developed by Anandamûrti. The Brahmachakra builds on Samkhya, Kashmir Shaivism and Patanjali's Yoga Sutras, but also makes these philosophies more aligned with evolutionary theory and modern cosmology. The beauty of the Brahmachakra lies in its representation of a perennial view of the world. Its wisdom resonates with all the world's wisdom teachings, while being perhaps the most detailed and 'contemporary' of any ancient cosmology.

The Brahmachakra expresses a holistic or spiritual view of the universe. This does not mean, however, that the Brahmachakra explains everything there is to know about creation, life, death and the meaning of life. But unlike many religious creation stories, the Brahmachakra does not oppose science or logic; rather it often complements science and adds a spiritual perspective to our understanding of the natural order of the universe.

The Brahmachakra teaches us that we exist in a living, breathing, thinking cosmos guided by a supreme intelligence. Some call it god, others call it goddess, and yet others call it great spirit. In tantra this cosmic intelligence is termed Brahma, and it has two aspects, two qualities: one is Shiva or cosmic consciousness, the other is Shakti or cosmic creative principle. According to the tantric cosmology, the fundamental stuff of existence is Shiva, and all things in existence are just different manifestations or modifications of that. The force which modifies Shiva is Shakti. She is therefore the Goddess of Creation.

Shiva and Shakti are unmanifest potentials. They are the primal seeds of consciousness and creation. Most importantly, they are not separate from creation, residing in some heavenly abode, but rather intimately and inherently part of the cycle of creation at all levels and through all created forms and beings.

The Cosmic Embrace of Shiva and Shakti

The inseparable and eternal embrace of Shiva and Shakti – often depicted in Indian mythology as two lovers in an ecstatic embrace – is of fundamental importance to tantric cosmology. Some religions, however, have divorced the male and female aspects of divinity or god. They have separated Shiva from Shakti, so to speak, or ignored them altogether. This subtle epistemological 'mistake' has resulted in the beliefs in which god and creation are seen as distinctly separate entities.

This trend is often termed as the path of the ascenders – the belief that the world was created by an otherworldly god. Such beliefs are usually puritanical and tend to devalue the body and the senses as impure. The ascending path glorifies god, heaven and the afterlife. In India, many ascetic yogis hold this view and look upon the world as an illusion. The descending path, on the other hand, glorifies the earth, not god. It celebrates the body, the senses and the material world. Any attempt at transcendence is looked upon with suspicion, for their only god is the world of nature, of matter.

Tantra strikes a graceful balance between these extreme paths. For tantra, god is both in the heaven and the earth, both in the body and in the soul. Hence tantra does not dispute the scientific explanation that mind developed from matter, it simply maintains that matter was in turn created from consciousness. So, metaphorically speaking, creation exists within the imagination of Brahma. More specifically, the material universe, or nature, is the visible thought-waves of cosmic consciousness or Shiva. And this manifestation of nature, of our world, is possible due to the benevolent aid of the creative principle or Shakti.

In tantra there is both a descending and ascending part of the creation story. Indeed, the best way to look upon the Brahmachakra is that it is a creation story, a map of the universe, a guide to better understand the workings of nature. The descending half-circle of this map explains the creation of matter from cosmic consciousness before life is created. The ascending half-circle explains the creation of mind and life from matter and the subsequent evolution of plants, animals and humans.

In this regard, it is important to note that in the Sanskrit language, 'Shiva' is masculine, 'Shakti' is feminine, and 'Brahma' is neuter. The dual nature of Brahma is symbolized by the two sexes. Yet Brahma is paradoxically also beyond all duality. Beyond all polarity, Brahma embraces and penetrates all with the omnipresent nature of its own oneness.

Shakti's cosmic embrace of Shiva makes him denser. She creates the manifest world of many from the deep, cosmic womb of the one. Thus, it is on account of Shakti alone that humans, animals and plants exist. But the word Shakti is not equivalent to the word 'nature' in the English language. As a matter of fact, nature is a property of Shakti, the manifest expression of Shakti. Whatever Shakti creates is commonly known as 'nature'.

Once again, the perennial philosophies and its mystic proponents agree. Meister Eckhart in *Sermons* suggests that the one has two distinct aspects, godhead and god. For him, the godhead is the transcendent cosmic consciousness of Shiva and god is that creative spirit of Shakti, which continually projects the universe in all its magnificent multiplicity. Likewise, in Taoism cosmic consciousness is called Tao and cosmic creative energy is called Teh. The Greek mystic Plotinus called them the One and Nous, respectively, and the Sufis referred to the dual nature of the one as Haqq and Khalq.

If you find the tantric cosmology to be complicated and abstract, do not worry, you have already become familiar with its core concepts. That is, the ultimate reality, Brahma, which has two characteristics, Shiva (cosmic consciousness) and Shakti (cosmic creative principle), who creates and is the essence of this world. Most importantly, Shiva and Shakti are not separate entities. Shakti has no existence separate from Shiva, and neither one are separate from Brahma. So we can conclude that tantra is based on non-dualism. Furthermore, Brahma is the essence of both the perceptible and imperceptible worlds. This concept is vital to understanding tantric spirituality. For according to tantra, we, as humans, have the inherent ability to know that we indeed are Brahma, the supreme intelligence. This simple truth, that you and the world around you are Brahma, is indeed the main lesson to learn from tantric cosmology. Indeed, all of tantra's wisdom is based upon this realization: *I am Brahma and the world around me is also Brahma.*

Cosmic Sisters: Shakti, Sophia and Anima Mundi

The concept of Shakti, the feminine operative principle, is not unique to tantra. The well-known American poet, storyteller and mythologist Robert Bly, who was initiated into tantric yoga in the 1970s, reminds us that it can also be found in early Gnosticism as the descent of Sophia. To the Gnostics, she embodied the feminine characteristics of god. 'In the Gnostic religion,' says Bly, 'which was a contemporary of early Christianity, Sophia looked down upon this dark planet of ours and decided to descend into it.' [37] Thereby she entered the earth itself – the stones, the trees, the birds and the water.

To the Greek philosophers, the Anima Mundi was a kind of cosmic courier or intermediary between the changeless being of universal form and the manifested denseness of the earth, or the lower world. She was mind embedded in matter, the force which created harmony in forms that otherwise would have been expressions of chaos.

These three cosmic sisters – Shakti, Sofia and Anima Mundi – are Western and Eastern concepts outlining the nature of the same creative force of cosmic intelligence. Through the cosmic force represented by each of these three concepts, the manifest world is created.

The Hidden Principle of Omnipresence

Although Shiva and Shakti are one, inseparably united as Brahma, they are made distinct by virtue of their functions and qualities.

Shiva is Brahma as motionless consciousness and Shakti is Brahma as the force that creates nature by the gradual metamorphosis of the motionless consciousness of Shiva. Thus both Shakti and Shiva are within and beyond nature. This concept thus creates a holistic cosmology which distinctly proclaims the omnipresence of Brahma. This subtle attribute of reality – which we also term God – is everywhere. In fact, the whole cycle of creation happens everywhere simultaneously. There is no point in asking where this cycle within the cosmic being of Brahma or god starts and where it ends. Merged in its own ocean of everywhere, it therefore embraces everything. God is in you, the reader; in this book; in the air you breathe and in the chair you sit on. God is indeed your closest friend and ally.

The vibrant colours and infinite forms of creation are a result of the cosmic embrace of the two divine lovers – Shiva and Shakti. Through their intimate relationship, the world around us is soaked with the cosmic intelligence of consciousness. As it is said in the Rig Veda, 'Behind all the manifestations in the universe, there is One, a Cosmic Magician, who controls all. Whatever has been or will be created is that One alone.' And, in the words of Anandamurti: '[Cosmic Consciousness] is present about us sometimes as sound expression, sometimes as thought or emotion, and then again sometimes as individual entities. There is [no] place in the universe where [it] ... is not manifest'.

Contemporary science does not support the concept of cosmic consciousness, of course. Nevertheless, many Western scientists and intellectuals, including prolific science writer Paul Davies, believes that 'a hidden principle seems to be at work organizing the cosmos in a coherent way.' [38]

Devolution: Shakti's Divine Descent

In tantra, Shakti is that very 'hidden principle' organizing the life of galaxies, stars, trees, flowers, animals and humans. But before trying to understand Shakti's cosmic, devolutionary dive into the manifest world, it is important to remember that Shiva and Shakti are simply different aspects of the same omnipresent consciousness, Brahma.

Shiva is the 'primary instrumental cause' of creation and Shakti is the 'secondary instrumental cause'.

Metaphorically, this can be compared to the relationship between a potter and the clay. The potter and the clay are both Shiva, but the energy exerted by the gentle, yet firm arms of the potter moulding the clay, her action, her creativity, is Shakti. She is the link between the potter and the clay, between the primary instrumental cause and the secondary instrumental cause, between pure consciousness and the objective world. Shakti is therefore also called the 'linking force'. She is the force that links the consciousness of Shiva with everything she creates. Consequently, everything in this universe is a manifestation of consciousness; even the inanimate rocks surrounding a flower garden are manifestations of Brahma.

Consciousness then – as created by the force of Shakti in the form of a tree or a horse – is not simply a separate part of that Almighty Force, as in pantheism. Rather, it is that Almighty Force's very essence. This visible world, this book, is not just matter, nor is it an illusion. As a result of cosmic devolution, through Shakti's divine descent, this book is Brahma, in the form of ideas, ink, paper and glue.

Imagine if this insight became part of how everyone views the world, including economists, ecologists, artists, farmers, politicians, writers and teachers. Yes, imagine if more people thought of the world in which we live as Brahma or God. I am sure we would be more inclined towards creating a better and more harmonious world.

The Cosmic Trinity

How does Shakti create the world around us? She 'creates all forms in the universe, while [Shiva] is the witness to this creation. [She] is primordial physical energy containing the three attributes, or *gunas*, found in all nature, the evolving cosmos,' explains Vasant Lad, a professor of ayurveda.[39] The philosophical meaning of guna is a 'binding principle'. It connotes the force of Shakti whereby she binds cosmic consciousness to various shapes or ideas. In English the word 'tendency' may also be used to express the spirit of guna.

In the primordial universe, Shakti expresses herself through a whirlpool of three forces called *sattva, rajas and tamas,* eventually forming a vast matrix of triangles, constantly transforming themselves into one another. Once again, it is important to remember that these three forces are not separate from Shakti; they are as much part of her as your hands are an integral part of you.

Gradually, and before creation has really started, these gunas begin to combat each other, to struggle for dominance. An imbalance is created in the triangle and from this imbalance a resultant force issues forth, and the splendid, cosmic show of creation begins.

The three expressions of Shakti:

1. **Sattva** (subtle force) creates the sense of cosmic existence, the perception of 'I am or I exist'. With the help of this latent cosmic force, Shakti gives birth to the first sense of 'other than' or 'separateness from'. It originates the pure state of potential mind, away from the essence of unqualified cosmic consciousness. This cosmic state of subjective 'I' existence within the cosmic mind, prior to creation, is termed *mahatattva.*

   In nature, sattva is the force which enables the graceful lustre of a flower to remain in full bloom. In humans, according to tantric and ayurvedic scholar David Frawley, 'It produces enlightenment and self-realization. Sattva is the divine or godly nature. It brings about internalization of the mind, the movement of the consciousness inward and the unification of the head and the heart.'[40] People endowed with deep spiritual insights, those who have advanced towards the realization of their higher self, are increasingly radiant with dispassion and a resplendent flood of light. This internal purity also becomes apparent in their external personality and activities. In other words, a saintly person is someone who has become the very embodiment of the effulgent force of sattva.

2. **Rajas** (energetic force) is characterized by action; it desires to keep the cosmic 'I' busy with activities and then enjoys

the fruits of those actions. Shakti, with the aid of this cosmic force, awakens the sense of doer-ship. Under its bondage, *ahamttatva* is created from mahatattva. In nature, it is the energetic force of rajas which enables a seed to grow and become a plant or a tree. In humans, rajas creates energy and vitality. Its shadow side is distraction, turbulence, agitation and desires. Through the vitality of rajas an intellectual is fed the necessary creative energy to solve problems and create new ideas. However, it is also due to rajas' turbulence that the same intellectual may suffer from absentmindedness or emotional distress.

3. **Tamas** (static force) creates a sense of objectivity in the cosmic mind; it originates the *citta*, this objectified portion experiences the reaction to the actions made by ahamtattva. Citta is cosmic mind-stuff, or ectoplasm. At this stage, cosmic consciousness is ready to be transformed into dense material forms. In nature, when the force of *raja guna* is used up, the *tama guna* predominates. A flower thus gradually withers and fades. The glow of *sattva* wanes and eventually the all-devouring hunger of tama transform it into a state of crudeness – that is to say, the flower dies. In humans tama represents 'dullness, darkness and inability to perceive. It is the mind clouded by ignorance and fear. It means heaviness and lethargy. It involves lack of mental activity and insensitivity, and domination of the mind by external or subconscious forces.' While raja mobilizes the energy needed to create, tama creates stability and allows fixed forms to take shape, thus it underlies the structure of matter and the physical body.

The Cosmic Mind

The appearance of these three forces, expressed as mahatattva, ahamtatva and citta, forms the transcendental cosmic mind of tantra. In alchemical terms, it is the macrocosmic 'brain' of the universe. But as noted earlier, it is difficult to make comparisons between mainstream science and the intuitional empiricism of tantra. The closest scientific formula which grants the creation of life a transcendental origin is probably the anthropic principle. Developed around the First World War by Harvard biochemist Lawrence Joseph Henderson, this principle assumes the existence of life largely based on the unlikelihood of a Big Bang resulting in the formation of planets, plants and humans without the help of some cosmic intelligence. British science writer John Gribbin calculates that if the parameters had been different than 'a decimal point followed by sixty zeroes and a one, life would never have appeared on Planet Earth, what to speak of it acquiring emotions and intellect'. [41]

As described earlier, Shakti's three forces – sattva, raja, and tama – first forms the three states of the cosmic mind – cosmic mahatattva (I am), cosmic ahamtattva (I do) and cosmic citta (I have done). Cosmic mahatattva is 'cruder' than Brahma. It is not infinite like Brahma but it is endless. It has a starting point but it is inexhaustible. Imagine cosmic mahatattva as if Brahma wakes up and says, 'I exist. I am'. Cosmic ahamtattva is Brahma realizing a sense of action. In this state, the cosmic mind has the potential to act. Cosmic citta is the state in which the cosmic mind of Brahma is an objective reality. Imagine that mahatattva and ahamtattva can take citta as their object and say, 'I have created this.' These three levels of cosmic consciousness make up the cosmic mind. The Indian sage Aurobindo called this the 'Supermind'.

Astronomer George Seielstad postulates that this cosmic mind might be a fundamental part of the universe, like time and space. In the absence of conscious life, nothing might exist. Hence, the goal of a universe in search of reality is to generate expression and ownership. In tantric terms, Seielstad's Anthropic speculations implies a cosmic mind, a subtle, godlike intelligence, prior to the Big Bang. Through various metamorphoses this intelligence reveals itself as the 'brain' of the universe. This magician imagines and creates in order to witness and play with the results of its own creations. [42]

The Convergence of Tantra, Plato, Tao and Chaos Theory

Thanks to Plato, these metaphysical concepts are not as foreign to Western cosmology as they may at first seem to be. The three gunas create a realm of incorporeal forms similar to this Greek sage-philosopher's geometrical universe. Without these forms, matter would be unintelligible if not completely non-existent – a reality of unrealized possibility. And these forms, in their universal, triangular tranquility, could have no connection to the temporal world of physicality without the aid of Anima Mundi. Like Plato, sage-philosopher Plotinus also believed that the Anima Mundi, the Shakti of the Western hemisphere, is the cosmic principle manifesting the divine within the mundane level of existence.

There are notable similarities between the Indian and the Greek understanding of the universe, and they do not appear to be accidental. Pythagoras studied in Egypt and Persia and is said to have had Indian teachers. Pyrrho visited India in 327 BC and returned to Greece to teach non-attachment and spiritual enlightenment. Plotinus – who was unable to visit India on his trip in AD 242 – taught, in true Eastern fashion, the importance of meditation as a means of discovering the immortal higher self within. And Plato was no stranger to Eastern mysticism, either. Reincarnation was a central theme in his teachings.

Knowing that many of the fundamental ideas of Chinese, Japanese, and Greek, philosophy had their origin in the tantric tradition of India, perhaps it becomes easier for Westerners to relate to this cosmology. Learning from a rediscovered and refined version of classical tantra does not have to represent an imposition of Eastern thought on the Western mind. Rather, it is possible this system may form the nexus in a conceptual universe where East and West again can merge.

The new scientific discovery of patterned chaos may also signify a link between East and West. Popularly, and somewhat misleadingly, known as chaos theory, this new science studies processes that appear to be chaotic, but in fact they are not. They are also determined, as one can predict an overall pattern or order in everything. Chaos theory has thus enabled us to see order within apparent random events. And because its mandala-like computer graphics looks like fine art, and its explanations of reality reads like poetry, this new discovery is a breath of fresh air in the otherwise humdrum world of science.

The fractal is an important symbol of chaos theory. A fractal can repeat itself with variation on scales large and small, in space or time or matter or energy. The most famous fractal is the Koch snowflake. In 1904, Helge von Koch described a triangle on which one 'grows' another triangle onto the back of each side, just like the old triangle, but only one-third its size. The first symbol that thus appears is the so-called 'Star of David'.

The synchronistic or 'chaotic' part of the Koch snowflake is that long before Koch described it mathematically, this so-called 'Jewish Star' had existed in the form of a *yantra* in India since the dawn of human civilization. A yantra is a geometric representation of the various energies of the cosmos. In other words, it is a microcosmic replica of the macrocosm. A yantra drawn in Nepal around AD 1750 consists of many Koch snowflakes or Jewish stars at its centre. In fact, this symbol has been central to tantric symbolism since the time of Shiva around 5000 BC. According to tantric legend, this yantra was brought to the 'Holy Land' by tantric sages around 4000 BC. These 'missionaries' supposedly visited Arabia, Abyssinia and Phoenicia. Eventually they settled in the mountains of an area which today is known as Israel. They named the place Shriishailam. In English 'shrii' translates as divine, 'shaila' means hill and 'ma' means shelter. This divine hilly shelter is today known as Jerusalem, the politically unstable birthplace of Jews, Christians and Muslims.

Thus through chaos theory the tantric or Jewish star has now become a central 'symbol' in Western science. Thus a remarkable cycle of mystical and scientific interconnectedness is completed. With these fascinating historical, philosophical and scientific connectives in mind, let us now continue to explore the spiritual descent of Shakti's three primordial forces.

The Five Building Blocks of Creation

Through the continued action of Shakti, through her creative, cosmic unfolding within cosmic consciousness, she further creates a conducive environment for the birth of the five building blocks of creation. First in subtle, or potential form, then in denser, perceptible quantities, the five fundamental factors – ethereal, aerial, luminous, liquid and solid – make up the basic elements of the manifest universe. In ayurveda and in Chinese medicine, these factors are commonly known as ether, air, fire, water and earth.

1. **Ethereal Factor** (ether): Through the influence of tama guna, consciousness is transformed and a portion of cosmic mind is metamorphosed into ethereal factor, or what we commonly term space. Ethereal factor pervades the entire universe. It is the ocean in which the material universe floats.

   - This subtle layer of the cosmos has the capacity to carry the most refined of all expressions, that of sound – even though at this stage it is not yet audible to the human ear.

   - The ear is the human organ linked to ethereal factor.

2. **Aerial Factor** (air): Tama guna continues to exert its influence on space and moulds a portion of it into aerial factor.

   - Sound and touch are the sensory perceptions related to this factor.

   - Air gives sound the ability to touch the air; hence, sound is audible at this level of creation. Atoms of hydrogen are formed, and the pressure exerted by the static force draws them together, forming hydrogen clouds.

   - The skin is the sensory organ linked to this factor.

3. **Luminous Factor** (fire): Due to the ever-increasing pressure of Shakti in the form of tama guna, these hydrogen clouds start to condense, which drives the atoms closer together,

causing friction and heat. Luminous factor is therefore related to the formation of stars.

- Luminous factor carries the vibrational qualities of sound, touch and sight.
- The eye is the human organ associated with this factor.

4. **Liquid Factor** (water): Tama guna continues to bind consciousness further, eventually condensing fire into liquid plasma. Liquid factor is the most common element in everyday human existence.
   - This factor carries the sensory qualities of sound, touch, sight and taste.
   - The tongue is the sensory organ to which this factor is related.

5. **Solid Factor** (earth): Further exertion of force on the liquid factor solidifies it, and the solid factor – carrying the vibration of smell – is born.
   - Commonly termed matter, this factor is the composite of all the other factors and the carrier of all the sensory perceptions – sound, touch, sight, taste and smell.
   - The nose is the sensory organ linked with solid factor.

The Emergence of Life According to Tantra

When all the five fundamental factors coexist in the universe as an endless continuum of potentialities, the force of tama continues to exert its pressure on solid factor, which, as we have seen, contains all the other five factors. For life to evolve from the body of the solid forms of matter, two conditions are necessary:

1. Due to the pressure of tama an opposing inertial force and a nucleus is formed within the material object.
2. The five fundamental factors must be in requisite proportion.

In contrast to the sudden explosion of the Big Bang, the

formation of life is a rather leisurely process. With the emergence of vital energy, or prana, a qualitative change takes place within the material structure. It converts from a lifeless, inorganic mass into organic cells and protoplasm – the living matter of plant and animal tissue – evolves. Evolution of life has finally begun. The holon of life has evolved, and it is now ready to become part of a greater and more complex series of animate wholes.

The path of the life-giving holon's or unit's journey is to express itself into increasingly complex forms which allows for greater expression of consciousness and unity. Until finally, as a human being, it has that exalted and rare opportunity of again becoming one with that ultimate Omega Point, that final whole. In the words of the Christian mystic Johannes Tauler, 'All creatures seek after unity; all multiplicity struggles towards it – the universal aim of all life is always this unity.'

A truly holistic philosophy is thus one which includes cosmic consciousness as the beginning and end of creation. But before reaching that all-embracing and greatest of all holons, that cosmic consciousness, that Brahma, all beings must first move along, step by step, on the ever-ascending journey of evolution. Thus, through the simple elegance and beauty of a circle, the devolution and evolution of tantric cosmology forms the one integral and whole cycle of creation.

Cosmic Truth in the Face of the Faceless

Our cosmic journey has taken us from cosmic consciousness to the denseness of matter. This centripetal journey forms one half-circle of the tantric circular universe. The other half, the ascending, centrifugal journey (which will be outlined in the next chapter), describes the universe from the creation of matter to the state of enlightened, human consciousness as it finally culminates in the spiritual realization and embrace of cosmic consciousness.

This cosmic cycle of creation – within the limited confines of philosophy and its circular diagram – describes the complexities of an unlimited and holistic system. This order of reality has no centre, no beginning and no end. It's a closed loop which creates, grows and dissolves at all times, in all directions, simultaneously and instantaneously. Actually, it has a centre, a beginning and an end – but they are all at the same place at all times, in all directions. As both Plotinus and the sages of India have pointed out, there is no 'this world' or 'other world'. In actuality, there's not even a 'going down' or 'coming up'. Cosmic consciousness is everywhere and simultaneously nowhere. In tantra, the universe itself is considered the mind of God – all the manifest objects of the physical universe are the thought projections of god's cosmic mind. Consequently there's no concept of heaven and hell in tantra. One is in heaven when one perceives the great spirit shining forth from 'one and all objects' at all times. One is in hell whenever one forgets that all is consciousness, whenever one forgets that consciousness is everywhere. In other words, heaven and hell is simply a matter of one's state of mind, of one's state of perception.

In the daily grind of the relative world there is a gap of time, place, and person, a gap between various manifest entities, between observer and the observed. So to the materialist, perceiving the world through his or her mind and sensory organs, with the help of microscopes or telescopes, the physical world naturally appears to be the only truth, the only observable God. And to the idealist sages, whose lofty minds remain in celestial heaven, this compact world appears to be an illusion. So what is the truth? Tantra solves this longstanding philosophical and epistemological conflict by pointing out that cosmic consciousness is absolute truth and the manifest universe is also truth, but relative. Cosmic consciousness is immutable and infinite – it is the ultimate reality within and beyond the relative world.

The universe, on the other hand, is the result of changes within that consciousness due to the influence of Shakti. She brings the transcendental oneness into the realm of manifest relativity, into the realm of ether, air, fire, water and earth. And thus under the bondage of time, place and person, the cosmic oneness becomes the world of many. Her embrace of Shiva finally gives birth to the children of inanimate and animate forms.

For today's Western mind, steeped as it is in its rational and materialist thinking, these 'abstract constructs' appears to be mere 'metaphysical speculations'. So how do we determine if this knowledge is real? For the mystic there are five ways to observe reality: rationality, sense inference, intuition, authority and mystical union. To deduce the nature of physical phenomena, sense inference and rationality are adequate tools. But to fully understand the subtle beginnings of the cosmic cycle theory, actual contemplative apprehension based upon direct experience achieved in a state of mystical union is necessary.

In its pre-creation stage, prior to the five fundamental factors, this holistic system cannot be experienced or deduced by the rational mind or through sense inference. But that does not mean it is beyond the scope of experience, hidden in some obscure metaphysical or mythological realm that cannot be verified cognitively. Such apprehension, conceived within the transpersonal or mystical mind of tantric sages represents empirical knowledge at its most sublime and comprehensive. To them it is not speculation, but nature as it reveals itself in its subtle, spiritual manifestations. In other words, they do not believe in spirit or god; they know, they perceive spirit or god.

The material scientists, who dismiss everything spiritual as 'otherworldly nonsense,' are therefore missing out on a fundamentally important part of reality. Faced with a mounting and authoritative body of contemplative knowledge of the spiritual domain – from Shiva to Buddha, from Plato to Plutonius, from Aurobindo to Anandamurti – they are, in many ways, displaying the same dogmatic attitude as those religious leaders who executed mystic and scientist Giordano Bruno, or those who refused to accept Gallileo's astronomical theories.

But it is equally simplistic or dogmatic, as is often common in New Age circles, to equate everything that is new and unexplainable in science or metaphysics to true mysticism. Although cosmic consciousness is the source of all 'material and metaphysical facts', and its existence can be experientially verified through meditation, that same faceless entity will forever remain an enigma to the material scientists. Such is the dynamic and beautiful dance of existence.

Cosmic consciousness cannot be described by the mathematical formulae of science. It can only be empirically perceived through transrational or mystical perception. However, there are scientists today, in the so-called intelligent design movement, who are attempting to describe the mechanism of evolution in nature as intelligent design rather than (as in Darwinism) a set of events based on chance mutations or traits developed over time by the survival of the fittest. The intelligent design movement insists that much of the solutions in nature, such as the creation of organs and organisms, including a lot of what is called macro-evolution, shows indisputable evidence of intelligent design. However, the intelligent designer is not an otherworldly force or god. The ID-movement is actually unable to say who the intelligent designer might be. The Darwinists, on the other hand, dismiss the intelligent design movement as some kind of pre-rational belief system, in large part because some of the movement's supporters are Christian creationists.

In tantra, the empirical also includes the transrational realm. Thus tantra can proclaim that nature and evolution are the footprints of Shakti's intelligent design work and that Darwinism and intelligent design in nature may be compatible.

Tantra sees no major conflict between these two views of evolution. Shakti's cosmic intelligence is at work both within and beyond nature. She is thus the primary cause of evolution. But there are aspects of evolution where Darwinistic mechanisms are also at work, because that is just another expression of cosmic intelligence. Tantra simply teaches us that nature in her totality is a result of Brahma's cosmic intelligence, an expression of Brahma's infinite and creative unfolding.

The Basic Elements of Tantric Devolution (Saincara)

Brahma: Cosmic Consciousness; formless; the source of all created things.

Nirguna Brahma: Brahma in unmanifest form, the state of Brahma in which the three gunas are dormant; prior to creation.

Saguna Brahma: Brahma in manifest form; that part of Brahma bound by Prakrti or Shakti.

Shiva: also called Purusha; cosmic consciousness, an integral aspect of Brahma; literally, 'in whom all things lie'.

Shakti: also called Prakrti; Cosmic operative principle, an integral aspect of Brahma; literally, 'ability to create something'.

Sattva Guna: subtle binding force; conscious.

Raja Guna: energetic binding force; active.

Tama Guna: crude binding force; inactive.

Mahatattva: 'I am' state of cosmic mind, created by sattva guna.

Ahamtattva: 'I do' state of cosmic mind, created by raja guna.

Citta: 'I have done' state of cosmic mind, created by tama guna.

Ethereal: ether; tanmatra – sound; gateway – ear; function – to hear.

Aerial: air; tanmatra – sound, touch; gateway – skin; function – to touch.

Luminous: fire; tanmatra – sound, touch, form; gateway – eye; function – to see.

Liquid: water; tanmatra – sound, touch, form, taste; gateway – tongue; function – to taste.

Solid: earth; tanmantra – sound, touch, form, taste, smell; gateway – nose; function – to smell.

Matter: a combination of all the five fundamental factors. Shiva, Shakti, the three gunas, citta, ahamtattva and mahatattva are inherent parts of matter in potential form. In other words, matter is simply Brahma in its most condensed form. Life, according to modern science, evolves, through evolution, from matter. Tantra agrees, but adds that life does not originate with matter, but originates in Brahma, in cosmic consciousness, which also creates matter.

In summary, the above elements in the tantric cosmology describes – from the subtlest Brahma to the crudest matter – the devolution of cosmic creation, from the state of non-dual consciousness to the state of dualistic forms, or matter. That is, from Brahma and Shiva and Shakti, from when Shakti binds Shiva and creates the three gunas, from when the cosmic mind is created to the creation of the five elements, ether, air, fire, water and earth. The earth element, which contains all the other elements, is what scientists call matter, of course, and the creation of matter gave birth to our own earth more than five billion years ago, long before life.

The point of devolution, the first half circle of the cosmic cycle in tantric cosmology, starts from Nirguna Brahma and ends with matter. And since consciousness lies dormant in matter, life starts from matter. That is, evolution begins with matter, and because matter is essentially 'frozen consciousness' it has consciousness inherently built into it. Matter thus gives rise to life. It creates life as a microcosmic expression of consciousness – just as it did on our planet with the momentous event when simple cells first developed more than 3.8 billion years ago. Tantric cosmology teaches us that creation is also God in the form of Shakti, and where there is Shakti, there is also Shiva. Hence, creation is all God, all Brahma. No matter which stage of creation we point towards – the most subtle or the most crude – we are always looking at God's sublime face.

Creating a Tantric Lifestyle

Tantric Philosophy: *Ota Prota Yogabhyam Samyukta Purushottama* – The cosmic nucleus (God) is connected with each entity individually and all entities collectively.

Daily Contemplation: God is not a distant entity in heaven. God resides in each and every heart and in each and every animal, plant and rock. Every entity has an atman, a soul and this soul is the reflection of God.

Daily Acts of Sacredness

One: Go to a lonely place and focus on a rock, a tree or an animal and feel that they are all reflections of God.

Two: Go to a busy park, café or waiting room and when watching the people around you think of them as god watching back at you.

Chapter Seven

THE SPIRIT OF EVOLUTION

 **S**ince childhood, I have always been mystically drawn towards nature. Growing up on a forested island, I spent most of my childhood and youth playing in nature, watching birds and animals in the forest and on the ocean. It was in nature that I first felt connected to a world of tranquility and beauty, a world mysterious and sacred. It was in nature that I first felt the presence of god, felt drawn to that cosmic attractor we call by so many names. Not surprisingly, according to tantra, nature is god made visible; nature is Shakti's form dancing on the sublime, ethereal body of Shiva. Nature is our direct, unspoilt link to the world of god, and it was in India and Nepal in my youth that tantric yoga practice truly awakened this awareness in me: that our body and nature is one body, one god.

Tantra maintains that nature and all beings are guided by the unseen force of god's cosmic mind. Quantum physicists are also open to the possibility of an unseen intelligence permeating nature and the world around us, including man-made things. As science philosopher Karl Popper once put it, in the new universe, 'matter has transcended itself'. What he meant by that was that the once-solid atoms have dissolved into waves, vibrations, patterns of mysterious activity – a world more akin to mind and consciousness than matter. That this world is literally the 'body of God', is essentially what all mystics claim. May be soon scientists will have to concede that Baruch Spinoza, a Dutch philosopher, was right: matter is an extension of God.

The Cosmic Attractor

Both before and after the creation of life, Shakti, as the cosmic designer, is at work. Everything expressed as microcosm, whether in the form of water, a tree or a tornado, is shaped on the drawing board of that unseen designer. All of the finished designs of nature clearly exhibit a self-organizing ability. Physicist and cosmologist Brian Swimme calls this unseen shaping capacity the 'self' of nature. Each being of nature, from the smallest amoeba to the largest African elephant, is guided by this self, this unseen shaping of the cosmic designer. In tantra, this self is the 'Cosmic I'. In the initial stage of evolution of mind, the living structures, with their underdeveloped ego, cannot function independently but act in accordance to the will of the cosmic I.

A tree or a tornado does not have the same self-awareness and ability to discern and act as a human being; its existence is guided and maintained by the unseen shaping of the cosmic I. As Swimme explains, 'A tree is a self: it is unseen shaping more than its leaves or bark, roots or cellulose or fruit. The tree, as a self, organizes all these millions of operations so that it can enter into relationships with air, rainfall and sunlight.' [43]

This incredible process, which is beyond the comprehension of the materialist or reductionist world view of mainstream science, again confirms the alchemical saying: 'As above, so below'. The macrocosm guides and reflects itself in microcosm, all the way from the unconscious, elemental womb of the supernova to the self-reflective consciousness of a human being. The same force that guides the stars in the heavens also guides the earth and all its magnificent creations. Indeed, it guides the very cells and blood in our bodies at this very moment! This force is the cosmic I of the macrocosm, and it acts within the crude mind of a tree or a tornado, and supplies these beings with requisite force for their growth and movement. As the crude mind develops further, this cosmic force or pull is increasing.

This force, this cosmic allurement or enchantment, is a fundamental mystery in all of creation. In its most basic expression this attraction is the desire for survival, for procreation and for expression. In a tree this allurement is manifested in its growth, protective strength, beauty of its flowers, and the sweetness of its fruit. A tree is cosmic allurement and creativity revealing itself in the graceful beauty of its form. Even a tornado wants to maintain its existence, its shape, its path of movement. Although very destructive to other life forms, the cosmic allurement moves the tornado forward. In its highest form, this attraction is the human expression of love for the mystery of life, spiritual love for that great cosmic enchanter. At every level of creation there is a movement forward, unconsciously or consciously all beings want to ascend back towards the source of creation, back towards the infinite bliss of cosmic consciousness. As Anandamurti once remarked, many years before Luke Skywalker popularized the concept, 'The force that guides the stars, guides you too'.

(The various expressions used above – cosmic I, cosmic nucleus, cosmic designer, cosmic attractor – are different names indicating the manifold creative capacities of cosmic consciousness, both as Shakti or the operative principle, and as Shiva or cognitive principle.)

The Evolution of Divinity

A century before Charles Darwin and Alfred Russel Wallace co-discovered the theory of Darwinian evolution, theories of cosmic and human evolution were literally springing up everywhere. Already by 1693 Gottfried Wilhelm von Leibniz understood the reason for past species extinctions and the 'transcreation' of others. Immanuel Kant claimed, as in tantra, that the original universe was simple and undifferentiated. Then, through evolution, it gradually grew more complex. Even matter, he claimed, has a natural tendency to organize itself into more perfect constitutions. Thus nature has a direction towards greater diversification. But not only that, each ascent into more evolved beings creates a higher union or integration.

This stunning vision found its most eloquent adherent in Friedrich Wilhelm Joseph von Schelling. He maintained that by superseding the intellect or reason, we will discover that both 'mind' and 'nature' are different movements of spirit. To him this spirit or god was both the 'first and the last ... the unevolved and the fully evolved'. Thus consciousness is present throughout creation, from the creation of matter to the development of the human mind.

So to both Schelling and tantric sages, it is this organizing principle, this Shakti, which makes the world a system, a self-organizing biosphere. And by 1810, naturalist Lorenz Oken claimed that the philosophy of nature is basically the science of the transformation of god into the creation of the world. This concept compares beautifully to the tantric notion that the world is the thought-projection of Brahma.

When Darwin carefully outlined his ideas about evolution in his famous book *The Origin of Species*, everybody – except, of course, the diehard believers of the Genesis myth – accepted his theory of natural selection through chance mutations. This theory has, since then, become scientific dogma and has allowed scientists to 'drive out' any connection between evolution and cosmic consciousness. Today, most philosophers of science openly admit that evolution has an intrinsic, self-transcending force within it. That force, according to tantra, is Shakti, and unlike Darwin, Wallace maintained in the true spirit of tantra, that evolution itself was the 'mode and manner of God's creation'.

Creation of Mind

Shakti can be considered the cosmic mother of creation. As such, she is a busy matriarch. Prior to creation she created cosmic mind. During creation she gives birth to billions of unit minds – from singular cells to human beings. Whether in the descending circle of creation, or in the ascending arch, it is Shakti who is responsible for the invention of all elements. She creates it all – matter, mind, plants, animals and humans. She is the eternal form. Shiva, on the other hand, is busy just being eternally aware and still. He is the dormant, witnessing consciousness with which Shakti creates. He is the eternal inside. She is the eternal outside. But in their totality they are always united. Embraced in each other's loving arms, they are nothing less than Brahma itself. Thus the whole of creation is suffused with the subtle nature of Brahma. There are no particles or beings, inanimate or animate, any place in this universe, whose body is not always saturated with Brahma's enchanted essence.

It is the cosmic designer or Shakti who – through her expression as the three elemental forces – exerts tremendous pressure on matter. Thus ectoplasmic particles or 'mind-stuff' evolves.

How something as ephemeral as consciousness can create something as dense as matter is not easy to reconcile with modern science. Brain researcher Dr Andrew Newberg, whose findings on the brain images of meditators have been published in the books, *The Mystical Mind: Probing the Biology of Religious Experience* (co-authored by Eugene d'Aquili) and *Why God Won't Go Away: Brain Science and the Biology of Belief* (co-authored by Eugene d'Aquili and Vince Rause), suggests that 'perhaps consciousness and matter are two ways of looking at the same thing'. This is exactly how tantra sees it – matter is nothing but a metamorphosed form of consciousness from which mind evolves. Thus, to tantra, even a stone has consciousness, but in a dormant state.

Cosmologically speaking, the main difference between a stone and a human being is that the consciousness of a stone is purely latent; it remains in a potential state and is unable to express itself. Thus evolution, from matter to amoebas to plants to animals to humans, is characterized by the gradual increase in expression of consciousness, complexity and unity, until the human mind is capable of experiencing the ultimate unity consciousness by becoming one with cosmic consciousness, Brahma, or god.

Matter, Mind and Brain

While reading this, the grey, tofu-like substance of your brain is busy firing off billions of neural messages to thousands of connector neurons. But is that all there is to the brain? What about the brain's relationship to the mysterious mind of ours? Are they the same? If not, where does the mind start and the brain begin? According to most neuroscientists, the brain and the mind are synonymous. Our mind, our consciousness, is nothing but neurological interactions in the brain. To these scientists, if there is a god at all, he or she is simply an image or an idea conjured up by the neurological fireworks within the walls of our bony skull.

On the other extreme of the spectrum are those dualist thinkers, like French philosopher René Descartes, who believe that the mind is entirely separate from the brain. 'I think therefore I am' was Descartes's famous proclamation. But what is it that does our thinking?

For tantra, the answer lies somewhere in between these two extreme views. The brain, like the rest of the body, is the outer or physical portion of the mind, since the body, or the anamaya kosha, is the sixth and most dense layer of a human being. The brain, then, is an interactive tool of the mind, but the mind is much larger and subtler than the brain. Some scientists, like biologist Rupert Sheldrake, maintain that the mind is an 'information field' that is connected to but extends far beyond the periphery and function of the physical brain.

Another way of explaining the mind/matter conundrum is offered by a range of thinkers and scientists through the theory of panpsychism. This idea, which is remarkably similar to tantra, is advocated by both theologians and scientists – from David Ray Griffin to David Chalmers. Panpsychism asserts that consciousness, as explained in the Brahmachakra, is found everywhere and is a fundamental property of the universe – all the way down to atomic particles. Thus rocks and salt crystals have what Chalmers call 'protoconsciousness'.

But perhaps the new science of complexity explains all this even more 'scientifically' by stating that, yes, consciousness does arise from the brain, but it simply cannot be reduced to the brain. As in tantra, the science of complexity acknowledges the biological roots of the mind, but it also maintains that we are more than our neurons. In other words, the complex and subjective experiences of our thoughts and emotions when we make love, read or listen to music cannot simply be reduced to neurological patterns in the brain. For, the human mind has a unique, interior experience all of its own. This becomes especially clear in regards to the realm of spirituality. Because it is universally accepted that people with mystical experiences report that these occurrences are 'more real' than anything else they have experienced.

In other words, the experience of spirituality cannot merely be triggered by sensory or neurochemical pleasures. These experiences are of a higher or deeper nature than that which we ordinarily encounter every day. They belong to the purely interior and subjective realm of the mind. But material science, that which is seen and studied by the eye of flesh, is simply not equipped to understand the subjective or spiritual part of reality, thus it regards such experiences as unreal or something produced by the brain itself. Therefore, to understand spirituality, science must, as Thomas Samuel Kuhn said, 'undergo a complete paradigm shift'. Otherwise science will not be able to embrace all of reality – from matter to mind to spirit.

The human brain and mind are constantly interacting. These two fine-tuned mechanisms are integral expressions – one lower and one higher, one external and one internal – of cosmic consciousness made perceptible at the highest or most complex state of evolution. Thus to paraphrase Descartes: 'I think because I am cosmic consciousness'.

In the beginning of this chapter, I mentioned that philosopher Jan Smuts reminds us that nature, and thus evolution, 'is an interlacing network of *wholes*'. Both the brain and the mind are perfect examples of these interlacing wholes, but the mind's whole is much larger, much broader in scope than the brain. Therefore the brain is enveloped by the mind, not the other way around.

In the book *The Mind and the Brain: Neuroplasticity and the Power of Mental Force*, Jeffrey M. Schwartz and Sharon Begley document how the mind is more expansive, powerful and creative than the brain by illustrating through positron emission tomography or PET scans that wilful meditation practice can actually alter the brain's physiology. They have proven that we can – as in fact yogis have maintained for thousands of years – will ourselves to become better human beings. Not only that, we can, in effect, even alter brain function through the use of mindfulness, through the practice of spiritual intention.

The brain and the mind are both exceptional and mysterious expressions of the cosmic unfolding of Shiva and Shakti. The brain and the mind are also perfect examples of nature's duality and oneness, of the interlacing relationship between matter and consciousness, between Shiva and Shakti. For, throughout evolution, on both the grand cosmic scale, as well as in the minutest expressions of matter, Shiva and Shakti are but two expressions of the one universal being.

The Three Forces of Evolution

The mind of living beings evolves largely through three stages of evolution:

1. Physical energy develops as a result of physical clash with the environment. At this stage living beings advance the first and crudest layer of the mind, the citta. Thus the mind of living beings develops in reverse order of the cosmic mind. The earliest stages of human society evolved due to physical clash with nature, which initiated the development of simple tools, etc.
2. Psychic energy develops as a result of psychic clash. Through this clash, living beings evolve the aham portion of the mind. Psychic clash often occurs when one comes in contact with more advanced ideas through education, etc.
3. Spiritual energy develops as a result of one's longing for the great, one's devotion to god. At this stage, human beings use their self-will to move towards union with Brahma, to return to the source of all beings. This effort is the sadhana or spiritual practice of tantra. The more spiritual practice one performs, the closer the proximity to Brahma, the more one evolves spiritually, until one finally merge in Brahma through the experience of Yogic samadhi or mystic union with god.

Through evolution, our dormant spiritual consciousness is awakened from its basic instincts of self-preservation and reproduction to the many higher expressions of human life. As humans we are on different evolutionary levels relative to our development of aham and mahat. Together, all three levels of mind – citta, aham and mahat – are termed 'unit mind'. This unit mind actually possesses all the qualities of the cosmic mind, thus we can, through spiritual evolution, when unit mind unites with cosmic mind, become one with god. We can, in a sense, become gods and goddesses in human form. And that indeed, says tantra, is the final goal of human evolution.

The Basic Elements of Tantric Evolution (Pratisaincara)

Prana: energy that is an inherent part of every material object in the universe.

Pranah: vital energy that evolves and creates life within solid factor (earth, matter).

Citta: ectoplasmic mind that evolves from solid factor or matter due to clash of energies; instinctual mind; Dominated by tamas guna.

Aham: a portion of citta that evolves into a subtler form of mind influenced by intellect and ego; Dominated by rajas guna.

Mahat: a portion of mahat evolves into a subtler state of mind influenced by the thought 'I want to know who I am?' Dominated by sattva guna.

Plant Mind: dominated by citta.

Animal Mind: dominated by citta and aham.

Human Mind: dominated by aham and mahat.

Chakras and Koshas: the human mind and soul can be further divided into five koshas and seven chakras, each one more subtle and integral than the other. The first five koshas and chakras are intimately related. The two highest chakras refer to the human soul – jivatman.

Jivatman: human soul. The human soul longs to be reunited with Paramatman, the cosmic soul of Brahma.

Brahma: when the human soul, through meditation is reunited with Brahma, the tantric cycle of devolution and evolution is complete. Both metaphorically and practically speaking, Shakti, expressed through the force of kundalini in the human body, has once again united with Shiva, her cosmic consort in a loving, cosmic embrace. They are both one in the 'One Brahma'.

In the evolutionary phase of the tantric cosmology, we see consciousness manifest life in matter because Shakti as prana (energy) and pranah (vital energy) are awakening life in matter, which in turn, through citta, aham and mahat gives birth to mind and consciousness in all life forms, from plant to animal to human. In other words, through evolution, life and the creation of mind, Brahma is seeing reflections of itself, and in the human mind, that reflection has the potential through spiritual practice to become self-conscious, to become aware – through love and spiritual awakening – that we are indeed god, we are indeed inherently Divine. Not only do we become intellectually aware of this reality, but also, through spiritual practice we reach the final stage of enlightenment, and thus actually experience god realization, the cosmic oneness with Brahma.

Creating a Tantric Lifestyle

Tantric Philosophy: *Brahma Satyam Jagadapi Satyamapeksikam* – Brahma is absolute and unlimited truth; the world is limited and relative truth.

Daily Contemplation: Brahma is unlimited, infinite and undergoes no change. It is the ultimate truth. The world is the result of changes in Brahma due to the force of Shakti, who brings the infinite realm into the realm of relativity. The materialist believes that only the world of relativity is real. The idealist (vedanta, for example), on the other hand, believes that the world is an illusion and only Brahma is real. Tantra philosophy strikes a wonderful balance between these two opposites by saying that both the infinite (Brahma) and the relative (the world) are real.

Daily Acts of Sacredness

One: Learn this saying from the Svachanda Tantra by heart: 'There is nothing that is not divine. To know all as illusion is ignorance, to know all as god is knowledge.'

Two: Imagine that each day is an opportunity to reveal the presence of Brahma, of god, in this world.

Chapter Eight

THE BODY-MIND-SPIRIT CONNECTION

Our human body is a microcosmic reflection of the macrocosmic universe. As we have learnt from the holistic cosmology of the Brahmachakra, our own body is in essence made of the same stuff as stars and galaxies. Our body is indeed nothing but cosmic consciousness in the form of the five elements: ether, air, fire, water and earth. This cosmic, ecological insight is also an integral part of Taoism, Chinese medicine, as well as ayurveda. In the human body, the five elements are regulated and controlled by prana, or vital energy, which controls the *vayus*, or vital airs, which are responsible for such organs and activities as heart, lungs, excretion, circulation, etc. These five elements are again linked to the psycho-spiritual vortexes, or subtle energy centres or chakras, located along the spinal column, through which the psycho-spiritual kundalini energy flows. Each chakra controls one of the various elements. Moreover, the chakras, which are also connected to the glandular endocrine system (which in turn is connected to the brain and thus the mind), are chiefly governed by five koshas, or states of mind.

In this brief description, many important details of the tantric or yogic approach to the body–mind are omitted. However, the detailed maps of this intricate and significant body–mind connection constitute a subtle science, one which some scientists have begun to study with great interest. This multilayered hierarchy of being, this intricate body–mind relationship – from cells to nerves, from body to brain, from mind to spirit – has been outlined in great detail over thousands of years by yogis and other spiritual mystics of many different traditions.

The basic premise of this gross and subtle body science is that while aspiring towards inner, lasting bliss, we cannot ignore our physical health and existence in the here and now. Tantra views the body as the base in which the spiritual current needed for transcendence is grounded, and thus a healthy body is an indispensable means to reach higher realizations. In recent times, no one has documented this subject more comprehensively than Esalen founder Michael Murphy. In his pathbreaking thesis *The Future of the Body: Explorations into the Future Evolution of Human Nature*, based in part on the yogic insights of Indian mystic Aurobindo, Murphy describes the importance of an integrated spiritual practice deeply rooted in a sophisticated understanding of the body–mind connection. Thus an integral body–mind practice may include a daily regimen of healthy diet (preferably vegetarian), sports (jogging, weightlifting, etc.), yoga, massage, tai chi and meditation. As it is said in the *Yoga Vashista*, an ancient Sanskrit text, 'For the ignorant person, the body is the source of endless suffering, but to the wise person, the body is the source of infinite delight.'

As all genuine integral sages will point out, the entire creation itself is our body. The body we walk in is made up of the same elemental stuff as the earth beneath our feet. Again we witness the alchemical analogy: As above, so below. We are indeed the earth and our own body is therefore a partner in a great ecology of being that constitutes the environment we live in. From this perspective, a healthy mind in a healthy body means to also lead an environmentally responsible lifestyle. We have bitterly experienced in recent years, that when we pollute the body of the earth, we ultimately pollute our own body, as well.

The Mind-Spirit Connection

In the cosmic scheme of things, matter evolved from consciousness. This view, that consciousness creates the various elemental factors which in turn materialize as matter is unique to the perennial philosophy. In tantra it is said that the five elements are created from the cosmic mind. This part of creation, which we may term 'the spectrum of cosmic-ness', has yet to be clearly explained by modern cosmology or science. On the other hand, both the wisdom of tantra and science agree that mind was created from matter. Tantra holds that because the entire mass of material structure has evolved out of the cosmic mind, the potentiality of mind will always remain latent in matter and under the right conditions it will resurrect itself.

Tantra sees mind as a latent part of all living cells. Where there is life, there is mind or cognition. This concept recently became part of science through the works of Humberto Maturana and Francisco Varela, who rediscovered, so to speak, that 'living systems are cognitive systems and living as a process is a process of cognition'.

In its most basic form, mind exists on a cellular level, residing within the body as oil in a seed. Mind is thus expressed as the most primitive, cellular sensations and instincts, and as it evolves to the human level, its capabilities radically expand through repeated experience. The human mind, as a culmination of this evolution, expresses itself through instincts, emotions and rationality, and is thus capable of expressing everything from speech to logic, from creative imagery to spiritual bliss. The human mind, then, is a microcosmic potential or reflection of the cosmic mind, or the mind of god.

On our brief journey through the micro- and macro-cosmos, we have finally arrived at a crucial aspect within the small chain of being, namely at the beginning stage of what we may call 'spectrum of consciousness'. This concept concerns another universal feature of the perennial philosophy: the human mind can be divided into various levels, spheres or koshas. According to tantra, 'the human being is composed of five layers of mind, just like the banana flower'. The body, or annamaya kosha comprises the sixth layer. Each one of these 'petals' envelopes the other and, depending on the perspective, progressively conceals or reveals the ultimate Brahma.

Similarly, in vedanta Hinduism, an individual is composed of five such sheaths. First is the *annamaya kosha* or the physical body. Second is the *pranamaya kosha* or the sheath composed of life force – it is the connecting link between the physical body and the mind; the sphere of emotions. Third, the *manomaya kosha* is the rational mind. Next is the *vijanamaya kosha* or the sheath of intuition; the subtle mind. Fifth is the *anandamaya kosha* or the sheath of blissful transcendence.

In Mahayana Buddhism, there are eight levels of consciousness. The first five represent the five senses. The next layer of the mind is based on sensory experience. The seventh layer, called *manas*, refers to both higher mind and the centre of the illusion of the separate self. The final level is the *alayavijnana*, the veil before *alaya* or pure Spirit. Later in this book, you will be introduced to yet another kosha model from Anandamurti's tantra that is perhaps more relevant in relation to modern psychology. The essential nature of this spectrum of consciousness model is both profound and simple: our individual mind rests within and is part of the soul. Through an integral body–mind–spirit practice such as tantric yoga, our mind expands through its various layers, and finally, with crystal-clear perception, we are united with the cosmic soul. We have thus realized the goal of tantric yoga, the unification between our individual soul with the cosmic soul.

The Steps Towards Spiritual Permanence

Genuine and permanent spiritual attainments, as demonstrated by Prince Gautama's interior climb through the koshas to final enlightenment and Buddhahood under the Bodhi tree around 600 BC, are not just an Eastern phenomenon. Through the writings of Western sages – such as St John of the Cross, Meister Eckhart, Plotinus, St Teresa of Ávilla, Hildegard of Bingen, and others – it has become obvious that spiritual enlightenment has and will always be a universal, global and human phenomenon. Enlightenment is, of course, not the monopoly of any path or religion. What is true, though, as partly documented by the above descriptions of the koshas, is that the Eastern traditions, and in particular the tantric, have demonstrated a more widespread and sophisticated reliance on a tested and proven spiritual practice. The mystical traditions of the East have shown, beyond a shadow of a doubt, that authentic transformative spirituality is real, and that it is empirical and repeatable. That is, it fulfills all the criteria of a bona fide science. However, as it is an interior science, it must be tried and tested in the deep, inward space laboratory of the individual mind. It must be experienced and verified by the eyes of mind and spirit.

Even though an intellectual understanding of the various states of mind (koshas) is educational, it is of course no substitute for real experience achieved through a genuine spiritual practice. These inner maps are truly only helpful as guides for one's practice. Even though 'accurate', without practice they simply mould into stagnant belief systems, remaining within the mental realm of the intellectual mind as mere rhetorical imitations of the real experience.

Spiritual transformation is beyond mere mental belief or faith; it is beyond the mental realm. Authentic transformative experience is distinguished by a state of direct knowing, a dependable state of subtle, or causal perception. However, and this is very important, the various states of mind, although authentic and realized through a genuine spiritual practice, are often characterized by being of a temporary nature. Such ephemeral jolts of inner rapture are commonly known as 'peak experiences'. These sudden surges of psycho-spiritual insights and ecstasies may last from a few seconds or minutes to a few hours, and they may occur in any of the subtle or causal states of mind, from atimanas to *hiranamaya kosha*. A common occurrence is to enjoy peak experiences during part or most of the meditation practice itself, and then return to a manomaya or kamamaya state once the practice has concluded.

Sometimes powerful meditative ecstasies or 'otherworldly' experiences are marked by visions of deities or ethereal sounds and voices. When these visions or voices are linked with certain pre-rational sentiments, they often give rise to various mythic beliefs. Consequently, many religions, and in particular the New Age movement, are teeming with such irrational or pseudo-spiritual myths. All tantric paths – whether Bhuddist, Christian mystic or yogic in nature – emphasize the importance of viewing such experiences as temporary mental distortions and not a true, inner realization of a subtle or causal nature. If spirit is the sun and the causal mind the blue sky, these experiences are the haze, clouds and smog of the mental and subtle mind covering the sun from cloudless view.

Sincere and prolonged practice will eventually transform the irregular peak encounters into a more prolonged plateau experience of divine oneness. At first they will ripen during meditation practice; then fill the day with a prolonged, blissful awareness, which may even carry over into sleep. Such states may last for days to weeks on end. Moving up from manomaya towards hiranamaya in successive order, each kosha is cleansed and the mind is established in each level. That is, one will not actualize a plateau experience in atimanas kosha before the lower (manomaya) kosha is cleansed. And thus the inner journey advances up the mental hierarchy, one more expanded and higher kosha enveloping and absorbing the lower.

It is very common that experienced meditators have a combination of intermittent peak and sometimes long lasting plateau experiences, thus making up for a colourful roller coaster ride of inner feelings and outer expressions. One moment one may act and feel like a saint, the next like a neurotic. Moreover, a person who has, let's say, advanced to a more or less permanent state of atimanas kosha or higher, may still have communication problems or health problems. A state of near sainthood does not automatically solve all of life's challenges. Despite this, the tantric approach is to see all expressions of life, good or bad, as the play (*leela*) of Shakti. Seeing it all as an expression of the drama of the cosmic joker liberates us from attachment and thus reduces our suffering.

After several years of prolonged practice, some seasoned adepts move towards that effulgent state of permanent attainment (*vashikara*). This state is characterized by the transmutation of one's base propensities (anger, jealousy, shame, etc.) into higher ones (love, discrimination, contentment, etc.) and by a perennial state of all-embracing and infinite bliss. It is from this sublime state the great masters have uttered:

'I and my Father are One.'

– Jesus Christ

'My Self has become the Truth.'

– Buddha

'I am the goal of the wise man, and I am the way.'

– Krishna

The inner journey is thus characterized in the beginning stages by belief and faith, then peak experiences, which consequently move into a prolonged plateau experience, until finally the meditator victoriously attains the state of permanent adaptation. In the tantric model, the first stage on the path of yogic science and introversion into pure spirit is called *yatimana*, and is characterized by a strong faith in achieving results in one's practice, and once in a while a direct sense of achievement or peak experience occurs.

In the next phase, *vyatireka*, a distinct sense of progress is felt through a mixture of peak experiences and a change in certain personal behaviours, yet other areas of the personality are still dysfunctional, and the lofty realms of the higher koshas still remain elusive peaks behind mental clouds of negative attributes and belief systems.

In the *ekendriya* stage, the meditator has achieved a sense of completion by transforming the *ashtapashas* (the eight bondages of fear, hatred, shyness, doubt, pride of heritage, pride of culture, vanity and backbiting) and the *sadripus* (the six enemies of lust, rage, greed, physical attachment, pride and envy) into higher attributes. There is often a sense of great spiritual achievement based on many powerful and prolonged experiences, yet the potential for pitfalls are greater. This, as has been documented in recent years, is the stage when many yogis or 'gurus' are falling like bad apples from the tree of grace.

Only in the final stage of *vashikara siddhi*, the phase of undivided fulfilment or permanent adaptation, is the meditator truly enjoying the state of complete inner liberation. The individual soul has finally merged with the cosmic soul. The mind soars in the oversoul Godlike, never to return back to the old habitat of its small self. This, then, is the stage of true holiness, the mark of the great yogis or yoginis.

The Body–Mind–Spirit Integration

The road towards permanent attainment, towards cosmic consciousness, or Buddha-mind, is complex and often full of pitfalls. The tantric transpersonal approach therefore would be to combine meditation with psychotherapy, exercise, yoga, tai chi, or whatever seems relevant to leading a balanced life. The bottom line is that in order to achieve self-improvement, not to speak of enlightenment, meditation alone is not enough.

The Eastern tantric approach to a balanced body–mind–spirit has traditionally been multifarious: to practice yoga; to adhere to certain ethical principles (tantric yogis observe yama and niyama, Buddhists follow the eightfold path, etc.); to study the perennial philosophy; to practice various meditation techniques, including pranayama (breathing exercises) and chakra visualizations, and to eat a balanced diet, and so on.

In the ashtanga yoga path, for example, which was formally advanced by Patanjali about two thousand years ago – and which is an integral part of the tantra yoga system (also called raja yoga) – a vegetarian diet, yoga and physical exercises are assigned to harmonize the physical body or annamaya kosha; the practice of yama and niyama balances the kamamaya kosha; and devotional practice (chanting and dancing), various visualization and meditation techniques and breathing exercises balance the higher koshas. In short, an authentic and effective spiritual path can be recognized by its integral nature, by its development of the whole being of body–mind–spirit.

To avoid the many possible pitfalls on the path, tantra advocates integrating another aspect of Eastern spirituality, namely the three main branches of yoga: karma (selfless action), jnana (knowledge), and bhakti (devotion). Through selfless action or service to the world, by seeing that all, both giver and receiver, are part of the one, the karma yogi's individual body is spiritually linked with the greater body of the society of people, plants and nature. As Mother Teresa recognized the face of god in the hearts of the dying lepers, prostitutes and beggars she served on the streets of Calcutta, the genuine karma yogis realize god through their service to the various manifestations of spirit in the objective world. Even the simple, mundane act of eating is, for the karma yogi, a sacred, spiritual act. For those who have not attained the sainthood of a Mother Teresa, the danger of the 'path of action' is that one can develop undue pride – selflessness may turn to self-importance.

The key to a balanced karma yoga practice is thus to feel that all aspects and objects involved in an action are but manifestations of the one and only Brahma. If environmental and social activists could agree, their actions would be infinitely more wholesome and effective for both themselves and society. Indeed, everyone's karma would be better off.

For the jnana yogi the supreme goal can be attained through discerning what is relative and what is absolute knowledge. A seasoned jnana yogi is one who has achieved a plateau experience of *viveka* (discrimination) and *vairagya* (non-attachment) of the *vijanamaya kosha*, and an accomplished jnana yogi is one who has realized that the mind's knowledge is only a poor carbon copy of the wisdom of the soul. Jnana yogis are certainly endowed with a brilliant and piercing intellect, but most intellectuals never attain the inner clarity of a true jnana yogi. Most intellectuals remain within the dusty confines of manomaya kosha's rational library. Thus, as the great Greek philosopher Plotinus can be considered a genuine jnana yogi, the great intellectual Karl Marx was certainly not, nor was his capitalist theorist and counterpart Adam Smith. The jnana yogic path has its own traps and potential detours, of course, as the pride and ego of the intellectuals are well known and often put blinders on the individual's potential panoramic view of the soul. But ideally, a jnana yogi serves the world of mind through his or her mental brilliance, supplying the world with lasting wisdom, and seeing the world of mind for what it truly is – nothing but an expression of the all-knowing mind of god.

One of India's greatest jnana yogis, the 8th century saint Shankaracharya, had to admit, however: 'Of all the ways to attain salvation the way of bhakti or devotion is the greatest.' The ecstatic life stories of renowned bhakti yogis like Ramakrishna and Mirabai attest to this path's passionate and poignant love for the divine. In the West, we have seen the supremely exquisite display of such love in many saints, including St Francis of Assisi. The path of devotion, then, is expressed through the intoxicating whirls of the dancing sufis, the earthy god-love songs of the wandering Bauls of Bengal, the otherworldly Gregorian chants of Europe, the trance-inducing bhajans and kirtans sung in village squares and on the roof tops of India, and the drumming, chanting and dances around the village fires of indigenous peoples the world over. The bhakti path is the way of praise, passion and joy. This path of transforming human emotions into sublime devotion is the most universal, ecstatic and probably swiftest way to contact spirit within. Everyone knows the language of love, and for the genuine bhakti yogis, spirit is nothing but true love, and true love is nothing but spirit. That love of spirit is what their hearts are filled with, and that love is what they in turn freely offer to the world. Bhakti yogis of the calibre of Ramakrishna and St Francis are the human embodiment of divine love.

Yet, this path of tender sweetness also has its potential pitfalls, as there is no guarantee that the alchemical mutation from emotion to pure devotion will occur. That is, the religious sentiment may never attain the non-dogmatic realm of spirituality. Suppose, for example, that the love for the chosen deity, mythological image, or prophet remains nothing more than unrefined and sentimental idolatry. Soon a romantic and irrational belief system takes the place of passionate, unadulterated, spiritual love. Indeed, there is nothing more confining for spirit's unfoldment than righteous, fundamentalist passion for what the chosen believers hail to be the one and only name of god.

The tantric spirit of integration thus calls for a harmonious balance of all of these practices. If we examine Ramakrishna's life and personality, for example, we will recognize all these three expressions of spirituality beautifully manifest in the life of this holy madman and village-sage from Bengal. This God-intoxicated bhakti yogi and deity mystic was a worshiper of Goddess Kali (another name for Shakti). In addition, Ramakrishna was a tantric adept who attained the highest state of non-dual realization only hours after receiving initiation by his guru Totapuri. Unlike some Indian yogis, Ramakrishna did not reject the world, retreating to a cave in the Himalayas. Throughout his relatively short life (1836–86) he served the world as a karma yogi in several ways: as a husband, a temple priest, a spiritual teacher and a servant of the poor. Although he went to school for about 12 years, he was not highly educated, but Ramakrishna was a jnana yogi of the highest order. His oral teachings

– based on personal experiences and further elucidated upon by his extensive knowledge of the vedas, puranas and tantras – were spoken in short, terse verses; a language that scholar Lex Hixon described as both 'primitive' and 'sophisticated'. 'Ramakrishna', Hixon writes, 'was constantly operating at the highest level of philosophical and religious refinement and universality .... In secular Western terms, he was a genius.' [44] Gracefully incorporating the three-pronged path of karma, jnana and bhakti yoga, Ramakrishna was a truly 'integral yogi', years before the term was invented by the great Bengali saint and scholar, Sri Aurobindo.

The path of body–mind–spirit integration thus involves incorporating many approaches, both Eastern and Western. The reasons for that are many: While a two-week intensive seminar in meditation may produce some great peak-experiences, you may still suffer from eating disorders. After a while, you may avoid incorporating daily meditation practices into your busy lifestyle, and at that time your past few glimpses of bliss are just that, glimpses of the past. While sports, yoga exercises and a balanced diet may keep you in great shape, from an integral perspective such a self-improvement programme represents just the beginner's first step to spiritual development. While psychotherapy may help you heal emotional wounds and increase your sense of well-being, from a tantric perspective, you may not at all have addressed the ethical aspects of self-improvement. In other words, your self-esteem may have increased, but you may still be both selfish and greedy, and your lifestyle may be far from socially or environmentally responsible. And, spiritually speaking, none of these approaches have even come close to the all-important climb towards the top of the hierarchy of the ever-expanding koshas.

Sure, you might try to pose as 'your own guru', shopping from one practice or path to the next. You might combine yoga and jogging, which will surely make you physically fit and even highly self-motivated. Yet, without other practices for the mind and spirit, you will, in the large context of perennial and integral practice, remain no more than a physically fit, yet spiritually inept beginner. Or worse, you may forget about your physical health all together and instead embark upon a purely ascending, mental journey through the world of books, and thus simply end up an unhealthy, aimless pilgrim in the unknown vastness of your own interior mind.

So the final lesson of all this is simple: it is highly recommended, indeed important, to support our spiritual journey with a perennial philosophy, authentic teachers, and a comprehensive body–mind–spirit practice – in short, an integral approach to the path of inner Enlightenment. In this regard, tantra has had thousands of years to prove its relevance and effectiveness.

Creating a Tantric Lifestyle

Tantric Philosophy: *Muktyakaunksaya Sadguruprapti* – Through the intense desire for liberation, the divine guru appears.

Daily Contemplation: It is said, 'When the disciple is ready the guru will appear.' And according to the sufi mystics, 'If you seek, you shall be found.' The divine guru is Brahma, always present as an all-pervading, omniscient, spiritual entity. For some, the divine guru appears in disguise. The great Indian intellectual Ram Mohan Roy once met a peasant on the road who gave him a leaf. When he came home, he discovered a mantra written on that leaf. He meditated on that mantra and attained the highest realization. My guru, Anandamurti, was a living beacon in my life for many years, and then he passed away. But his teachings and his spirit are more alive than ever. He embodies the meaning of a true guru, and he still guides his disciples to realize the 'Infinite Self'.

Daily Acts of Sacredness

One: The one and only guru is Brahma.

Two: The one and only Brahma will appear in the form of a living teacher and practice if you so desire.

Chapter Nine

TANTRIC ANATOMY:
THE PSYCHOLOGY OF THE SUBTLE BODY

 The idea that we humans are mirror reflections of the universe is quintessentially the essence of the tantric worldview. What is 'out there' in the universe is also 'in here' in the body. The alchemical principle 'As above, so below' is reflected in the idea that the five fundamental factors – ether, air, fire, water and earth – are physical expressions of cosmic consciousness and the basic building blocks of the cosmos as well as the human body. Hence, the tantric worldview is thoroughly ecological and holistic: there is no physical manifestation that is not an integral part of the whole while also simultaneously being an expression of cosmic consciousness. On the human, micro-cosmic level, this integral and holistic worldview is vividly expressed in the relationship between our physical body and its subtle, anatomical counterparts: the luminous wheels of chakras, the psycho-spiritual power of the kundalini, the subtle, energetic nerves of the *nadis*, the vital, energetic flows of the vayus, and the psychological mindscape of the koshas. In this chapter, we will explore all these elements of the subtle anatomy of tantra.

The Cave of the Nine Chakras

How long have the Indian yogis conceived of an ethereal body beyond flesh and blood consisting of chakras and nadis? According to my guru, Anandamurti, the earliest knowledge of these estoteric sciences is as old as human civilization itself.

The ancient Rarh area of West Bengal, the region between the Western plateau and highlands and the Ganges Delta is rich in the history of ancient tantra and has been the home to many great yogis and scholars, including philosopher-yogis Patanjali and Kapila, poets Chandidas, Jaidev, Rabindranath Tagore, and many others. Today, however, this area is neglected and one of the poorest districts in all of India. When spending a few months there some years ago, I was told that this area holds many secrets about tantra and about the wisdom of great men and women, including the Bauls. The following story about the ancient history of chakras, told by the late Kirtanananda Swami, corroborates what I also learnt from other yogis.

'There are many hills in Rarh, with many caves. Once my guru, Anandamurti, told us that if we studied the inscriptions and pictures on the walls of these caves, we could learn much about the ancient history of Rarh, and we would realise that its civilization is over 20,000 years old.

During the Early Stone Age, more than 2 million years ago, Anandamurti said, the humans who lived in caves had not learned how to use fire, so the mouths of their caves were wide enough to receive the warmth and light of the sun. After they had discovered fire, the mouths of the caves became small, since the people living inside had fire for light and heat. After people gave up the habit of living in caves, they often visited the old caves. The great saint Maharishi Kapila [who developed Samkhya philosophy, perhaps as early as 1500 BC] lived in a village in the area, but he composed his philosophy and his theorems of algebra in nearby caves, and he always went to caves to meditate. Even as late as the Buddhist Age, artists painted their paintings on the walls of caves; for they knew they could be preserved there for long periods of time.

Once Anandamurti was sitting on a hill, and he said that on top of this hill there was a large cave with a wide mouth dating back to the Stone Age, and another cave at the foot of the hill, more than fifty feet deep. He told us to go inside that lower cave and look for inscriptions on the walls and floor of the cave. It was very difficult to enter the cave because it was quite narrow in many places and stinking with the excrement of bats, but when we shone our torches we saw, just as Anandamurti had said, inscriptions etched on the walls. As we sketched those designs, we realized that they were the symbols of the subtle nerve currents (nadis) and nerve centees *(chakras)* of the body, including the *ida, pingala,* and *shushumna nadis.*

When we brought our sketches to Anandamurti, he said that these are the symbols of the nine chakras [the two additional chakras are on the tip of the nose and right below the crown chakra]; in that cave ancient yogis used to meditate and with stone implements they drew Tantric symbols on the walls. Anandamurti said that Lord Shiva had systematised *Navachakra sadhana,* the meditation on the nine chakras, which is the oldest sadhana of the world. He said, "I am naming this cave Navachakra Guha, the cave of the nine chakras." If you search you will find more inscriptions inside. You should do more research here, for this is the oldest cave of spiritual sadhana – it is more than 7,500 years old. And it is the most important cave in the history of spirituality and culture on earth.

The tantra of Rarh, Anandamurti said, is even older than Shaiva Tantra, the tantra of Shiva, because when Lord Shiva came to Rarh, tantra was already in existence there. He merely systematised it. Anandamurti said there are many such tantric caves in that area.'[45]

This story alludes to the antiquity of tantra in India as represented by the oral tradition of the yogis, and some day science, through carbon dating and other research methods, may corroborate Anandamurti's assertions as conveyed to his disciple Kirtanananda Swami in the above story.

Chakras, Glands and Healing

While tantra commonly divides human existence into the levels of body, mind and spirit, these divisions are rather artificial and do not reveal the organic and integral relationship between them.

Nor do these divisions adequately account for the fourth level of existence, the subtle energetic level, represented by the chakras, koshas, kundalini, nadis and vayus. These energetic channels are the psychosomatic pathways and bridges linking the body, mind and spirit realms. These elusive nerve channels make us feel the physical reaction in the navel region when we are stricken by fear or intense worry. These subtle pathways also enable us to feel the lightness of being, the psychological insights and creative bursts of energy when kundalini rises to the higher chakras.

Much has been written and speculated about the chakras and kundalini in recent years, especially in many New Age books. Some of this information is very insightful, while some is outright misleading and wrong. It is therefore important to keep in mind that it was the tantric yogis who first discovered the location and function of the chakras in the subtle or astral body, and it is therefore wise to consult this tradition in order to gain a deeper understanding of this fascinating science.

While modern scientists have recently begun investigating this fascinating field of reality, this complex realm of the interior body is still primarily understood, investigated and experienced within tantric yoga. And because tantra is as much an intricate art as it is a complex science, the various yogic schools may explain, emphasize and interpret this knowledge slightly differently. One example of this, and which has led to considerable confusion, is that the colours and shapes of the chakras are some times described differently. The simple answer to this discrepancy is that these colours and shapes are not descriptions of the chakras themselves but rather symbolic representations (yantras) used during concentration exercises, such as in the *tattva dharana* practice (the sixth limb of asthanga yoga), which helps in controlling and balancing the chakras. In other words, these shapes and colours, in conjunction with certain mantras, are used in meditation practice to access, balance and purify the chakras – the physical, mental, as well as energetic wheels of consciousness in our bodies.

Tantric yoga thus functions within the intersecting matrix of the body–mind–spirit continuum, where its goal is to establish physical harmony, mental well-being and spiritual bliss. Experimenting with physical exercises, such as asanas, the tantric yogis realized that the body and mind could be healed and harmonized by affecting various glands within the endocrine system.

Here is a relevant example of the integrated effect of asana practice: While performing shoulder stand (sarvangasana), the legs are raised into the air by resting the body primarily on the shoulders and thus locking the neck and chin, and pressure is mounted on the thyroid and para-thyroid glands. When combining this exercise with the fish posture (matsyendrasana), in which these glands are stimulated by opening and stretching the throat area, one will balance the production of thyroid and para-thyroid hormones and thus regulate physical growth, weight, energy and anxiety levels. The thyroid gland, for example, participates in these processes by producing thyroid hormones, principally triiodothyronine (T3) and thyroxine (T4). These hormones regulate the rate of metabolism and affect the growth and rate of function of many other systems in the body. T3 and T4 are synthesized utilizing both iodine and tyrosine. The thyroid gland also produces a hormone called calcitonin, which plays a role in calcium homeostasis. The parathyroid glands, on the other hand, balance our nervous system and our level of energy. In other words, imbalanced parathyroid glands can leave us fatigued, they can make us nervous, and they can make us become obese, or make us lose weight.

Some years ago, an Italian friend of mind who had been suffering from weight problems due, in part, to an imbalanced thyroid gland, started practicing these exercises regularly. Within a few months, he started losing a significant amount of weight, until he finally regained the youthful look he had in his twenties. I recently met him at a yoga conference in Sweden; now in his late 50s and still practicing yoga asanas, he is still youthful, slim and trim.

Similarly, the psychosomatic interchange between body and mind can also start from the mental and spiritual planes, as many diseases have their karmic cause within the human soul. Thus physical change and healing can take place within the subtle anatomy of the astral body before manifesting changes within the physical body.

While living in a yoga ashram in Copenhagen I had a close female friend who suffered from an 'incurable' illness that some doctors today would likely diagnose as 'chronic fatigue syndrome'. She was always tired and finally became bedridden with multiple symptoms that no doctor, neither holistic nor allopathic, was able to properly diagnose, nor cure. One day, her husband came to our yoga ashram to inform us that he thought his wife would soon die. She had been bedridden for months, and was often unable to walk to the bathroom. Desperate for help, he asked if an older tantric yogi and I could visit their apartment to 'pray and meditate for her'.

The very next day, we found ourselves sitting next to her bed meditating intensely for several hours. The sincerity and appreciation expressed by our friend, who was lying feebly in bed, in regards to our resolute response to her 'last wish' was clearly palpable, and this only increased the intensity and power of our meditative concentration and ecstasy. We finally concluded our meditation by doing guru puja, the singing of Sanskrit mantras surrendering all our actions and spiritual efforts to the divine guru. During this devotional practice, one offers all actions, dreams and hopes to the divine guru – Brahma. When this practice is performed with selfless sincerity, with the idea that 'God knows what is best', one will experience a deep sense of freedom, detachment and grace. Unbeknownst to us, these simple gestures of spiritual service and devotion had a great impact on our friend's well-being and state of mind. Indeed, a few days later her health started improving quite dramatically, and within a few weeks she resumed her normal life as a housewife and mother.

So what caused this mysterious and spontaneous healing? Even though our friend was not able to directly partake in the meditation practice, nor the Sanskrit guru puja prayer, she was psychically and spiritually very much connected to and moved by our actions. So, the tantric explanation is, in part, that change on the subtle level can be instantaneous if the person is 'karmically ready' and open to receive spiritual grace on the energetic plane. Once the healing, psychic energy pattern has 'filtered down' to the physical level, it effects bodily changes. Spiritual energy can thus remove energetic blockages and alter the energetic damages manifested within the subtle body.

Unexplainable illnesses are often manifestations of past karmic seeds embedded in our psycho–physical bodies. Once ripened, these karmic seeds may be surrendered to the higher power of cosmic consciousness and spontaneous healing may take place, through radical, internal, psychic changes within the patient, without the use of medicines. However, if healing does not take place, that is not necessarily because we are any less spiritual, it simply means that we must increase our effort to regain balance by the use of medicines and spiritual practice. Our life's karma is very complex, and sometimes physical healing does not occur, not even to the most spiritual of us. It is therefore best to surrender the results of our efforts to heal and change to the divine guru. Ultimately, it is our inner state of being that truly matters.

This is beautifully illustrated by the life of Ramakrishna, who said in his customary candid manner when he had developed cancer and a pandit named Sasadhar urged him to cure himself, 'This mind has been given up to God, once and for all. How can I withdraw it from him and make it dwell on this worthless body?' For this great tantric sage – who at this point in life remained in a perpetual state of non-dual ecstasy – death was nothing to fear. Not long afterwards, the great saint died peacefully of throat cancer at the relatively young age of 50. Like all great sages before him, Ramakrishna had awakened his crown chakra (*sahasrara*) and discovered the absolute freedom of the formless and the eternal spirit within. Even while in pain and facing death, he was transcendentally awake and free, for he had long realized the spiritual truth spoken by the European mystic Meister Eckhart hundreds of years earlier: 'God is a being beyond being and a nothingness beyond being. Therefore, be still and do not flinch from this emptiness.'

Another sign of a god-realized soul, who has activated his kundalini to the highest level of existence, is the ability to arouse this spiritual force in others (*shaktipath*) and replicate the experience of cosmic consciousness or samadhi. During the last months before his own death, Ramakrishna enabled Vivekananda, his soon-to-be world famous disciple, to experience samadhi. In a terse voice, Ramakrishna told Vivekananda: 'Now Mother has shown you everything. But what she has shown will be hidden from you. It will be shut up in a box, like a jewel – and I'll keep the key. When you have finished doing mother's work on earth, then the box will be unlocked and you'll know everything you knew just now.'

Another common ability for one who has raised his kundalini and controlled the higher chakras, is the god-realized soul's gift for prophecy and clairvoyance. Shortly after Vivekananda experienced samadhi, Ramakrishna told the other monks in the ashram: 'Naren [Vivekananda's name at the time] will give up his body of his own free will. When he knows who he really is, he'll refuse to stay on this earth. Very soon, he's going to shake the world with his intellect and his spiritual power. But the veil is so thin; it may be torn at any moment.'

A few years after Ramakrishna's death, Vivekananda was acknowledged world-wide as an intellectual giant and recognized for introducing Indian culture and tantra in the form of raja yoga and vedanta to the Western world. He was acknowledged by his school teachers as a genius and publicly as a fiery and brilliant speaker. The French Nobel Laureate Romain Rolland is reported to have said: 'His words are great music, [with] phrases in the style of Beethoven.' As the first Indian yogi to visit America, he quickly inspired the young nation's learned elite with his lectures and infectious enthusiasm. But as prophesized by Ramakrishna, his rich and influential life was short-lived. Vivekananda entered mahasamadhi (great union) at his ashram in Belur Math in Calcutta (now Kolkata) at the young age of 39. Not only that, as he had prophesied a few months earlier to his American disciples while travelling in Egypt, Vivekananda died on 4 July, the day when America celebrates Independence Day.

Tantra recognizes that there can be no perfect state of balance on the physical and mental planes as this manifest world is in a continuous state of change. We are affected by our past karma, both genetically and psychologically; we are effected by our environment, by the demands placed upon us our by family and work, and eventually by the physical limitations of old age and illness. Hence, tantric yogis are well-aware of the importance in balancing this onslaught of challenging energies by maintaining physical and mental well-being through yogic exercises, vegetarian diet, tantric medicine (ayurveda) and meditation. However, tantra does not recommend retreating to a cave in the Himalayas to escape the world to find enlightenment. It is possible to seek enlightenment and maintain personal *prama* or dynamic equilibrium, while still living a life deeply involved in the affairs of this challenging world. But, as we have seen in the examples of Ramakrishna and Vivekananda, great tantric yogis do not live forever; when their work on this earthly plane is complete, they fearlessly and willingly renounce their physical existence to be gracefully united with spirit. Thus, our life is ultimately not just measured in how accomplished we are in the relative world, but mainly in how realized and fulfilled we are in the inner realm of spirit.

Chakras as Luminous Wheels of Consciousness

When a group of yogis practice tantric meditation, one may sometimes hear the sound 'Hum!' loudly exclaimed by one of the meditating yogis. His or her body may shake as if struck by a current of electricity from within. This shouting and shaking is due to the awakening of the kundalini or Shakti, as this cosmic force in human form attempts to climb upwards through the luminous wheels or chakras along the spine, upwards towards the sahasrara. For someone not accustomed to the strong current, the force may be too much to handle and the meditator falls to the ground, or rolls on the floor laughing loudly. At other times, someone may become very emotional and experience tears of sadness or tears of deep joy and devotion. But most often, the meditation room is quiet and people are simply engaged in the silent breathing that takes place during group meditation. Indeed, it is not always the kundalini that manifests its energetic climb through the chakras in audible or visible outbursts. Most of the time, the awakening of the chakras is a rather quiet affair, manifesting itself in internal insights, such as feelings of love, deep conscience or empathy, or simply an inner sense of stillness, peace and bliss.

Equally often, the beginning meditator will experience unsettling emotions, such as confusion, anger, unease and stress, because meditation brings us in contact with our shadow self – the darker world of *vrittis*, our mental tendencies or instincts acquired from previous unwholesome actions, either in this or previous lives. Through the power of the siddha mantras employed in meditation, our past karmas are released more quickly when on the tantric path. But it is even more common that the mind is simply busy making plans for the future, anxiously thinking about the many tasks waiting at work tomorrow, or excitedly musing about a trip to the beach next month. No matter the state of mind, if one stays centred on the mantra, concentrates on the chakra prescribed by the teacher, and lets the mind flow in harmony with the deep breathing while allowing these feelings to just come and go, one will gradually become awake and at peace in the moment. With regular training, the breathing cycle gradually slows down to just a few breaths a minute, and the mind settles in the depth of the breath's invisible silence. Thirsty for revelation, the student inhales deeply from the tranquility of its cool and long pause, awakened by its depth of peace and wisdom.

Tantric cosmology teaches that our body, mind and spirit are micro-cosmic mirrors of the macro-cosmic universe. The cosmic force and creative principle of Shakti, which created the universe with all its stars and galaxies, is also the creative principle within us humans in the form of the kundalini force. Indeed, the kundalini force is the cosmic Shakti in human form. As the human body replicate the currents of the cosmos, the first five chakras, or subtle energy centres of the human body are the controlling points of the five fundamental factors of creation in the human body.

One of the main tantric meditation techniques to awaken and control the chakras is called *tattva dharana*, the elemental body concentration method mentioned above. Through this practice, we are not only getting in touch with the subtle anatomy of the chakras and its inherent link to the functions of the endocrine system, we are also getting in touch with the various levels of the mind (koshas), as well as the ecological nature of the body and its relationship with the cosmos. In effect, we link up with the basic elements of nature, with ether, air, fire, water and earth and these elements' corresponding levels in the human mind in the form of chakras and koshas. In this way, we tune in to the dynamic relationship between ourselves and the spiritual ecology of the universe in which we live.

Science and the Chakras

Dr Hiroshi Motoyama bridges the world of both science and spirituality – he is both a scientist and a Shinto priest. The founder of the International Association for Religion and Parapsychology, he was recognized by the United Nations Educational, Scientific and Cultural Organization (UNESCO) as one of the world's ten foremost parapsychologists. As a scientist with a keen interest in chakra research, he has developed a chakra instrument designed to detect minute electrical, magnetic and optical changes occurring in the immediate environment of his laboratory subjects. Using this instrument, Motoyama found that when an advanced yoga practitioner who regularly meditated on the Anahata chakra (heart chakra) was tested, the heart centre showed considerable intensification of measurable activity during the period of concentration. This measurable activity corresponded to the subject's regular spiritual practice. If the subject did not generally use the Manipura chakra (solar plexus chakra) as a focal point for meditation, there was less measurable activity in that region. Experiments such as these, conducted with over 100 subjects led Motoyama to conclude 'that mental concentration on a chakra activates it'. [46]

Professor Emeritus of Physiological Science at the University of California, Los Angeles, Dr Valerie V. Hunt, has measured human electromagnetic output in the body using an electromyography (EMG) instrument. Such an instrument normally records the electrical activity of the muscles, but Hunt, like Motoyama, used it for chakra research. Using the EMG instrument, Hunt recorded radiations emanating from the body at the sites traditionally associated with the chakras and discovered that certain types of consciousness are related to certain frequencies. Yogis and healers registered the highest number of cycles per seconds, over 900 characters per second (cps), while those whose consciousness was 'more anchored in the physical world' only registered 250 cps. [47]

Perhaps the most intriguing form of research into the subtle anatomy of the body and its relationship to the brain has been conducted by Dr Candace Pert, a physiology and biophysics scientist at Georgetown Medical University in Washington D. C. Like the tantric yogis, she claims we are all 'hardwired for bliss'. Indeed, this esteemed scientist thinks we are all biologically programmed for happiness, which is exactly what tantra has claimed and made into a science for thousands of years. Her research over the last 30 years has led her to conclude that this bliss is created by major endorphin pathways that lead from the back of the brain to the frontal cortex, where we have the most opioid receptors – the cellular bonding sites for endorphins. Endorphins are naturally occurring opioids that dull pain and produce euphoria when they bind with opioid receptors. They literally alter our mood on the cellular level. These morphine-like substances are linked to the pituitary gland, or the third eye in yoga terminology. Endorphins are also produced by runners' high, relaxation, acupuncture, laughter, playfulness and breast feeding. We may call them peptides for bliss, bonding and attachment. When we lack these feelings of bliss and bonding, drugs often become a substitute, and we develop substance addiction, which, in turn, suppresses the natural production of endorphins. We become depressed and end up in a vicious cycle where more drugs are needed to feel good. [48]

Generally, our more positive mental tendencies are linked to the heart chakra and above. Thus when chakras are prescribed for concentration during meditation, we generally focus on the four top chakras, as such practices produce an electrical and hormonal activity that synchronizes our feelings of love, belonging, harmony and expansion of the mind. There are also chakra meditations, however, such as *chakra shodana*, which creates balance and harmony between the chakras, and this practice focuses on all the chakras in a dynamic and circular fashion.

The endorphins produced in the third eye, where the pituitary gland and the hypothalamus are located, are especially created when the mind is focused on the third eye between the eye brows. This *ajna chakra* (third eye) is therefore a highly important focus of concentration and meditation in tantra. But when sitting down to meditate, we do not immediately start the focus of our attention here; we actually start in the lower chakras and gradually, through the process of concentration and sense withdrawal, move towards the higher chakras and finally focus our attention on either the anahata (heart), ajna (third eye) or the sahasrara chakra (crown chakra) to meditate. The selection of either chakra is not accidental and is generally prescribed by an experienced teacher.

The heart chakra is the place in our body in which we feel and express love and cooperation, positivity, hope and attachment. This chakra is also the abode of intuition, conscience, repentance and self-esteem. Some of the negative tendencies associated with this chakra are vanity, arrogance, anxiety, worry, greed, avarice, hypocrisy, deception, nervous breakdown and argumentativeness. Thus, tantric meditation and yoga has two purposes: to overcome and control the negative tendencies associated with a certain chakra and to increase the positive sentiments. In addition, tantric practice guides us further in moving beyond both the positive and negative sentiments towards the non-dual realm of the third eye and the crown chakra, where there are no expressions of negative emotions. Therefore, the highest tantric meditations are always associated with the application of energy, with psychic and spiritual force, in order to move from the static, dull and limiting energy of the lower chakras, and the negative mental tendencies associated with them, towards these two higher chakras. In fact, this is tantra's unique contribution to yoga: to empower us with techniques to embrace our dark propensities and to unreservedly transmute these negative energies into positive energy. It is for this fundamental and revolutionary faculty that tantra is referred to as a path of transmutation and liberation.

The Subtle Anatomy of the Chakras

When we are fearful, we know it by the feeling of panic and unease we experience in our stomach, in our third chakra. When we are in love, we feel the warming petals of euphoria opening our hearts in our fourth chakra. These feelings are not accidental; they are related to the psychic concentration of fear and love located in these respective chakras. Scientific research has also confirmed the existence of energy fields in the areas of the chakras, as we saw from the research done by Dr Valerie V. Hunt and Dr Hiroshi Motoyama. Furthermore, the late Dr Candace Pert, a leader in the field of psychoneuroimmunology, discovered a high concentration of a specific neuropeptide at the location of the classical chakras. This neuropeptide, called vasoactive intestinal peptide (VIP), is critical in regulating the neural immune switches between the brain and the immune system.

Anandamurti asserts that chakras are related to nerve plexus – networks in the autonomic nervous system that run near the spine. These are places where nerves converge and form a network, allowing for complex communication between nerve cells and the generation of more complex, functional activities. These nerve plexus are the physiological counterparts of the subtle energy body of the chakras.

Anandamurti and other yoga masters have also pointed out that chakras are associated with endocrine glands. Science has recently recognized the close functional relationships between the endocrine system and the nervous system – so much so that both systems are referred to as the neuroendocrine system. The relationship between mood and the nervous system has long been understood and has even entered the vernacular with expressions such as 'It gets on my nerves' or 'You've got some nerve!' Hormones secreted by the endocrine glands also have a profound effect on our moods – as any woman who has experienced premenstrual syndrome (PMS) or anyone with low thyroid function can attest. The yogis understood that when the nerve plexus and endocrine glands functioned properly, the mind was balanced, the body felt better and meditation became easier – in other words, balanced chakras equals a balanced mind. By doing specific yoga postures regularly, we can regulate the function of the neuroendocrine system and thereby balance the chakras.

The tantric yogis taught that each chakra was like a lotus flower surrounded by a specific number of petals. They called these petals *vrittis.* A vritti is a mental tendency or propensity – a potential state of mind. You have probably seen drawings of yogis sitting in lotus position with the seven, many-petalled chakras drawn on their body, from the bottom of the spine to the crown of the head. This image gives us a symbolic idea of the energy patterns the chakras and vrittis create.

The six lower chakras have a total of 50 petals. These petals represent the 50 main vrittis or vortices of psychic energy. Some of the 50 Sanskrit terms can be roughly translated as 'fear', 'irritability', 'greed', 'hypocrisy', 'hope', 'affection', 'surrender'. The four petals of the first chakra represent all the desires of human life: physical, mental, psycho–spiritual and spiritual (kama, artha, dharma and moksha in Sanskrit). The second chakra's vrittis express the darker side of human nature such as pitilessness, indifference, self-indulgence and cruelty. The third chakra's vrittis, such as irritability, shame, lethargy and craving, are perhaps the biggest challenge to our human potential. The fourth chakra's vrittis reflect our higher capacities for both beauty and destruction such as hope, love and effort and conversely greed, arrogance and hypocrisy. The fifth chakra contains vrittis which elevate us to the sublime, such as altruism, universality and surrender to a higher power. The sixth chakra's vrittis speak to our capacity for limitless knowledge.

These chakras, with their distinct vritti petals, create specific patterns of psychic energy. A person with a problem with depression, for example, would manifest a specific distorted pattern of energy within different chakras, depending on which vrittis contribute to their specific state of depression. [49] Since different people manifest depression in different ways, each person would have a distortion in their energy pattern based on his or her own specific way of manifesting that imbalance.

Samskaras: Imprints from Past Lives or from Yesterday

So now that we have looked at chakras and vrittis, let us look at the word samskara. Samskara is a Sanskrit term which means 'reactive-momentum'. Why do two people who face the exact same challenge respond differently? Why does losing a child cause one person to create a support group, develop a scholarship fund, volunteer at a local school, and find a deep inner peace while it causes another person to sink into deep despair, become bitter and withdraw from his or her relationships? Why, when these two people have experienced the same event, are the patterns of psychic energy they express so different? It all depends on our samskaras.

According to tantra, we bring certain samskaras into the world with us when we are born. People often call this concept karma, and it is much the same idea. We all come into this world with different sets of challenges, or different samskaras. These samskaras helps dictate which vrittis will be activated and cause mental imbalances. The two people who lost a child have come into this world with very different samskaras, therefore they react very differently to the same event.

So what is happening when you find yourself continually having challenges around a particular emotion? Say for example, you find yourself getting irritated at all sorts of insignificant issues which normally would not bother you. Or perhaps you have suddenly developed a tremendous fear of public speaking. Both of these scenarios are symptoms of a mental imbalance. The psychic pattern of chakra energy, distorted by the samskaras and activated vrittis, have created imbalances in the emotional state, which then causes us to act nervously or angrily.

Western science has given us the ability to look at how these energies relate to our physiology. Candace Pert's research on psychoneuroimmunology has been groundbreaking in showing how mental/emotional states are produced all over the body and are not confined to the brain. Pert explains that nerve cells have long finger-like endings which reach out and send neuropeptides to other cells. When we are sad, the nerves produces neuropeptides that promote sadness and send that chemical to all the cells in the body, so that every cell in the body becomes sad—your skin is sad, your bones are sad, your toes are sad; literally, the whole body becomes sad. [50]

Similarly, according to tantra, an imbalance in the chakra due to vritti activation creates an energy field that is picked up by very subtle nerve currents (*nadis* in Sanskrit). The mind becomes perturbed, which in turn stimulates or inhibits the secretion of the endocrine gland associated with that particular chakra causing an over- or under-secretion of hormone, which in turn activates a certain physical or emotional response.

Specific yoga postures can help strengthen the endocrine glands and nerves associated with the particular imbalanced chakras. If you have an imbalance of the fear vritti, you can use postures which primarily balance the third chakra, such as the mayur asana (peacock pose) which put tremendous pressure on the third chakra. The peacock asana is especially good for people who have fear of public speaking. By practicing this asana regularly for a few weeks or months, one may overcome this inhibition. Specific asanas held for specific periods of time put sustained, alternating pressure on the endocrine glands and help them to function better through facilitating blood circulation. The better functioning glands begin to shift the energy field of the chakra, helping to bring the disturbed vrittis into balance. Moreover, the tantric meditation technique *chakra shodhana*, in which a mantra is recited repeatedly in each chakra in a specific sequence, creates a harmonious flow between each chakra and thus balances our emotions and creates a deep sense of peace and bliss.

There is a deep need, both individually and collectively in our world, to achieve balance in our body and mind. So much of the pain and suffering people experience today is due to the lack of peace which yoga can bring to our lives. The biopsychology of yoga can give us the tools to change the underlying factors that bring us unhappiness and dissatisfaction. All of us humans are consciously or unconsciously seeking to unblock the energy of our fourth chakra, our heart chakra, and to allow compassion, magnanimity and love to flow freely. There is a deep, collective force within us that wants to surmount our lower vrittis and merge our hearts and minds with other peoples' hearts and minds, indeed, with all of life. This is both the greatest desire of the human heart and its greatest challenge. And tantra has many of the answers to unlock and awaken that possibility.

If we are essentially one with Brahma, what causes us not to experience this oneness at all times? Why are we humans different from each other? Why does one person feel shy, while another has a sense of pride, and a third person a strong propensity for anger? The reason, according to tantra, is that we have different mental make-ups, different karmic backgrounds, and different samskaras. In addition, our personal nature depends on the condition of the various glands in our body, because these glandular imprints are part of our karma or samskaras from earlier times, even from past lives.

The various types of mental tendencies in human beings are caused by the different *vrittis*, or propensities, which are rooted in the human glands surrounding the various chakras in the body. The sahasrara chakra, or pineal gland, is the controlling point of all these vrittis. Hence, the goal of tantra is to gain control over this so-called crown chakra by elevating one's kundalini (Shakti) through the practice of hatha yoga and meditation. This subtle elevation, from the first chakra to the seventh chakra, is both the path and goal of tantra.

The Chakras: A Map of the Subtle Body

Below is a detailed blueprint of the chakras, their related locations, organs, shapes, colours, glands and sounds. Please note that the *Muladhara Chakra*, which is often termed as the lowest chakra, is, in a sense, actually the 'highest' chakra. Why? Because it contains all that we need to become god-awakened human beings, namely the four basic propensities for success in life: dharma (psycho–spiritual longing); artha (psychic longing); kama (physical longing); moksha (spiritual longing). Indeed, it is because of the existence of these beautiful and powerful longings in the lowest chakra that we have an innate urge to survive and to proceed on our spiritual journey towards the highest chakra, the crown chakra of enlightenment. Finally, please also note that the pronunciation of each root sound is important and rarely, if ever, as done here, taught correctly in books.

Muladhara Chakra

- Anatomical location: In males between the scrotum and the anus; in females on the posterior side of the cervix.
- Root sound: Lam' (pronounced *lang*. For best effect, the root sound is pronounced silently during meditation)
- Tanmatra: Smell
- Organ: Nose
- Corresponding Kosha: Kamamaya Kosha (conscious mind)
- Element: Earth
- Plexus: Terranean Plexus
- Gland: Testis
- Vrittis: 1. Dharma (psycho-spiritual longing); 2. Artha (psychic longing); 3. Kama (physical longing); 4. Moksha (spiritual longing)
- Corresponding Sanskrit letters: Va, Sha, S'a, Sa

Svadhistana Chakra

- Anatomical location: At the base of the spine, at the level of the coccyx or tailbone. In front of the body it is at the level of the pubic bone.
- Root sound: Vam' (pronounced *vang*)
- Tanmatra: Taste
- Organ: Tongue
- Kosha: Manomaya Kosha (subconscious mind)
- Element: Water
- Plexus: Fluidal Plexus
- Gland: Ovary
- Vrittis: 1. Avajna (indifference); 2. Murcha (psychic stupor); 3. Prasharya (indulgence); 4. Avishvasa (lack of confidence); Sarvanasha (terror); 6. Krurata (crude manners)
- Corresponding Sanskrit letters: Ba, Bha, Ma, Ya, Ra, La

Manipura Chakra

- Anatomical location: Navel
- Root sound: Ram' (Pronounced *rang*)
- Tanmatra: Sight
- Organ: Eyes
- Kosha: Atimanas Kosha (unconscious mind)
- Element: Fire
- Plexus: Ignasus Plexus
- Glands: Thymus, pancreas and adrenal
- Vrittis: 1. Lajja (shyness); 2. Pashupati (sadism); 3. Iirsa (envy); 4. Susupti (lethargy); 5. Visada (melancholia); 6. Kasaya (peevishness); 7. Trsna (yearning for acquisition); 8. Moha (infatuation); 9. Ghrna (hatred); 10. Bhaya (fear)
- Corresponding Sanskrit letters: D'a, D'ha, N'a, Ta, Tha, Da, Dha, Na, Pa, Pha

Anahata Chakra

- Anatomical location: Heart, centre of the chest.
- Root sound: Yam' (Pronounced *yang*)
- Tanmatra: Touch
- Organ: Skin
- Kosha: Vijanamaya Kosha (subliminal mind)
- Element: Air
- Plexus: Sidereal Plexus
- Gland: Thymus
- Vrittis: 1. Asha (hope); 2. Chinta (anxiety); 3. Chesta (effort); 4. Mamata (hope); 5. Dambha (vanity); 6. Viveka (conscience); 7. Vikalata (mental numbness); 8. Ahamkara (ego); 9. Lolata (avarice); 10. Kapatata (hypocrisy); 11. Vitarka (argumentativeness); 12 Anatupa (repentance)
- Corresponding Sanskrit letters: Ka, Kha, Ga, Gha, Una, Ca, Cha, Ja, Jha, Ina, T'a, T'ha

Vishuddha Chakra

- Anatomical location: Throat
- Physiological concomitant: Pharyngeal and laryngeal nerve plexus
- Root sound: Ham' (Pronounced *hang*)
- Tanmatra: Sound
- Organ: Ear
- Kosha: Hiranmaya Kosha (causal mind)
- Element: Air
- Plexus: Sideral Plexus
- Glands: Thyroid and parathyroid
- Vrittis: 1. Sadaja (sound of peacock, first note in Indian musical scale); 2. Rasabha (sound of bull, second note); 3. Gandhara (sound of goat, third note); 4. Madhyama (sound of deer, fourth note); 5. Panchama (sound of cuckoo, fifth note); 6. Daevata (sound of donkey, sixth note); 7. Nisada (sound of elephant, seventh note); 8. Om (cosmic sound); 9. Humm (sound of kundalini); 10. Phat (practication); 11. Vaosat (mundane service); 12 Vasat (psychic service); 13. Svaha (psycho-spiritual service; 14. Namah (surrender); 15. Visa (repulsive expression); 16. Amrta (sweet expression)
- Corresponding Sanskrit letters: A, A', I, II, U, U', R, Rr, Lr, Lrr, E, Ae, O, Ao, Am', Ah.

Ajna Chakra

- Anatomical location: Between eyebrows
- Physiological concomitant: Pineal
- Root sound: Tham' (Pronounced *thang*)
- Tanmatra: None
- Organ: none
- Kosha: Above the koshas, atman
- Element: None
- Plexus: Lunar Plexus
- Gland: Pineal and pituitary

- Vrittis: 1. Apara (mundane knowledge); 2. Para (spiritual knowledge)
- Corresponding Sanskrit letters: Ks'a, Ha

Sahasrara Chakra

- Anatomical location: Crown of head
- Root sound: None
- Tanmatra: None
- Organ: none
- Kosha: Above the koshas, paramatman
- Element: None
- Plexus: Macro-propensive plexus
- Vrittis: This chakra controls all the lower chakras, koshas and vrittis. Hence yogis whose mind is constantly within the realm of the two highest chakras are above the influence of lower human tendencies and indeed living saints.
- Corresponding Sanskrit letters: None [51]

Creating a Tantric Lifestyle

Tantric Philosophy: *Vadha Sa Yusamana Shaktih Sevyam Sthapayati Laksye* – An obstacle is a helping force which brings one to the goal.

Daily Contemplation: Anandamurti often said that obstacles and difficulties are not to be feared or avoided; rather they should be embraced as if they are our greatest friends. By facing our challenges, we face our past samskaras, and we become free of their mental and physical bondages.

Daily Acts of Sacredness

One: Make a vow to overcome a challenge you have avoided for some time.

Two: Make another vow to overcome another challenge you have avoided for some time.

Chapter Ten

TANTRIC PSYCHOLOGY:
KOSHAS, CHAKRAS, KUNDALINI AND KARMA

How the Secret Sounds of the Chakras Created Sanskrit and Indian Music

According to the subtle science of tantra, every vibration in this universe has both colour and sound. Every vibration also represents a particular idea, and therefore each idea, too, has a vibrational sound and vibrational colour. Moreover, each of the 50 vrittis, from muladhara to ajna chakra, has a vibrational sound called a bija mantra or root sound. Each of these inaudible, core sounds were discovered by tantric yogis in deep meditation and constitutes one letter in the Sanskrit alphabet. We are normally not able to hear these root sounds, because many vibrational waves are not audible to the human ear. These fundamental matrixes are subtle vibrations emanating from each chakra and when the Sanskrit language is spoken, chanted in kirtan or recited as a mantra during meditation, these sounds vibrate from within the corresponding chakras. This subtle wisdom science is the reason that Sanskrit is considered a sacred language and the most suitable language for healing, meditation and spiritual chanting.

According to Anandamurti 'The sound *a*, is the acoustic root of creation, and thus is the controller of the seven notes of Indian music'. [52] These seven notes are located in the throat, or vishuddha chakra. Although the sound 'a' indirectly controls the seven musical notes, it chiefly controls the first note, *śad–aja*. The letter 'a' is thus the first step in the learning of music. In Occidental music, the octave (do-re-mi-fa-so-la-ti-do) has evolved in a similar way. The main variance between Occidental and Oriental music is that in the former, the first note, śad–aja (or 'do'), is repeated at the end to form an octave. Thus in Oriental music, it is termed *surasaptaka* or musical 'septave' (collection of seven notes) whereas in Occidental music we term it 'octave' (collection of eight notes).

According to the Shiva Puranas, it was the great tantric sage Shiva who arranged these sounds in the form of the *septave*, which contributed both to the acoustics of tantric science and the rhythmic phonetics of music. 'Hence', writes Anandamurti, 'in the study of music we cannot afford to forget [Shiva's] unique contribution'. [53]

Through the ingenious combination of different sounds, Shiva created six basic ragas and thirty-six raginis. This revolutionary contribution to the world of music earned Shiva the epithet Nádatanu (embodiment of divine sound) in the vedas. However, it was Maharishi Bharata who, several millennia after Shiva, popularized these ragas and raginis amongst the Indian intelligentsia.

The Secret Origin of the Om Sound

Of the many names for god, Om is most likely the oldest and one of the most widely used throughout the Indian sacred traditions. Om's significance as a celestial syllable in Indian spiritual culture is illustrated by this simple story.

There was once a sadhu who owned nothing but a water pot and a book. Every day he would worship the book with offerings of flowers, and then he would read the book with intense concentration for hours on end. One day, a curious onlooker asked the sadhu what book he was reading. Without answering the sadhu simply handed him the book. When the onlooker opened it, he discovered the book contained only two words written in bold red letters on every page: Om Rama. The sadhu explained: 'What's the use of reading many volumes of books? God is the origin of all sacred books and scriptures, and there is no difference between God and His name.'

In the vedas we are told: 'In the beginning was the Lord of creatures, and second to Him was the word ... the word was truly the supreme Brahma.' And in the Christian Bible, which uses the word Om in the form of Amen, it is stated in the first verse of the *Gospel of John*: 'In the beginning was the Word, and the Word was with God, and the Word was God.' In other words, it is commonly understood throughout human sacred history that the idea of god and the word that symbolizes god are inseparable, that some words truly are what they express.

The sacred sound Om is commonly understood in tantra as the cosmic sound vibration that originates, maintains and reabsorbs everything in the universe. What is not so commonly recognized, however, is that the Sanskrit letter 'Rr', which is located in the throat, or vishuddha, chakra, is the acoustic root of the sacred Om sound. This revered sound is often chanted at the beginning and conclusion of yoga practice and so many other sacred ceremonies. But how can the letter Rr be the acoustic root of the famous Om sound? Indeed, what is actually the origin of the Om sound?

According to tantric philosophy, the physical universe constitutes three elements: creation (A), preservation (U) and destruction (M). Hence the letters A + U = O, and the letters A + U + M = OM. But that is not the end of the story; the dot (.) and the crescent that forms part of the Om symbol are also important. The dot represents the unmanifest universe; the crescent represents the principle of transmutation from the unmanifest (nirguna) to the manifest (saguna). Hence, Om is the acoustic root of creation, preservation and destruction, plus the principle of transmutation, the devolution from pure cosmic consciousness to the physical world.

Even though the sonic sound Om (which symbolically includes the dot and the crescent) constitutes the acoustic root of this universe, the Om sound is nevertheless a combination of sounds, thus it requires an acoustic root of its own. In Sanskrit, the acoustic root of another root sound is called *atibija*, or *mahabija*. So the letter Rr is the mahabija of Om. Hence, from the point of view of phonetics and the science of combining sounds (*sandhi*), the Rr sound is an integral part of the Sanskrit alphabet and the acoustic root of the sacred letter Om.

There is also a more down-to-earth explanation for using Om as the most sacred syllable. Om is simply the most comprehensive and most complete word to be found, simply by the way it is pronounced. When pronouncing Om, we combine all possible positions of the throat, mouth and tongue. You start with A, the root sound, in the back of the throat without touching the tongue or palate. You continue with the O sound by rolling through the mouth from throat to the lips. And you conclude pronouncing the sacred syllable with M by closing the lips. Hence, that is how Om, tantric yoga's most sacred and complete word, is produced.

In his bestselling book, *Light on Yoga*, world-renowned hatha yoga teacher B. K. S. Iyengar describes the psychological and spiritual reasons for chanting Om. 'The letter A symbolizes the conscious or waking state,' Iyengar writes, 'the letter U the dream state, and the letter M the dreamless sleep state of the mind and spirit.' In its totality as a symbol, Om stands for the 'realization of man's divinity within himself.'

Layers of Consciousness: The Tantric Kosha Model

The science of the chakras is intimately linked to the creation of language and music, and these chakras also form the basis of tantric psychology. Simply put, each chakra represents a state of mind, a state of consciousness, which we refer to as a kosha, or a layer of mind. In Jungian psychology, the first chakra represents the conscious mind, the second the subconscious mind, and the third the unconscious mind. The fourth and the fifth chakra represent, according to tantra, the causal mind, the deep recesses of the transcendental mind of spirituality. We will now take a closer look at how modern tantra divides these koshas or sheaths of the mind and thus beautifully complements the more commonly known vedantic kosha model of yoga psychology:

1. *Annamaya Kosha*: The physical body, composed of the five fundamental factors or elements. Controlled by the crudest layer of mind, the *kamamaya kosha*.

- **Tantric practices to develop this kosha:** yoga asanas, bandhas and hatha yoga pranayama, vegetarian diet, exercise.
- **Natural habits developing this kosha:** Vegetarian diet, exercise.

2. Kamamaya Kosha: This state of mind is the 'desire' kosha; also known as conscious or crude mind. It has three functions: a) sensing external stimuli from the outside world through the sense organs of the body; b) having desires on the basis of those stimuli; and c) acting to materialize those desires by using the motor organs. This layer of the mind controls the motor organs and the instincts; it activates the body to satisfy the basic instincts of hunger, sleep, sex and fear, but it also contains an inherent spiritual impetus for personal growth and enlightenment. The kamamaya kosha interacts with and controls the first chakra, the root chakra.

- **Tantric practices developing this kosha:** yama and niyama, or yogic ethics (first and second limbs of asthanga yoga).
- **Natural means of developing this kosha:** environmental challenges, overcoming illness, physical exercise, travel, etc.

3. Manomaya Kosha: The mental layer of mind also called the subconscious or subtle mind. This state of mind controls the conscious mind. It has four functions: a) memory; b) rationality; c) experience of pleasure and pain based on reactions from past deeds; and d) dreaming. This kosha interacts with and controls the second chakra, the genital chakra.

- **Tantric practice developing this kosha:** rajadhiraja pranayama (fourth limb of asthanga yoga in which a breathing exercise is infused with spiritual ideation using a mantra).
- **Natural habits to develop this kosha:** physical challenges and exercise.

4. Atimanasa Kosha: The supra-mental or subtle mind, the layer of direct knowing, creative insight and extrasensory perception. Although most people spend the majority of their lives in the kamamaya and manomaya koshas, sometimes this layer is accessed through deep contemplation, artistic inspiration, or intellectual discovery. In this layer a deep yearning for and sometimes an experience of spirit is felt very intensely. This kosha interacts with and controls the third chakra, the navel chakra.

- **Tantric practice developing this kosha:** *pratyahara* or sense withdrawal, through particular meditation techniques in which the mind is turned inwards in preparation for higher meditation (fifth limb of asthanga yoga).
- **Natural habits to develop this kosha:** contact with spiritual people, exposure to sacred cultures and ideas, self-study and education, etc.

5. *Vijanamaya Kosha*: The first layer of the causal mind, also called the 'special knowledge' kosha. In this level of mind one is able to pierce through the veil of the gross, objective reality and get a glimpse of the world as it really is – simply spirit. Many divine attributes are expressed through this state of mind – mercy, gentleness, serenity, non-attachment, steadiness, success, cheerfulness, spiritual bliss, humility, magnanimity and more. This kosha has two main functions: a) discernment (viveka); and b) non-attachment. True discernment means to be able to discriminate between relative and absolute truth. True non-attachment does not mean to escape the world but rather to embrace it as spirit, to see that all is divine. This kosha interacts with the fourth chakra, the heart chakra.

- **Tantric practice to developing this kosha:** *dharana* or concentration technique (sixth limb of asthanga yoga); when the mind is focused in one point, such as a chakra, and we go beyond thought into consciousness itself.
- **Natural habits to developing this kosha:** by overcoming mental and emotional challenges without suppressing or bypassing them.

6. *Hiranamaya Kosha*: Subtle causal mind, also referred to as the 'golden' kosha, because of its effulgent, blissful expression. Here the feeling of 'I' is only latent, only a thin veil separates the spiritual practitioner from the atman, where there is little or no distinction between the human mind and god's mind. One has approached the dawn of true awakening and the predominant feeling in this state of mind is the intoxication of pure bliss and an intense attraction to merge in the atman. This kosha interacts with and controls the fifth chakra, the throat chakra.

- Tantric practice to developing this kosha: *dhyan* or flow and absorption meditation (seventh limb of asthanga yoga) when the mind, through concentrations, flows into a deep state of absorption in consciousness.
- Natural habits to developing this kosha: through attraction and love for the divine.

The relationship between the chakras and the koshas outlined above is like the relationship between the mind and the body. We know that the mind in many ways control the functions of the body; but not always. If your leg is lame, the mind will not be able to make you run up a hill no matter how strong the intention. Similarly, while the mind is extended into the lofty realms of a higher kosha in deep meditation, you may still be affected by the allure of a lower vritti in a lower chakra. That is, a psychic or clairvoyant person may frequently experience states of deep insight in the unconscious mind of atimanas kosha, but the same person may sometimes be neurotic, negative and unpleasant in daily life. Likewise, a saintly person may still sometimes experience anger or lust due to the influence of a vritti in a lower chakra. But because of the practice of meditation, the saint is not attached to these lower vrittis and does not act them out in unconscious or impulsive ways.

In other words, how we act and feel depends to a large extent on which kosha our mind is predominantly associated with and to a lesser extent on how strong and stubborn the samskara is. The regular practice of meditation will help us venture into deeper states of mind from which we develop a broader, more detached perspective on life, no matter how troublesome the samskaras dictating our life are. We may not be able to change or prevent these troubling samskaras from expressing themselves, but through meditation and contemplation in the higher koshas, we may gain the power to choose how we react to these samskaras. Even though fate may bestow upon us many trials and tribulations, spiritual practice will grant us both power of detachment and depth of compassion, and thus the freedom of mind to chart a happy and fulfilling path through life. But if meditation is not enough to give us insight into overcoming or controlling a disturbing feeling or behaviour, we may seek psychological counselling. Indeed, psychology and meditation, just like posture yoga and meditation, can work hand in hand in awakening us towards deeper psychological healing and spiritual freedom.

Atman: Beyond the Layers of the Mind

Deep beyond these koshas, as each layer is enveloped by a more subtle layer, the tantric yogi experiences the thin veil of the last kosha and unites with the atman, the yogic soul. The 16th century Christian mystic St John of the Cross explains this highest state of God-consciousness: '... the soul appears to be God more than a soul. Indeed, it is God by participation.' [54]

This exalted state of being corresponds to the two highest chakras, the brow chakra and the crown chakra. It is in these chakras, when the kundalini has reached the eyebrows and enjoys the sublime nectar of the pineal gland, that the yogi experiences the atman. In this stage, there is the feeling of ecstatic oneness with God. In the last stage, when the kundalini reaches the sahasrara, or crown chakra, the yogi enters complete absorption in God, the stage described as the void, nothingness, or Nirvana in Buddhism.

Although each tradition explains these layers and this inward journey somewhat differently, it is a natural and universal process of gradual unfolding and eventual full awakening. As John Caird said so beautifully in his *An Introduction to the Philosophy of Religion*, the enlightened minds 'appropriate that infinite inheritance of which we are already in possession'. But, perhaps none could have expressed this simple yet remarkably advanced process better than the poet and artist William Blake: 'If the doors of perception were cleansed, man would see things as they really are – infinite.'

Anandamurti echoes Blake by emphasizing that the cosmic state of mind reveals itself by cleansing one's perception by converting 'the mind into a real mirror'. He continues: '[Every] kosha has to be made transparent and crystalline .... Thus through the medium of Kosha-wise [meditation] ... the fuller [the spiritual practitioner's] entire entity will become [one] with Divine radiance, with Divine bliss.'

While the kosha model above is from tantra, as taught by Anandamurti, the inner process of the gradual unfolding and deepening of the mind into more subtle levels of existence, through spiritual practice, is part of all mystical paths. The universal aspect of this process is illustrated by the writings of many mystics and saints from various traditions. With keen, spiritual insight, Christian mystic St John of the Cross resembles the tantric sage Anandamurti when he writes: 'A soul makes room for God by wiping away all the smudges and smears of creatures, by uniting its will perfectly to God's ... When this is done the soul will be illumined by and transformed in God. And God will so communicate his supernatural being to the soul that it will appear to be God himself and will possess what God himself possesses.' [55]

Karma and Samskaras: How to Become Free from the Reactions to Our Actions

The word karma describes the natural law that every action has a reaction, and that we humans are a product of our past actions from this and other lives. The word samskara, however, is much more descriptive and pertinent in describing and understanding why we are who we are. The tantric concept of samskaras gives us deep insight into one of our lives biggest mysteries and frustrations: why do bad things happen to good people? The answer lies in our samskaras.

Sir Isaac Newton famously said that 'For every action there is an equal and opposite reaction.' The same law of karma holds true with the physical as well as mental level of existence. More precisely, a samskara is formed from the latent potentials in our chakras, the vrittis, when they give expression to our actions based on our previous actions. Hence, when we express a vritti, let's say anger, a portion of our mind (citta) receives this action as an imprint, or memory. This impression is our samskara, a reaction in potentiality that sooner or later will again need to be expressed and experienced. If we have mostly positive and only a relatively few negative samskaras from the past, our lives will be relatively harmonious and happy. But if we acquired some deeply negative samskaras, our life may be filled with many unexplainable conflicts and retributions.

One of Anandamurti's relatively wealthy disciples once came to him to seek counsel on how to rectify his rebellious and mischievous son. While the elderly man led a pious life practicing yoga and studying the scriptures, his son was exactly the opposite. He spent most of his time ridiculing his father, partying and wasting his hard-earned money, buying fancy clothes and cars. After Anandamurti listened to the man's story, he simply said: 'Do you know why your son is doing this to you?'

'No, but I really want to know,' the man answered. 'In your previous life, your son was your best friend,' Anandamurti continued. 'When he was on his death bed, he called you to his house to angrily remind you that you had not paid back your huge debt to him. Now, in this life, he has come back as your son, and he is unconsciously but happily spending the money you owe him.' This simple story humorously illustrates the nature and complexity of our samskaras, and why, without the omniscient ability of a guru like Anandamurti, it is often difficult to know exactly why bad things happen to good people. But it's all a result of our samskaras. As Jesus said, 'As ye sow, so shall ye reap'.

There are two kinds of actions: original and reactive. An original action is carried out by free will, and it is on the basis of such an action that we accrue samskaras, which again are experienced through reactions later in this or our next life. That is, the old man in the story above was undergoing the consequence of his past actions in this life. And so was his son. As Anandamurti told the man: 'Your friend died an unhappy man, longing to take revenge, and now he has come back to fulfil his desire in the form of your son.'

So, how can we determine or anticipate the degree of reaction an action will cause? This depends on the nature of the original, free-willed action. There are four possibilities:

1. **A mental action causes an equal reaction:** Let's say you think ill of a friend or your spouse, then you will receive an equally negative vibration of ill-will directed back at you (but not necessarily from your spouse or friend). To avoid a reaction of ill-will, we can simply offer or surrender our negative thoughts to God, to Brahma, to that infinite source in which all negative reactions dissolve.

2. **A psycho-physical action not affecting the mind:** Let's say you are unconsciously sitting in a chair moving your leg up and down. Since your mind was not affected or distorted by this action, there will be no reaction.

3. **Psycho-physical action affecting someone physically:** Let's say you become angry with someone and think of hurting him, and then you actually carry out the action and punch him on the nose. In that case, the reaction will be much more severe than if you simply thought of hitting someone. By sincerely apologizing to the person, we will minimize the reaction and also help prevent ourselves from repeating it again. Moreover, we can repeatedly surrender the action to that infinite source (Brahma) who willingly receives all our pain and suffering. While doing so, we may also undertake a short fast by skipping meals for a day while we mentally, through inner prayer, surrender the action to that infinite source (Brahma). While this will reduce the effect of the reaction, there will be some reactive momentum left in the form of a samskara, and we will, sooner or later, suffer some of its consequences.

4. **Actions performed with spiritual ideation, with 'honey wisdom' (*madhuvidya*):** These actions, in which we mentally surrender the action to Brahma, will cause no reactions, no samskaras. When we take the ideation that Brahma, not our petty ego, is the performer of the action, then the reaction, its imprint, will be expressed in the vastness of Brahma, not in our own mind, which was not at all associated with or affected by the action. Thus, before performing any action, repeat a mantra, take the name of god, and surrender the action to that infinite source. Gradually, all our actions become more self-less and spiritual, become part of our meditation, become as sweet and effulgently transparent as honey. It is for this reason yogis are urged to keep repeating their mantras not only during deep meditation, but all day long. By seeing the spirit of Brahma in all that we do, we practice *madhuvidya*, we lighten our karmic imprints, and we become happier, more easy-going and liberated.

Living in this world, we cannot stop our actions lest we quickly perish from hunger, thirst and inactivity. As it is said in the Bhagavad Gita: 'Without action one cannot attain knowledge, and without renunciation of action one cannot attain spiritual achievements.' Thus, rather than inaction, a yogi will go on acting by relinquishing the desire for the fruits of those actions, by abandoning all vanity related to an action, and, as mentioned above, by surrendering all actions to Brahma. For a tantric, the goal is not good karma, but rather no karma! And how does the yogi achieve that? Not by identifying his or her thoughts with the ego, but by identifying the thoughts and actions with his or her atman, with his or her inner divinity.

Three types of samskaras

We all marvel at the young boy who can play like Mozart at the age of four. We are all saddened and existentially frustrated by the young girl who is killed by her father at the age of six. How is it possible, we ask ourselves, that innocent young children can meet such radically different fates at such an early age? The answer, the yogis say, lies in our inborn samskaras.

Of the three different types of samskaras – inborn, acquired and imposed – our inborn samskaras (*sahajata*) are those we have inherited from our past lives and which, by and large, determine whether we become a genius musician or a victim of murder. There are no accidents, as the saying goes, only incidents, and our inborn samskaras fall in that category. There is no independence in action when we are undergoing the reactions of previous actions; we are merely mechanically propelled by those reactions. Therefore, there is no use blaming or praying to God to save us from such bad actions or praise His glory for the good that happens to us. For good or for worse, we are bound to undergo their effects and the best attitude towards our inborn qualities is to humbly accept them as a result of the actions in our past lives, whether good or bad. This does not mean we become fatalistic about our fate, or accept the injustice of the caste system as something pre-ordained by god. Since it is impossible to know the complete nature of our inborn samskaras, we adopt an attitude of surrender and dynamic action: we surrender the past and the future, and we try to act in the present with self-lessness and ego-lessness.

Our acquired samskaras (*pratyayamulaka*) are those we inherit from our independent actions. That is, all our so-called free willed or original actions, will acquire reactions either to be experienced in this life or in the next. That is, unless we surrender these actions through the process of madhuvidya.

Finally, the imposed samskaras (*aropita*) are those we acquire from our family members, our education, the society we live in, the responsibilities we perform in society, and those that are the result of habituated behaviour and thus become part of 'our personal nature'.

Through the combination of our inborn and our imposed samskaras, we are as individuals broadly a product of our environment. So how many free willed actions do we actually perform? Not so many. Moreover, each new, free will action will again form new samskaras, from which we have to suffer in this or in our next life. Thus as Buddha said, human existence is an endless 'wheel of birth and death' that turns ceaselessly. There is a way out of this wheel of death and suffering, however, and that is through the practice of meditation and *madhuvidya* – to live in this world, but not be of it, to act in this world, but not be attached to it.

Imagine, then, our life as a movie. As long as the film goes on, our life is enacted on the screen before us. Millions of samskaras can pass before us in mere seconds. This phenomenal world appears as real, of course, just like we believe our samskaras are real, and thus we suffer. But the film has an end, and when it ends, all we see on the screen is the light from the projector: there is no action, no death, and no drama. There is nothing but the pure light, the same light as the yogi experiences in deep samadhi; there is only the effulgence of the soul. The movie is over, only the liberated, awakened soul exists. This is the analogy of enlightenment. In tantra, the highly elevated and liberated souls, the *jivanmuktas*, are able to view the world as a film and be the projector's light at the same time. That is, an awakened, liberated soul is able to live like a beacon of light in this world, but not be of it; to act in this world, but not be affected by it.

How our Samskaras Mature

Our samskaras from the past, what we have sown, cannot be fully reaped until they undergo an intermediate stage of ripening or attainment of maturity. This process of ripening occurs when the mind is dissociated from the body through the following means:

1. **Senselessness or fainting:** In 1975, during a thunderstorm, author Dannion Brinkley was talking on the phone. He was suddenly hit by a bolt of lightning that sent thousands of volts down through his brain and body. Literally thrown across the room, he later reported seeing his lifeless body on the ground. He saw auras around everybody in the room except around his own body below. That is, a sign that he was, in fact, dead. As doctors soon afterwards pronounced Brinkley dead, he

experienced himself travelling through a dark tunnel towards an angelic being who led him into a 'crystal city'. Most importantly, Brinkley's life completely transformed after this near-death experience. His samskaras had been 'ripened and burnt' to such an extent that he now completely dedicated himself to spirituality, writing, lecturing and service. His remarkable life story, documented in the best selling book *Saved by the Light*, is an example of the life transformations many people go through when they become unconscious due to disease or accident for a prolonged period of time: their samskaras ripen and their lives undergoes a dramatic shift for the better. [56]

2. **Death:** In tantra it is said that death is a like a long sleep, and during this long sleep between lives, our samskaras ripen, and we are reborn to reap those ripened samskaras from our past lives. Thus we get what we deserve, or said more positively and concretely, the circumstances into which we are born – the family, the culture, the environment – is psychologically the perfect place for us to experience and burn our samskaras from our previous life. This is not fatalism and does not mean that we should not actively strive to change our life and struggle against all kinds of social injustices, because to change our lot in life is also part of our karma, part of our acquired, free-willed karma. Thus, without no one to blame, there are only constructive possibilities for positive change.

3. **Spiritual practice (sadhana):** Through deep meditation, when the mind is associated with higher chakras and koshas, when the mind, with the help of a mantra, temporarily enters into the realm beyond the mind, into the atman, then many samskaras ripen and we are free to experience their reactions. Moreover, many samskaras are not only ripened; their seeds are also burnt in this process, and thus their reactions need not be experienced at all – they are instead experienced on the inner plane. Hence, two experiences become evident in a tantric yogi's existence: life becomes very dynamic, but also

more peaceful and free. While one will undergo many more rapid changes and self-transformations than an ordinary person, sometimes even experiencing great suffering, one will also gain the inner peace and stamina to undergo those dynamic changes without undue pain. The end result: spiritual awakening, detachment, and a deep sense of bliss, love and freedom.

Two Types of Enlightenment: With Samskaras and Without Samskaras

Samskaras can be likened to mental seeds that can be ripened or burnt. The mental seeds from a previous life are ripened during the period of death, and when we are born we start our journey to burn these seeds by undergoing the reactions to our inborn samskaras. If we are karmically supposed to die young, there is nothing we can do about it. What we have power over is how we experience our life during the short stay we have on this earth. Some people with a terminal disease become depressed; others see this ultimate challenge as a positive opportunity. 'We are all going to die,' they think. 'Now, it is my turn, and I will make sure I enjoy the rest of my short life.' That is, the more spiritual our life is, the more detached we become to the reactions of our past samskaras, whether those are in the form of a serious disease or a gift of sudden wealth.

As mentioned earlier, we may also burn the emotional or physical seed samskaras during deep states of meditation or during states of unconsciousness due to disease or, as in Dannion Brinkley's case, a near-death experience. As the tantrika progresses along the spiritual path by leading an ethical life, performing self-less service to family and community, and diligently practicing his or her *sadhana*, one may eventually experience enlightenment, first spontaneously, then temporarily and finally regularly. The second highest form of enlightenment in tantra is *savikalpa samadhi*, or qualified enlightenment, when the overwhelming bliss experience is a constant feeling that 'I am one with the Universe; I am one with God.' The highest state is *nirvikalpa* samadhi, or unqualified enlightenment, when there is no I-experience at all, when there is complete non-dualism, only the awareness of being the ocean of oneness exists. The Buddhists aptly term this ultimate state the 'void' or the 'great nothingness'.

After many lifetimes as a great yogi, you may finally experience nirvikalpa samadhi after having burnt all your samskaras in this life time through intense spiritual practice. In this state of *nirbija*, where there are no seed samskaras, one will achieve moksha or final liberation and enlightenment. In that unparalleled peak of spiritual achievement, some great yogis make a final vow or sankalpa, to remain alive in the body to serve humanity. These rare yogis are the so-called living gods, the *jivanmuktas*, the liberated souls, the true gurus. It is still rare, but more common, that a great sage regularly experiences nirvikalpa samadhi in meditation while a few deep karmic seeds remain. In this state of *sabija*, he or she continues to live and serve humanity until all the karmic seeds, until all the samskaras, are burnt in the purifying and effulgent fire of spiritual practice.

Experiences beyond Our Samskaras

Our samskaras are like the grooves in a vinyl record, and these mental and physical grooves make up who we are. Just like the grooves in the record when played repeats the sound recorded in a groove, we are programmed to look, feel, think and experience based on the grooves of our samskaras. In other words, our samskaras help us understand and orient ourselves in the world based on past experience, but they also prevent us from experiencing the world as it simply is. That is, they prevent us from truly living in the moment. They prevent us from seeing the world as spirit, as magical, as sacred.

In terms of the psychological model of tantra, this means that we experience the world mostly through the lower chakras and koshas. Our samskaras are stored in these lower states and thus mechanically and subconsciously predispose our experiences and make us slaves to our emotions and thoughts: We are not free; we are not living in the moment. The way out of this predicament is to move the mind beyond these lower levels and into the higher states of mind through spiritual practice, through meditation. By lifting the mind above these predisposed experiences we have a much broader, detached perspective. We will not prevent our samskaras from playing out the meaning, sounds and sights of their grooves. We will not radically change who we are, but we will radically change the *experience* of who we are. This will occur because we are no longer affected by our samskaras; we experience them much like a film on a screen. We become a witness. We become free. We enter the power of now. And there is no better way to experience the power of now than through the use of a mantra.

Creating a Tantric Lifestyle

Tantric Philosophy: *Na Svargo Na Rasatalah* – There is no heaven, no hell.

Daily Contemplation: The great Indian mystic poet Kabir said, 'What is found now is found then.' Or as they say in America, 'Wherever you go, there you are.' We cannot escape from our samskaras by offering money at the temple. We will not go to heaven by soaking our heads in the Ganges. There is no afterlife in heaven to escape to. There is no burning in hell if you have been a sinner. If we care to read all the great spiritual masters carefully, they all say the same thing – heaven and hell is all fantasy. So, live your life to the fullest now! Find heaven within your heart and spirit now!

Daily Acts of Sacredness

One: Feel heaven appearing in your heart and through everything you do!

Two: Realize that hell is here on earth in the form of poverty, ecological destruction, fear, ignorance, hatred, and so on!

Chapter Eleven

SONG OF THE UNIVERSE:
THE GRACE AND POWER OF MANTRA MEDITATION

Mantra Power: Awakening the force of positive thinking

Science has shown that during an average good day, more than 30,000 thoughts move through our brains and minds. During an average bad day, however, our negative, self-talk increases to more than 60,000 thoughts. No wonder positive thinking and positive self-talk is important in how we feel. As the saying goes, we are what we feel, because our thoughts influence how we feel. Using a mantra throughout the day will not only reduce our busy minds to think fewer distracting thoughts, but using a mantra also helps us think more positively. Indeed, mantras are very powerful. They focus our mind on the most positive aspect of life – divinity. Therefore mantras are the ultimate in positive thinking and self-talk. Using a mantra is to constantly remind ourselves of who we are – not just a bundle of samskaras, but an expression of divinity. Using a mantra allows us to witness our thoughts and actions more dispassionately and calmly. By linking our mantra to the flow of our breath, we calm down and become more peaceful.

Mantras are based on an ancient science of sound. Their inherent vibration awakens powerful and healing energies in us. Earlier in the book, I told the story of how the silent repetition of a mantra caused a young man to fall over backwards and experience a state of superconscious trance (samadhi). This story clearly illustrates the immense power of mantras to not only gradually awaken us, but to sometimes dramatically catapult us, even physically, into a state of ecstasy. While such experiences are rare and depend, in part, on our own karmic readiness, they illustrate the extraordinary ability of tantric mantras to awaken the spiritual force, or kundalini, located at the bottom of the spine. When the kundalini is aroused, we are spiritually awakened as from a deep slumber. We are awakened by the gentle repetition of the mantra, and we gradually, or suddenly, start to realize our true nature, our authentic divine self.

According to tantra, the cosmic energy of Shakti binds Shiva's consciousness and transforms it into the very essence of nature, as creation itself. So the goal of tantra is to realize what we and everything around us is truly made of – divine Shakti energy. In philosophy, this divine Shakti energy is represented by the dot (*bindu*) in the letter Om. From that point where creation starts, Shakti emanates herself in the form of the cosmic mind, as the three energies of nature – sentient, energetic and static – as the five elements of nature and finally as nature itself with all its plants, animals and people. In human life, Shakti is particularly and most potently expressed as the enigmatic and powerful kundalini. Thus the first chakra, at the base of our spine, is the originating bindu point of human life.

This first chakra is the starting point of our spiritual life, and it contains four longings: psycho–spiritual longing, psychic longing, physical longing and spiritual longing. The purpose of mantra meditation is to awaken and channelize the latent potency of these longings, to literally awaken the latent power of the kundalini so that we can delve into the deeper and higher states of mind and experience positive, divine thoughts, even feel peace, bliss, sacredness and divinity. But how is that extraordinary feat accomplished with the mere silent repetition of a word?

The Power and Quality of Mantras

Nandikeshvara, one of the early tantric masters, said that all the sounds of the Sanskrit alphabet came for the cosmic drum of Shiva; that is, from creation itself. This sound of creation, this sound of the universe is the Om sound, and it is from the inner, ancestral vibration of this root sound that all the sacred mantras are born. And when we humans repeat these sacred mantras, we re-unite with that ancestral vibration; we become one with that vibration, that elemental sound of creation.

We have learnt that the cosmic energy of Shakti is expressed in the human form as the enigmatic and powerful kundalini, which is a key component of the vital energy system of tantra that regulates our health, vitality, thinking and emotions. The goal of tantric meditation is to awaken this latent spiritual force, and we do that primarily with the help of mantra meditation. A mantra literally means *a sonic sound which liberates the mind*. The goal of tantric meditation is to raise the kundalini Shakti upwards and through the various psychic energy centres, the chakras. As the kundalini force moves upwards inside the spinal column, it pierces through the various chakras and thus revitalizes them, until it finally reaches the crown chakra, 'the abode of Shiva'. There, when the two archetypal lovers, Shakti and Shiva, unite as one in Brahma, one experiences enlightenment, the highest samadhi, the experience all yogis long for: the non-dual bliss of superconsciousness, oneness with God.

Why are all tantric mantras in Sanskrit? This sacred language, discovered by yogic seers in deep trance, is based on the esoteric science of the 50 sonic sounds within the various chakras. Hence, the Sanskrit alphabet has 50 letters. Each one of these acoustic root sounds corresponds to a psychological propensity, a vritti – love, ecstasy, anger, hate, etc. – which in turn is intricately linked to our glandular system. Each of these propensities and acoustic root sounds is controlled by the various chakras. A tantric mantra is thus a composition of sounds that stimulate certain internal vibrations. During meditation, we employ those mantras that are conducive to balancing body and mind and in fostering spiritual growth stimulating feelings of love and ecstasy rather than anger and hatred.

There are three types of mantra meditation:

1. **Chanting and prayer (vedic meditation):** These mantras are recited or chanted to invoke a sacred feeling, to invoke a longing for god or a mythical deity, and to create an ambience that is conducive for spiritual transformation. It is important to note here that the deities used in tantra are 'psychological or spiritual archetypes' for objects of concentration and

contemplation and not literal gods or goddesses outside the mind.

2. **Silent meditation (tantric meditation):** After the practice of chanting, and sometimes dancing (bhakti yoga), the yogi will sit down for meditation. First one practises a technique called sense withdrawal (*pratyahara*), which enables the meditator to calm and focus the mind. A meditation mantra is then repeated silently while one focuses on a particular chakra (*dharana*). As per tantra, the yogi will also engage in breath meditation (pranayama) and deep flow meditation (dhyan). The primary goal of these meditation techniques is to attain yoga, a state of union in luminous oneness.

3. **Walking meditation (*japa*):** While active during the day at work, driving a car or a bicycle, while walking, or sitting at your computer, you can engage in mantra repetition in harmony with your breath and thus stay in touch with and act from that deep spirit within.

Two Effective Powers of a Mantra

To be effective, a mantra must have two qualities:

1. Torch power (*Dipani Shakti*): spiritual power awakened through the personal effort of the meditator.

2. Consciousness power (*Mantra Chaitanya*): spiritual power ignited by the spiritual force of an enlightened teacher.

To achieve torch power, we cannot simply mechanically repeat the mantra unconsciously like a parrot; the mind needs to be engaged in unison with the flow and meaning of the mantra. This is absolutely essential in order to invoke the latent power of the mantra. In other words, while the mind is engaged in reciting and pronouncing the correct sound of the mantra, the mind is also engaged in invoking the feeling and meaning of the mantra. This torch power quality marks one of several differences between Buddhist mindfulness meditation – in which the meditator simply observes the breath, his thoughts and feelings – and tantric meditation. In Transcendental Meditation (TM), the meditator repeats a mantra without any particular meaning; nor is this mantra, as in tantric meditation, synchronized with the breath. While mindfulness and TM meditation certainly are relaxing, there is little or no torch power quality in them. Nor are they invested with the second quality of a tantric mantra with consciousness power.

Consciousness power is, in part, achieved by the student of tantra himself, but first by the guru's deep proficiency in the sonic science of tantra. The tantric master knows that every meditation mantra is a sonic vibration that vibrates simultaneously in the cosmic body as well as in the individual human body. This gives the guru the ability to move the collective ectoplasm through the medium of his own ectoplasmic rhythm. That is, through his own spiritual power, the guru is able to invest a mantra with renewed spiritual potency by awakening these mantras with cosmic vibrations directly from the cosmic mind itself. In other words, by using his spiritual power, much like a magnifying glass focuses the sun to create fire, the guru concentrates potent cosmic energy into the sound of a sacred word. Such mantras are called *siddha mantras*, and in tantra it is said that a spiritual aspirant can, through proper instruction and practice, achieve enlightenment through the medium of such mantras. The creator of such mantras is called a *Mahakaola*, someone who can not only raise his own kundalini, but who can also help to raise the kundalini of someone else to the highest level of enlightenment.

To fully awaken the consciousness power of a mantra, however, the meditator must also do his part by establishing parallelism between his own mind's vibration and the vibration of cosmic mind as represented by the mantra. In fact, the mantra has two syllables, one representing the individual vibration of the person and the other representing the cosmic vibration of consciousness. Thus, when these four elements – breath, chakra concentration, mantric sound and meaning – are synchronized during meditation, the spiritual vibration of kundalini is stirred and the meditator starts to experience its force. Then, gradually, through months and years of disciplined practice, the kundalini unfolds into spiritual awakening.

Mantra Awakening

You may have heard stories about how meditation makes you calmer and more centred. A peaceful meditation experience, however, can sometimes be the calm before the storm, because, as mentioned earlier, meditation brings us deep into our subconscious where our unreleased samskaras are stored; especially when you practice tantra meditation.

Tantra meditation, which combines mindfulness with other techniques, ripens our samskaras quicker than when only practicing mindfulness meditation or hatha yoga. This is because of the penetrating power of tantric mantras. So, when the samskaras ripen and are being expressed, and the psychological storm engulfs us, we may not be prepared to face it. We may find it too uncomfortable and decide to discontinue the practice. Many people therefore stop meditation, seek a therapist, pick up a self-help book, or simply continue a less psychologically confrontational hatha yoga practice with renewed inspiration and vigour. These are all very good complementary choices. But they cannot replace the effectiveness of a regular meditation practice in creating spiritual awakening.

So, if we desire awakening, then we must calmly and bravely face our samskaras head on. That is the spirit of tantra: to openly embrace our weaknesses and the darker side of our personality. Since these physical and psychological reactions are stored in our pain body, the armour we, according to Eckhart Tolle, surround ourselves with, the armour of our false self, they need to be seen for what they are, without attachment, and then released. And that work can be accomplished through mantra meditation.

In other words, mantra meditation helps us release all the repressed, unconscious material the father of modern psychology, Sigmund Freud, said we invented religion in order to escape. According to tantra, however, Freud had it wrong. Religion, or spirituality, and in particular meditation practice, was not invented to escape anything, but rather to transform our repressed samskaras into a spiritual force. That is indeed the specialty of tantra, its power of transmutation: To transmute darkness into light; to transmute negative feelings into positive feelings; to harness the energy of that which brings us down to lift us up; and to shift our reality beyond the contradictions and duality of life, beyond our samskaras, into the bright realm of synchronicity and spirituality. And when these shifts happen, we can stay present and happy even during difficult times. We can stay in the heart of love even when love seems utterly impossible.

We often don't see who we really are because we are so wrapped up in the image of ourselves coloured by our mental imprints, our samskaras. Meditation helps us to gradually gain the insight that being in the now is a condition of freedom beyond contradictions and limitations, beyond our samskaras. This state of inner union or wholeness that comes with prolonged meditation practice is a state where there is no need to resolve the contradictions of our life, because all opposites have already been solved. We are then in that state where everything begins and everything ends, in wholeness, in union, in bliss, in love. We have truly awakened in the 'Power of Now'.

Part III
Tantric Sex, Healing and Ethics

Chapter Twelve

SEX, KUNDALINI AND TANTRA

Many mystics and sages, including the Christian scientist and mystic Pierre Teilhard de Chardin, have described the close relationship between sexuality, kundalini and spiritual love. 'Some day', he once wrote, 'after we have mastered the winds, the waves, the tides and gravity, we shall harness ... the energies of love. Then, for the second time in the history of the world, man will have discovered fire.' This profound observation stems from the mystical realization that our sex drive, our creative impulses, our longing for spiritual union, our feelings of love and pleasure are all related to the force of kundalini, the impulse for spiritual union. Indeed, all of these deeply human feelings and longings are expressions of Shakti. In other words, they are universal, they represent the creative forces of nature itself. Various writers have therefore described this force of Shakti as the World Brain, a Supra-Sexual force, or as the Indian sage Aurobindo called it – Superman and Overmind. In tantra, this force is called Shakti on the cosmic, global and biological level and Kundalini Shakti on the human level.

This correlation between physical, psychic and spiritual energies is, as described earlier, clearly illustrated in the tantric system. Indeed, all of these longings – physical, physico-psychic, mental and spiritual – are located as four vrittis in the first chakra. In other words, we are by nature – due to the force of Shakti in the form of kundalini – as programmed for physical, sensual and sexual pleasure as we are programmed for mental creativity, spiritual bliss and extrasensory transcendence. That is, our human journey is as much driven by sex hormones, as it is driven by poetic metaphors, geometric logic and spiritual awakening. Thus the urge to unite with a cosmic god, and the urge to merge with a beloved from the opposite sex comes from the same human force. They are just different levels of expression. Spiritual bliss is the energy of the kundalini reaching a transcendent climax in the highest chakras. Sexual pleasure is the energy of the kundalini attempting to reach the higher chakras, but the sexual climax is not usually felt as transcendence but rather as a powerful and pleasurable climactic release, which is often followed by tiredness.

This is not to say that one cannot have spiritual experiences during sex, but it is not the same as full-blown spiritual ecstasy, which is followed by an indescribable and long-lasting heightened sense of energy, awareness, perception and love. The reason for that is that the kundalini uses the sexual organs, nerves and brain chemistry much like it uses the nervous system, the immune systems, the endocrine system, the lymphatic system and the digestive system – to climb the body–mind–spirit ladder towards transcendence. And it is for this reason that the tantric yogis developed hatha yoga: to prepare the body and refine and balance these biological systems to better facilitate the ascent of the kundalini. In other words, the practice of posture yoga, breathing exercises and eating a wholesome vegetarian diet, is for the tantric not a goal in itself, but a preparation for the spiritual ascent of the kundalini. Simply put, a balanced body can better facilitate and withstand the current of the kundalini. Otherwise, just like a weak electric wire is unable to carry a strong electric current, a weak, unhealthy yogi will not be able to withstand the power of kundalini and may therefore experience both physical and mental imbalances when kundalini is aroused.

In ayurveda, the medical system developed by yogis, we further learn how intricately linked our sexual and spiritual energies are. The three subtle energies of prana (life force), ojas (vigour), and tejas (radiance) are all nourished by the reproductive fluid (*shukra*), and together they give us the necessary life energy, dynamism and sparkle to lead a vibrant, spiritual life. Without proper exercise, sleep and nutrition – which all contribute to the formation of reproductive fluids, we will become deficient in these three energies. Moreover, if we drain our reservoir of reproductive fluid with excessive sexual activities, these energies will also be depleted. It is for this reason, and not at all due to moral squeamishness, that many yogis recommend abstinence from sex if you are a celibate monk or nun, or to have sex no more than four times a month if you are a householder. That is, the more prana, ojas and tejas a person acquires, the more of these energies is available for spiritual growth.

While this level of sexual activity may seem way too conservative for some, for others, especially those who are engaged in intense intellectual, creative and spiritual work, even less sexual activity is desired. If you are married or in a relationship, what ultimately matters is the level of love and harmony experienced by the partners – and love can be expressed in so many ways, both emotional and physical, without engaging in ejaculatory sex. Moreover, when sex is not just based on self-gratification, compulsion and addiction – as it so often is in our over-sexual Internet culture – it is an expression of a natural need for intimacy and becomes a unique, celebratory occasion between two partners in love. In other words, the tantric view on sex is not about morality, but about finding the right dynamic balance for experiencing love and spiritual union.

Kundalini power develops from all three of these energies, but primarily tejas. The inner fire of tejas enables the pranic force to move kundalini by the sustained energy of ojas. In other words, the union of all these forces combines into the spiritual energy required for deep meditation, sustained concentration and higher states of yogic ecstasy. We can also aid in this process by certain physical, mental and spiritual practices.

We can increase ojas by eliminating fish and meat products from our diet and eating wholesome meals rich in legumes, whole grains, vegetables, sweet fruits, yogurt, seeds and nuts, especially almonds. In addition, we may use tonic and nutritive herbs such as *ashwagandha* and *amalaki*. Sexually, we increase ojas by reducing our sexual activity to four times per month, or to a lesser extent by practicing so-called tantric sex without orgasm. The reason these practices are not as effective as abstinence or sex at once-a-week intervals, is that once the sexual fluid has been produced it needs to be released from the body through orgasm or through the urine. It is a myth that sex without orgasm means that you can preserve the reproductive fluid in the body to nourish the kundalini and the brain. The fact is, once reproductive fluid has been produced for orgasm, it must naturally leave the body, either rapidly during orgasm or slowly through the urine if orgasm is withheld.

So what are the great secrets about tantra and sex that so many modern authors write about and promote through workshops? There are no doubt complex sexual rituals in the left-handed schools of tantra in India ranging from testing one's temptations by meditating in front of a naked consort, rituals involving the man smearing semen and menstrual blood on his chest, and also intricate initiatory techniques in Kashmir Shaiva tantra involving the ability to not have a sexual orgasm but instead have a whole body–mind– spirit orgasm. Very few people in the Western world, and even in India, have ever experienced these practices outside a few secretive adepts and gurus. Most modern teachers of so-called sexual tantra teach practices that resemble sex therapy more than they resemble authentic tantric practices. Moreover, they are misguided in teaching that these sexual practices can lead to enlightenment any more than eating, walking, or having regular sex can. So, by and large, there are only two great secrets to know regarding tantra and sex.

These secrets are: to learn the balanced and dynamic use of energy and love. That is, to use our energy in a dynamic and balanced way through the proper cultivation of prana, tejas and ojas so that the kundalini force may ascend, and to cultivate madhuvidya, or sacred love – not just before and during sex, but before and during all of life's daily activities. Remember, tantra is not just the yoga of sex, tantra is the yoga of everything. Tantra is not just about cultivating the impulse for sexual love, tantra is about cultivating the impulse for universal love. Tantra is seeing and feeling the love of the divine in everything.

Sexual Repression and Addiction

Two monks were once crossing a shallow river when they were approached by a woman who asked them if they could help her across. Even though it would mean to break one of the rules of the monastery by helping her, one of the monks nevertheless lifted the woman on his back and carried her across the shallow but forceful currents in the river. When they arrived on the other side, the woman thanked him generously, while he simply bade her farewell. After a few miles of walking, the other monk said angrily, 'How could you commit such a sin and break our rules by touching that woman?' The monk who carried the woman replied calmly, 'I simply carried her across the river, and I left her there by the riverside, but you are still carrying the woman in your mind.' While he had realized that discipline was necessary and sometimes bendable tool to achieve freedom from desire, the other monk experienced discipline as a repressive and rigid force that produced fantasies of longing and retribution.

It is well-understood by psychologists and has often been reported in the media, that repression of sexual energy in families or monastic communities leads to unconscious expressions of those same energies in the form of sexual compulsions, addictions, abuse and paedophilia. Moreover, it is common in our modern, oversexed and pornographic world that our sexual fantasies turn people of the opposite sex, especially women, into objects of desires and thus prevent us from seeing them as who they truly are: friends, co-workers, strangers, mothers, fathers. These fantasies are products of our conscious and subconscious minds; they cloud our ego-minds and prevent us from experiencing the world with a loving heart.

Many people on the spiritual path are unable to deal with their subconscious fantasies, and they see them as disturbing and unspiritual distractions. Therefore, they impulsively suppress these 'sinful' longings. These longings are natural and harmless, but if they are suppressed, they become stronger and may turn into addictive and compulsive behaviour, sometimes requiring therapy and/ or intense spiritual practice to overcome. A better attitude than suppression is to accept these feelings, and to work with them as neutral energies that, like all thoughts and emotions, arise and then pass away. In fact, when they arise, they can become fuel for our spiritual longing. The genuine power and inner essence of tantra lies in its ability to embrace all feelings, all desires, no matter how strong or distressing, and to transmute these energies and desires and using them as fuel for concentration and surrender in meditation. Yes, the key is to transmute. Not to indulge, not to cling, but to alter, transform and metamorphose our desire–samskaras in meditation until non-attached, free-flowing and mind-blowing bliss-feelings arise naturally from our hearts.

In the words of the Buddhist tantric teacher, Thubten Yeshe: 'There is no reason at all to feel guilty about pleasure; this is just as mistaken as grasping onto passing pleasures and expecting them to give us ultimate satisfaction.'[57] So to conclude our short journey into the world of tantric love: sex is a natural, passing pleasure; spiritual love is the lasting, all-embracing satisfaction.

The Yoga of Tantric Love

Some of the vedantic ascetics of India, the Christian mystics of Europe and the Mediterranean Gnostics looked upon the body as an obstacle and the emotions of the heart as an hindrance to enlightenment. Indeed, many ascetics despise the body and view it as filthy and sinful. The tantric adept, on the other hand, has a radically different view. To him, divinity is everywhere, even in the body; he understands that attraction is the law of the universe, and that desire, even the desire for worldly pleasure, can be a road to god realization. Indeed, desire and attraction is part of our very nature. We are attracted to inspiring art, romantic sex, beautiful music and poetry. Bees are attracted to pollen, some lilies have a romantic relationship with the moon, and mystical poets, such as Rumi, Kabir and Mirabai, were insanely attracted to the divine. In Vaishnava tantra, the path of bhakti yoga or the yoga of divine love, spirituality is expressed through longing and love for god. Bhakti yogis see emotions as a great vehicle to enhance spiritual devotion. Through spiritual longing, they open their hearts for greater union, ecstatic bliss and communion with the divine.

Tantra cannot be divorced from the inner essence of its own spiritual heart, from the experience of Bhakti, from the expression of spiritual love. American poet Robert Bly aptly describes bhakti yoga as the path where 'the bee of the heart stays deep inside the flower, and cares for no other thing.' [58] This focus on passionate love is integral to tantra as it turns desire and attachment, the very antidotes of spiritual liberation, into an alchemical fuel for love and the emancipation of spirit by worshipping all as god. Thus the bee of the heart goes so deep into what it loves that it transforms into love itself. To become that love is the goal of the love-intoxicated path of tantra.

Tantric love is about creating spiritual oneness and union. Tantra is about feeling connected to the spiritual essence of the universe. And what is this essence? It has many names: God, Spirit, Godhood, Tao, Allah, or simply the One.

In tantra, this essence is called Brahma, or cosmic consciousness. And this Brahma is composed of Shiva and Shakti, the dual expressions of Brahma, just like light and heat are inseparably one with fire, yet also its dual expressions. Shiva and Shakti, like a wave and a particle in quantum physics, are never separate. They are always together, always the same. They are simply two different expressions of the same universal Brahma. Remembering these primal aspects of the world, we open up to see and experience oneness in duality everywhere. We open up to feelings of spiritual connectedness and love.

The primal, evolutionary force of Shakti – which is both real and symbolic – is that which inspires us towards illumination and wisdom. Yet the same force has the capacity to blind us, to drive us away from truth and self-realization. In other words, the duality of wisdom and ignorance, vidya and avidya Shakti, exists at the very root of creation and life itself. Thus, no matter at which stage we are on the spiritual path, there is always the possibility of making mistakes. Hence, there is always a need for spiritual vigilance, always a need to personify a deep, spiritual ethic, and always a need to transcend our own limitations and ignorance.

The path of tantra is about experiencing spiritual bliss, to soak the human heart with divine spirit. Thus, it is often said that bhakti yoga, the path of ecstatic love, is the best and safest path. This yoga of love is beautifully exemplified in the life and poetry of Rumi, who said, 'The taste of milk and honey is not it. Love instead that which gave deliciousness.' [59]

In other words, love that which is within and beyond all physical forms and expressions. Love that which is within and beyond food, sex, fame and money. As the tantrics will say, when you cultivate love for that which gives you all that is delicious in life, namely Brahma, you will eventually experience love in everything. That is the spirit of tantra. That is the alchemy of tantric love.

From the Yoga of Sex to the Yoga of Everything

On some yogic and spiritual paths, the attitude to life is via negativa – the world is negated and seen as a cause for suffering, as giving us a sense of false identity when we are attached to it. So the yogi's task becomes to disengage, to free him from suffering, or from attachment, and to become a witness to it all. But that is not the attitude of tantra. In tantra, we actually want to get engaged, to get tangled up in the world, but with our spirit still shining.

Tantra, therefore, does not deny the world of pleasure or sex. But, contrary to popular opinion, tantra is hardly just about sex. Yet most Western books on this subject inform us that tantra is simply some form of esoteric sexual practice. These books forget to mention, though, that most of the writings on sex–tantra have been lifted straight from the pages of the *Kama Sutra*, a Hindu text on lovemaking, which no doubt has its own sensual beauty to offer, but this book is essentially not at all part of tantric literature.

Since health is not gained by gorging on organic food and true wealth is not found in the desire for more money, tantra is not the path of indulgence, either. Nor is tantra the path of mere sensual gratification. Hence, on the subject of indulgence in drink and sex as a path to liberation the Kularnava Tantra speaks with a straightforward voice: 'If [you] could attain perfection (siddhi) merely by drinking wine, all the wine-imbibing rogues would attain perfection. If mere intercourse … would lead to liberation, all creatures of the world would be liberated …'

Tantra is about finding balance in all aspects of our lives. In its essence, it is about seeing and realizing that everything we do can become a sacred, spiritual act – including sex. Even our suffering, our attachment is our yoga, our spirituality. In tantra all problems are potential friends and allies, a support system for deeper understanding, deeper love. The key to being a tantric yogi or yogini is to embrace duality and then go deep into and then beyond duality. How? Because for tantra, duality is just another expression of non-duality. In other words, there is spirit, god, awareness, consciousness in everything – even in suffering and pleasure. This knowledge, this wisdom of madhuvidya is the idea that 'the bees of sprit' can turn everything we do and feel, even failure, into nectar.

Here are seven ways to experience madhuvidya – love and sacredness everywhere:

1. Tantra embraces the idea that attraction is the law of the universe. And then, like a tai chi master, tantra moves with the energy of attraction towards freedom from attachment and suffering. We are attracted to inspiring art, romantic sex, beautiful music and poetry; we are attracted to the divine.

    When we are attracted to the divine, it is called *prema* or spiritual love. When we are attracted to money, land, fame, sex, it is called *kama* or desire. In tantra, the yogi is advised to turn kama into prema – to see everything as sacred, as divine.

'For those pure in mind, everything is pure.'

Georg Feuerstein, *Tantra: The Path of Ecstasy*

In bhakti yoga, the yoga of divine love, we express our spirituality through longing and love for god. Bhakti yogis see emotions – even anger and sadness – as great vehicles to enhance spiritual devotion. Through spiritual longing, we open our hearts for greater vulnerability and union, greater ecstatic bliss and communion with the divine. That is, if we really and truly long for sacred communion.

'In truth there is neither purity nor impurity. Therefore he who is free from such notions is happy.'

– Vijñāna Bairava Tantra

2. Tantra sees everything as sacred. Everything is god or goddess. The consciousness within everything, the latent intelligence in the universe is god, or Shiva. The latent energy, the creative force of the universe is goddess or Shakti. Together in cosmic union, these alchemical lovers unite as Brahma, the ultimate consciousness beyond name, form or attachment.

'Jagadananda, or world bliss, is the understanding that the realization of the Self includes everything, within and without.'

– Abhinavagupta, from the *Tantraloka*

So, in tantra, everything is Brahma. Everything we experience is an opportunity to practice yoga; to be a yogi or a yogini. Tantra represents our universal quest for truth within and beyond the world of science and religion. Based on a spiritual worldview and yogic practices, the tantric lifestyle helps us to invoke the sacred in everyday life.

3. Tantric love is a form of bhakti yoga. Tantra, which often is termed tantra yoga, cannot be divorced from the inner essence of its own spiritual heart, from the experience of bhakti, from the expression of spiritual love.

One early morning a couple of years ago, while waiting for the poet and translator Robert Bly to get ready so I could drive him to the airport after a poetry reading and a workshop I had organized for him, he asked me: 'Do you know what this country needs?' And without letting me get much time to suggest an answer, he simply said: 'Praise!'

Then, wide awake at around 6, he started reciting from memory various sacred poems satiated with the fierce sweetness of bhakti; including these lines by Kabir, from his popular book

Kabir: Ecstatic poems.

'When the Guest is being searched for,
it is the intensity of the longing for the Guest that
does all the work.
Look at me, and you will see a slave of that intensity'.

– Robert Bly, *Kabir: Ecstatic Poems*

This focus on passionate love is integral to tantra as it turns desire and attachment, the very antithesis of spiritual liberation, into an alchemical fuel for love and the emancipation of spirit by worshipping all as God. Thus the bee of the heart goes so deep into what it loves that it transforms into love itself. To become that love is the goal of the love-intoxicated path of tantra.

Tantric love is about creating spiritual oneness and union. Tantra is about feeling connected to and be awed by the spiritual essence of the universe. Kevala Bhakti is considered the deepest form of bhakti yoga in tantra. The devotee simply loves the divine without asking anything in return. *Kevala* means only, so the devotee loves for the sake of love, only love. That is, Kevala Bhakti is revealed in the heart when the alchemy of longing has been exhausted and turns into pure love, pure being.

'Kevala Bhakti is not attained by baths, exercises, or efforts'.

– Shrii Anandamurti, *Subhasita Samgraha*

4.   Tantra is cosmic union. Tantra is worldly union. In tantra, the essence of the universe is called Brahma, or cosmic consciousness. And, as mentioned above, this Brahma is composed of Shiva and Shakti, the dual expressions of Brahma. How? Just like light and heat are inseparably one with fire, yet also its dual expressions.

Shiva is Brahma as pure cosmic consciousness, and Shakti is Brahma as cosmic creative energy, the force behind creation, the force that created you and me. Shiva and Shakti, like a wave and a particle in quantum physics, are never separate. They are always together, always the same. They are simply two different expressions of the same universal Brahma. Remembering these primal aspects of the world, we open up to see and experience oneness in duality everywhere. We open up to feelings of spiritual connectedness and love.

Hence, tantra is worldly union when we truly experience the world as spirit, as sacred.

'The real knowledge issues from the mystic unification of Shiva and Shakti. It is the cause of liberation'.

– Tantraloka

5. Tantra is not about indulgence, not about more sex, more money or more vitality. That's the trap tantra can lead you into. Lead you into thinking that, if all is sacred, then more of everything is better – more sex, more money. Actually, tantra warns you that everything in this world can be a trap and can lead to pain. That's because the duality of wisdom and ignorance, vidya and avidya Shakti, exists at the very root of creation and life itself. Thus, no matter at which stage we are on the spiritual path, there is always the possibility of being a total failure.

Tantra is about being aware, being connected to god/goddess when you are making love and money. But that takes practice. That takes discipline. Tantra is not about indulgence but about deep practice, deep meditation and deep love. Hence, there is always a need for spiritual vigilance, always a need to personify a deep, spiritual ethic, and always a need to transcend our own limitations and ignorance.

'Those who let the body decay, destroy the spirit;
And they won't attain the powerful knowledge of truth.
Having learnt the skill of fostering the body,
I fostered the body, and I nurtured the soul.
The Perfect One has entered the temple of the body.'

– Tirumular (seventh century Tantric sage)

6. Tantra is the path of sacred love and (sometimes) the path of sacred sex. The path of tantra is about experiencing spiritual bliss, to soak the human heart with divine spirit. Thus, it is often said in the yogic scriptures that bhakti yoga, the path of ecstatic love, is the best and safest path: In other words, love that which is within and beyond all physical forms and expressions; love that which is within and beyond food, sex, fame and money; especially when eating, having sex, attaining fame and earning money!

'Just as the waters enter the ocean, full and of unmoving ground, so all desires enter him who attains peace, but not the desirer of desires'.

– Bhagavad Gita

7. Tantra is seeing love in everything. Tantra is the path of via positiva. Tantra is an affirmative path; the path of embracing life's challenges.

    As the tantrics will say, when you cultivate love for that which gives you all that is delicious in life, namely Brahma, you will eventually experience love in everything. That is the spirit of tantra. That is the alchemy of tantric love. This, then, is the path of tantric love – the path that leads us to experience the unity of Shiva and Shakti in our own hearts and minds, and, hence, to the realization that the divine can be experienced everywhere.

'When salt dissolves, it becomes one with the ocean. When my ego dissolved, I became one with Shiva and Shakti'.

Jnaneshvar (tantric sage)

Tantra is the yoga of transformation and of transmutation. Through the spiritual practices of posture yoga, mantra meditation, pranayama, and chanting, a tantrika churns longing into love and melts separation into togetherness. This form of alchemical spirituality, where even our failures can become 'honey knowledge', is the essence of tantric love.

Tantra and Kundalini: Uncoiling the Sacred Snake of Sex and Liberation

We humans are hardwired for sex, sadness and liberation. The proof of that, says tantra, lies coiled up in the kundalini, deep in our first chakra, the Muladhara.

In his book *Gods of Love and Ecstasy: The Traditions of Shiva and Dionysus*, Alain Daniélou links the spiritual hearts of the Indian God Shiva with the Greek God Dionysus. In these two divine characters of magic and transcendence, East and West meet, both literally and symbolically. When mystical labyrinths appeared in the earth of Crete some four thousand years ago, Shivaism (tantric yoga) had already existed in India for thousands of years. 'Since its remotest origins, Shivaism has been inseparable from Yoga,' writes Daniélou. He also claims that Shivaism as a sacred, yogic culture stretched over a vast area – from India way into Greek and Celtic Europe. Perhaps that is why archaeologists have found sculptures of naked women in lotus pose in ancient France and a Viking yogi on the so-called Buddha Bucket from a Viking ship in Norway from AD 800.

In other words, the inner labyrinth of yoga, the kundalini, which is a coiled up snake of creativity, sex and spiritual liberation at the bottom of our spines, also manifests as exterior labyrinths of the earth, as symbolic representations of the inner journey of yoga. And Daniélou believes these shamanic and yogic snakes crawled to the West from India and can be found in caves and earth circles from the Ganges to England.

When you walk a labyrinth counterclockwise, you symbolically unwind the cosmic coil of kundalini, you liberate yourself from the earth cave of the Muladhara chakra. And this spiritual uncoiling from the inside is the awakening of Shakti, the kundalini, so that she can unite with Shiva in the Sahasrara, the crown chakra. This whole inner enterprise of uncoiling the inner labyrinth is what we call yoga. And it is an enterprise that's been going on for a few thousand years longer than the world's oldest yoga mat, since when people did their asanas on dirt, sand and rock, since when people did their meditation naked in rain and frigid weather in the Himalayas.

All energy is lodged in this first chakra, the abode of the Shakti. Indeed, as mentioned before, there are four fundamental vrittis, or human longings, associated with this chakra:

Dharma: psycho-spiritual longing
Artha: psychic longing
Kama: physical longing
Moksha: spiritual longing

In other words, the first chakra is not the 'lowest' chakra; it is actually the seat of our spiritual longing for both liberation and dharmic action. Indeed, our thirst for both physical and spiritual love comes from this inner labyrinthine cave. Thus, according to tantra, we are hardwired for spirituality, for dharma, for bliss. We are hardwired for lust, as well, but in equal measure, we are also hardwired for liberation, for spiritual union, for yoga. As it is said in the Kularnava Tantra, 'There is no fulfilment without the body. Hence obtaining the wealth of the body, engage thyself in works of merit.'

That is why in India, people literally worship vaginas and penises made of stones. The vagina, the yoni, or Shakti, is the earth labyrinth, the energy from where everything is created. This coiled female energy surrounds the male phallus, the linga, or Shiva, the self-born consciousness erect and alive in all things. That is why in India, people worship snakes as snakes represent the coiled inner serpentine, the kundalini Shakti, in nature, in the body, and in the cosmos.

Tantric yoga was not created by puritans, nor by the faint-hearted, but also not by the purely hedonistic. For these yogis of old, they knew that above the first chakra, there were numerous challenges ahead. These challenging vrittis, including hatred, deceit, possessiveness, cruelty, fear and arrogance, and many more, are located in clusters of six, ten, twelve, sixteen and two, around the other chakras.

As you can see, most of these vrittis are more psychologically challenging than the four primary ones located in the Muladhara chakra. But there are also positive ones, including hope, effort, discernment and perhaps the most important of all, the love vritti located in the heart chakra. Furthermore, there is the human capacity for awakening spiritual knowledge, the famous para vritti located in the Ajna chakra (eyebrow).

The tantric science of kundalini, chakras, and vrittis – and how these esoteric, inner expressions are awakened, balanced and alchemically tuned by hatha yoga and meditation – is complex and beyond the scope of this book. But the heart of this science is reflected in both the coiled labyrinth of the earth and the coiled kundalini of the body. In other words, the spiritual energy labyrinth inside us, the kundalini, is reflected in the sacred revelation of the earth labyrinth. As inside, so outside.

Our spiritual practice, our yoga, helps us uncoil and liberate the kundalini labyrinth and thereby free us from its containment in the earth chamber of the first chakra, raise the kundalini upwards and reach union with Brahma. That is true lovemaking, Tantric style. As it is said in the Kularnava Tantra, 'The rush of bliss that ensues upon the meeting of the Pair, the Supreme (Shakti) and the Self (Shiva) above, is the real Congress. All else is mere copulation.'

Creating a Tantric Lifestyle

Tantric Philosophy: *Visaye Purusavabhasa Jivatma* – The reflection of cosmic consciousness, or paramatma, in the unit body is known as jivatma, the unit soul.

Daily Contemplation: The human soul, or jivatma, according to tantra, is a reflection of god's soul, or paramatma. The meaning of yoga in tantra is thus the unity between jivatma and paramatma, the oneness of the individual soul with the cosmic soul. Tantric meditation was developed to experience this yoga, this union.

Daily Acts of Sacredness

One: Practice posture yoga daily, or asanas, and imagine yourself preparing your body and mind for the ultimate unity, the ultimate yoga.

Two: Practice meditation twice daily with the aim of experiencing yoga, inner union.

Chapter Thirteen

TANTRIC SECRETS ON ECOLOGY, HEALTH, ETHICS, LONGEVITY AND PERSONAL SUCCESS

Yoga and Ecology: Why Yogis Eat Carrots Rather Than Cows

To live a life according to the wisdom of ecology is the most urgent task for humanity today. What can the philosophy of tantra contribute to this critical challenge? How can we develop an environmental ethics according to yogic principles? What would a sustainable ethics based on tantra look like?

Mind in Nature

For science, viruses represent the smallest accumulation and diversity of molecules which is recognized as 'life'. May be in the near future, when more advanced scientific techniques are employed, we will recognize the sentience of smaller aggregations of molecules. For now, viruses personify the boundary between life and non-life according to science.

According to the so-called Santiago Theory of Cognition, developed by Francisco Varela and Humberto Maturana, the process of cognition is intimately linked to the process of life. Hence, the brain is not necessary for the mind to exist. A worm, or a tree, has no brain but has a mind. The simplest forms of life are capable of perception and thus cognition. For the tantric sages of India, it is impossible to draw a final line between animate and inanimate beings. According to tantra philosophy, Shiva (consciousness) and Shakti (energy) are everywhere in creation; hence, there is 'mind' even in the so-called inanimate world of rocks. This type of 'mind' is dormant, as if asleep, because there is no nervous system in rocks. And it is this dormant consciousness that, according to tantra, is the intelligent life force giving birth to evolution's numerous life forms. In other words, while scientists claim random events created consciousness and life from matter, the tantric cosmology holds that matter is condensed consciousness and thus life and mind are inherently part of matter.

The tantric cosmology is supported by many indigenous worldviews. Native Americans, for example, experienced mind in nature, in plants and trees and animals. In the international best-seller, *The Secret Life of Plants*, Peter Tompkins and Christopher Bird report that, when cutting down a tree, some Native American tribes have a heart-to-heart conversation with the tree. In no uncertain terms, they let the tree know what is going to happen, and finally they ask for forgiveness for having to commit this unfortunate act of violence.

In the same book they document scientific experiments on plants with a modified lie detector. The instrument would register when a plant's leaves were cut or burnt. Not only that, when a plant 'understood' it was going to be killed, it went into a state of shock or 'numbness.' Thus, the scientists explained, the 'warnings' possibly prevent the tree from undue suffering. [60]

Such laboratory tests may sound outrageous to materialists, but not to the ancient, animist peoples from all over the world, nor to Indian yogis or Westerns mystics. For thousands of years, they have taught us that we do not live in a dead and meaningless universe.

'High' and 'Low' Consciousness in Nature

Since mind or consciousness is part of all living beings and lies dormant, even in so-called inanimate objects such as rocks, sand or mud, there is an intrinsic, spiritual oneness in all of creation. Thus, according to the tantric worldview, we should grant existential rights or value to all beings, whether soil, plants, animals or humans. In principle, all physical expressions of cosmic consciousness have an equal right to exist and to express themselves, but some beings have higher consciousness than others and thus 'more rights'.

Evolution is irreversible – amoebas eventually evolve into

apes, but apes never transform into amoebas – thus tantra also acknowledges 'higher' and 'lower' expressions of consciousness. This differentiation is crucial, and it is on the basis of this that tantra philosophy and some ecologists differ.

Deep-ecology and Tantra

Deep-ecologists, for example, believe that no beings are 'high' or 'low', all are part of an 'egalitarian web of life'. The tantric ecological worldview, on the other hand, is both egalitarian and hierarchical. According to tantra, evolution proceeds by expressing more and more complex beings that are able to express higher levels of consciousness. On this evolutionary ladder, amoebas are at the 'bottom' and humans are at the 'top'. Within this hierarchical system there are various levels of egalitarian cooperation, but the system as a whole is hierarchical.

This notion is also supported by the new systems sciences, which proclaim that one cannot have wholeness without hierarchy. In an evolutionary context, this means that a new stage of development has extra value relative to the previous stage. An oak sprout is more complex and therefore endowed with a fuller expression of consciousness than an acorn. A monkey has a more evolved nervous system and mind than an insect, and a human has a more evolved brain and intellect than an ape.

This crucial definition of subsequent higher stages of consciousness, of a hierarchy of being, is central to tantra cosmology. But this insight is often overlooked by many ecologists. They often equate hierarchy with the higher exploiting the lower by transferring human pathological experiences of hierarchy – as fascism, for example – to the study of nature. But the ecological universe of nature could not exist without hierarchy, and humans, for good or for worse, are, as the most advanced expression of consciousness in evolution, stewards of the natural world. Hence, according to tantra, we need to acknowledge both unity and oneness as well as high and low (or deep and shallow) expressions of consciousness when developing an ecological world view.

Heterarchy vs Hierarchy

We need to emulate nature in advancing what Riane Eisler calls 'actualisation hierarchies'; we must learn to maximize our species' potential, both in relation to ourselves and to nature. In other words, a self-actualized humanity can learn to integrate itself in relation to nature. Learn to realize our oneness with the 'other'. Learn to recognize that being on top of the evolutionary ladder does not give us humans the right to destroy and exploit those lower than ourselves. According to the evolutionary philosophy of tantra, there is an ongoing movement towards greater complexity and higher consciousness in evolution, while at the same time there is, on a deeper level, ecological cooperation and spiritual unity amongst all beings. We are indeed one with all beings and our ecological outlook needs to acknowledge this insight if we are to live in harmony on this planet.

Unity and Diversity in Nature

In other words, there are both heterarchy and hierarchy. To disprove the hierarchical flow of evolution by saying that all of us – whether leaf, tree, monkey or human – are equal partners in the great web of life, is to impose on nature faulty and limited concepts. It reduces the wondrous complexity of creation to a lowest common denominator, and that serves neither nature nor humans well.

Tantra says that there is unity of consciousness amongst all beings, because we all come from, and are created by, the same spirit, the same cosmic consciousness. But nature is also infinitely diverse, and thus consciousness is also expressed in various ways, both 'high' and 'low'. Hence, a seedling is more complex and therefore more conscious than an acorn, and an oak is more complex and conscious than a seedling.

Ecological Ethics According to Tantra

Another way of expressing this is that a dog has more capacity for mental reflection and self-consciousness than a fir tree. Both are conscious beings, both are manifestations of cosmic consciousness, both have mind, and both have equal existential value but because of the difference in expression of depth and quality of consciousness, the dog is higher on the natural hierarchy of being than the fir tree. So when we develop our ecological ethics, both the 'low' and the 'high' expressions of nature must be valued and accounted for.

Non-human creatures have the same existential value to themselves as human beings have to themselves. Perhaps human beings can understand the value of their existence, while an earthworm cannot. Even so, no one has delegated any authority to human beings to kill those unfortunate creatures. But to survive, we humans cannot avoid killing other beings. So what to do?

Tantric Vegetarianism: A Spiritual and Ecological Perspective

To solve this dilemma, a tantric selects articles of food from amongst those beings where development of consciousness is comparatively low. Vegetables, corn, bean and rice are selected instead of cows or pigs, as these animals will have to be slaughtered and thus undergo much suffering. So, as a general rule, a tantric yogi will not kill any animals with 'developed or underdeveloped consciousness,' because it is clearly possible to live a healthy life without taking such lives.

In addition to existential value, various beings, based on their depth of consciousness, have a variable degree of what is often termed 'intrinsic value'. The more consciousness a being has, the deeper the feelings, and the more potential for suffering. Eating plants is therefore preferable to eating animals. As the Irish novelist and playwright George Bernard Shaw once said, 'Animals are my friends ... and I don't eat my friends.'

It is also ecologically more sustainable to extract nourishment from entities lower down on the food chain. Vast land areas are used to raise livestock for food. These areas could be utilized far more productively if planted with grains, fruits, vegetables and legumes for human consumption. It is estimated that only 10 per cent of the protein and calories we feed to our livestock is recovered in the meat we eat. The other 90 per cent goes literally 'down the drain'.

In addition to existential value, and intrinsic value, all beings have utility value. Throughout history, human beings usually preserved those creatures which had an immediate utility value. We are more inclined to preserve the lives of cows than of bats, for example. But, because of all beings' existential value, we cannot claim that only human beings have the right to live and not non-humans. All are the children of Mother Earth; all are the offspring of cosmic consciousness.

Sometimes it is difficult to know what the utilitarian value of an animal or a plant is; therefore we may needlessly destroy the ecological balance by killing one species without considering the consequences of its complex relationship or utility value to other species. A forest's utility value, for example, is more than just x number of metres of lumber. The forest serves as nesting and feeding ground for birds and animals; its roots and branches protect the soil from erosion; its leaves or needles produce oxygen; and its pathways and camp grounds provide nourishment for the human soul. As a whole, the forest ecosystem has an abundance of ecological, aesthetic and spiritual values which extends far beyond its economic benefits in the form of tooth picks, planks or plywood.

All of nature is endowed with existential, intrinsic and utility value. This hierarchical and ultimately holistic understanding of evolution and ecology, formulates the basic foundation for a new, and potentially groundbreaking ecological ethics deeply grounded in the philosophy of tantra. If we embrace the divinity in all of creation, the expression of our ecological ethics will become an act of sublime spirituality. Our conservation efforts and our sustainable resource use will become sacred offerings to Mother Earth, and ultimately to cosmic consciousness, to both the Shiva and Shakti within and beyond nature.

Secrets of the Tantric Diet

There is a close relationship between ayurveda and tantra, but their dietary prescriptions are not exactly the same. An ayurvedic diet is generally prescribed for someone who wants to rectify an ailment, to rebuild the constitution, to reduce weight, or to build strength after an illness. The ayurvedic diet is based on balancing the three bodily forces, the three doshas: vata, pitta and kapha – ether/air, fire/water and earth/water humours, respectively. These doshas impact us on two levels: they are responsible for the building of our physical bodies, and they also constitute our mind–body type. Therefore we speak of people as predominantly vata (thin, short or tall, and with a restless, creative mind), pitta (medium build with a strong, focused mind), and kapha (strong, heavy body with a calm mind). In real life, we all have some of each of these qualities, of course, but when any of them are out of balance, we can balance our doshas with a dosha-pacifying diet, with herbs, meditation and yoga. The tantric diet, on the other hand, is more general for all three types and its predominant aim is to create calmness and lightness of body and mind.

The interrelationship between body, mind and spirit has a direct correlation to physical health and longevity. The food we eat, for example, affects not only our body but our mental well-being as well. As is the quality of our food, so becomes the quality of our consciousness. If we want to change our state of mind, we must begin by changing our food habits. A daily diet consisting of meat, calorie-rich desserts, alcohol and soft-drinks may induce short-term sensory satisfaction, but in the long run, such a heavy diet will cause irritability, dullness and depression. Foods that are light, however – fruits, salad and cooked vegetables – will also make the mind light, but can, in excess, cause lightheadedness and insomnia. Perhaps the worst impediment to health, however, is to overeat. No matter if we eat predominantly healthy foods, overconsumption of food, especially sweet, starchy and fatty foods, will sooner or later cause acidity, obesity and disease. Therefore the tantric yogis recommend to drink water when hungry between meals and only to fill half the stomach with foods, while the rest of the space is reserved for water and air.

Food, like all things in the tantric universe, consists of three cosmic qualities: sattva (balance, lightness), raja (agitation, aggression), and tama (resistance, crudeness). These primal, cosmic attributes of the cosmic creative energy, or Shakti, are expressed throughout nature and form the physical nourishment and mental impressions gained in the food we eat.

A sattvic diet, which in ayurveda is prescribed for yogis, as well, is helpful in keeping our minds balanced and at peace. It has been particularly designed for the practice of yoga and the development of higher consciousness. A sattvic diet is also an expression of tantric ethics, of ahimsa (non-harming), and does not involve the killing or intentional harming of animals. While it is practically impossible not to cause any harm at all, since many animals such as snakes, insects and rodents die during farming, we will try to cause as little harm as practically possible. A sattvic diet consists of the following: nutritive vegetarian foods such as legumes, fruits (especially sweet fruits), vegetables, whole grains, seeds, nuts, milk, ghee and yoghurt. All of these foods help to build brain tissue, bodily strength, mental lightness and peace. In particular, these types of foods develop ojas, the subtle substance in the reproductive fluid which promotes longevity, physical and sexual endurance, mental power and clarity.

Rajasik foods, such as coffee, chocolate and black tea, develop energy, but if consumed in excess their consumption will lead to nervousness, high blood pressure and addiction. Tamasik foods are generally not good for either the body or the mind, and they consist of foods such as fish, meat, alcohol and garlic. These foods have a dulling and negative effect on the mind. The famous yogic canon, the Bhagavad Gita, sums these teachings up beautifully by stating that sattvic foods are good for body, mind and spirit and 'promote vitality, health, pleasure, strength, and long life'. Meat, fish, and alcohol, or tamasik foods, on the other hand, cause 'pain, disease and discomfort'.

The Origin of Vegetarianism in Indian Culture

Some scholars point to the early vedic peoples and their culture's lust for animal sacrifices – therefore, they argue, not all yogis were vegetarians. Other scholars point out, of course, that the tantric yoga culture actually had little in common with early vedic culture.

The nomadic vedic people were hunters and herders who brought their sacrificial practices with them from outside India. When they arrived, as early as 5000 BC, some Indians already practised yoga, grew rice and dwelled in urban cities, such as Mehrgarh (7000 BC), now believed to be one of the oldest cities in the world.

In other words, since the early tantric tradition had developed independently of the vedic tradition, it had advanced its own peculiar sensibilities, including an aversion for meat and a penchant for steamy dishes of rice, chapatti, samosa, and lentils. India was, after all, the rice and vegetable basket of the world during that time. Consequently, India also had the majority of the world's population, estimated at being only about 15–20 million people.

Indeed, according to the puranas, Shiva, the royal teacher of yoga himself, instructed even the common people to reduce their intake of meat and wine, what to speak of the cave-dwelling, navel- and breath-watching yogis. Hence, it is safe to assume that, for several millennia, the ancient yogis and tantrics lived, for the most part, outside of the vedic Brahmin priest culture, and that they learnt to abhor animal slaughter. Over time, as some Brahmin priests adopted yogic ways, they also became vegetarians.

The Buddha and his friend Mahavira – who founded the Jain religion in fifth century BC, and in which ahimsa is a cornerstone tenet – were two such yogis. On their path to religious fame in India and beyond, they were known for protesting against the vedic slaughter and sacrifice of animals; instead, they promoted vegetarianism. Consequently, India has the highest percentage of vegetarians of any country in the world – about 31 per cent of the population eats a purely vegetarian diet, while only 30 per cent eats meat regularly. [61]

Raw Food vs Cooked Food

There are many vegetarians today, especially vegans in Europe and the United States, who advocate a 100 per cent raw food diet. They proclaim that a raw, vegan diet is healthier, less cruel towards animals and more ecological, and that it contains the most vitamins, prana and phytochemicals of any dietary regimen. There is much truth in this, and throughout history many tantric yogis also lived on a raw food diet for long periods of time, as well. They found raw foods to be sattvic, nutritious, as well as enhancing the development of prana, tejas and ojas. For a yogi accustomed to simple living, regular fasting on lemon water, and a raw food diet seems quite natural. Once, while travelling in India, I met a yogi who only consumed sprouted moong beans, lentils, a few fruits and occasionally some milk. He seemed incredibly healthy, vibrant and strong. 'There is nothing better for the earth, the body and the mind than simply consuming what falls from the trees and grows in the soil,' he told me. Moreover, raw food is excellent for detoxification and especially beneficial if you are sick, need to lose weight, or control your insulin.

Tantrics, however, are practical people, not fanatics or dogmatists. They know from thousands of years of experience that cooked foods have some qualities that are superior to raw foods: it makes nutritious foods digestible that otherwise would be difficult to digest, and it builds stamina. Cooked food is also better suited in colder climates, so a mixture of cooked and raw foods is often the best choice for the majority of people. Thus, once someone has gone through a detoxification and healing regimen of raw foods and juices over a period of months, it will be beneficial to introduce some cooked food to build strength and prevent the doshas, especially vata (ether and air), from accumulating. In other words, unless you practice a lot of meditation and yoga and live in a tropical climate, a 100 per cent raw food diet can increase nervousness of mind and weakness of the body, especially for those who have a thin, restless, vata constitution. Therefore it is advisable to experiment and see how much raw food you can tolerate, but up to 50 per cent raw food is generally digestible for any constitution.

Tantric Ethics for Self and Society

As the proverb goes, one falsehood can spoil a thousand truths. Right conduct is therefore considered the foundation for living a life imbued with sacredness. Ethics is the soil and water we all need in order to sprout and grow so that we can openly bask in the sunshine of spirituality.

The practice of tantra embraces all aspects of our lives, and so our ethics – our guiding principles of conduct – are seen as essential stepping stones towards spiritual growth. The guidelines that follow are thousands of years old. They are not commandments but rather teachings to be contemplated and rationally adjusted as we are faced with the struggles, compromises, paradoxes and beauty of daily living. Their historical origin is uncertain, but they were first mentioned in the tantric–inspired puranas thousands of years ago, and later in Patanjali's *Yoga Sutras*. My tantric teachers, however, claimed that Shiva developed all of the eight limbs of asthanga yoga, including the yamas and niyamas. So, since ancient times, these guidelines have been an integral part of yoga practice. Those students of yoga who are already familiar with the yamas and niyamas will notice that the tantric interpretations of them are refreshingly insightful and free from dogma.

Yamas – acts of integrity

1. **Ahimsa:** the least harm possible. The essence of the practice of ahimsa, which literally means 'no harm', is to refrain from causing undue harm to other living beings. Made famous by Mahatma Gandhi's non-violence movement, this yogic decree is actually not a principle of absolute non-violence, which is practically an impossible goal to uphold. Sometimes the lesser of evils must be chosen. Sometimes a ruthless dictatorship inflicts more harm than does a violent uprising against it. So, a choice to struggle, even with weapons, while it cannot be called non-violence, may still uphold the principle of ahimsa. Indeed, our very existence causes violence and death every day. Even if we are strict vegans and our diet consists of only fruits, grains and vegetables, we must destroy life to live, including insects, rodents, etc.

2. **Satya:** honesty. Practicing satya is to speak truth with a spirit of welfare and kindness. Hence, a 'white lie', if it helps another person in need, can be satya.

3. **Asteya:** not stealing. On the face of it, asteya seems like a simple principle but it also refers to what we withhold from others. It speaks directly to our greed. Do our riches deprive others of their rights?

4. **Brahmacharya:** follow God, follow love. In many schools of yoga, Brahmacharya refers to leading a chaste life; to be a celibate. However, tantra interprets this concept differently. In Sanskrit, the word *Brahma* refers to God, and *charya* means to move. Hence, Brahmacharya has nothing to do with sex; instead it means 'to move with God, to follow God'. In other words, Brahmacharya reminds us that Brahma or God permeates every atom of the universe. It is a true principle of sacredness. It advises us to love everything all the time.

5. **Aparigraha:** simplicity. While Brahmacharya inspires our subjective realization of the oneness of God, aparigraha reminds us of the objective adjustments we must make in order to live as if all beings matter. Hence, we do not let greed dominate our actions; we lead simple, sustainable lives.

Niyamas – healthy practices

These principles help us build a lifestyle that supports the values of yama. They are steps we can take to make our lives richer and more sacred.

1. **Shaoca:** clarity. Often termed 'cleanliness', tantric yogis define Shaoca as 'clarity' instead, because it also refers to such values as being clear, simple, and direct.

2. **Santosha:** mental ease, balance. Santosha is the contentment that comes from accepting ourselves and others just the way we are. When we connect to the love we feel from within and the love we feel in others, we become content and at peace. We feel and act from a place of sacredness. More importantly, santosha is our ability to be at peace even during stressful situations. To be in balance when the world is not.

3. **Tapah:** giving of ourselves. When we practice tapah, we are willing to undergo sacrifices in order to help others and to serve a spiritual cause. We are willing, for example, to spend less on ourselves in order to help someone in need. We are willing to live simply, so that others may simply live. Ultimately, tapah means to truly serve the other as we would like to be served in return.

4. **Svadhyaya:** spiritual understanding. Understanding the spiritual gems hidden deep in the scriptures is a genuine, spiritual practice. Hence, we read and contemplate sacred scriptures every day.

5. **Ishvara Pranidhana:** spiritual practice. The literal meaning is 'to take shelter in the Supreme Being'. In tantra, spirituality is both a practice and an experience. Meditation is a spiritual practice, and as a result, we have spiritual experiences. Hence, we practice sitting meditation twice a day, in the morning and in the evening. The rest of the day, we take shelter in god by repetition of a siddha mantra, and through the madhuvidya practice (seeing God in everything); we become a conduit of sacredness. Hence, by practicing ishvara pranidhana, all of life can become a spiritual practice.

All of these timeless, ethical guidelines – which here are interpreted from a tantric perspective – can be applied in daily, personal life and also when we confront contemporary issues and problems related to ecology, parenting, politics, economics, etc.

Seven Tantric Secrets of Success

Material wealth and fame do not guarantee inner success; nor do they guarantee peace and enlightenment. Whether we are rich or poor, true success is a spiritual achievement. It can be measured only by the depth of peace and harmony we gain from within, and by the benevolent acts we perform for other living beings.

On the path of tantric sacredness, there are seven secrets to spiritual success. These seven secrets are over 7,000 years old and were taught by Lord Shiva, who developed tantra into a systematic spiritual science. These secrets are as important and effective today as they were at the dawn of human civilization. They are:

Secret # 1 – Firm determination: In order to be successful, one must believe one will be successful in one's mission. And in order to keep one's faith alive, one must have a clear goal, keep one's resolve, and face one's obstacles boldly.

Secret # 2 – Pursue universal truth: We gain universal truth through meditation practices that are both focused and expansive. By employing an inward, focused gaze combined with a panoramic vision beyond dualistic thoughts, we gain access to our own boundless reservoir of perennial wisdom. As we gain self-knowledge and awareness rooted in universal truth, this will compel us to seek self-realization and the welfare of all beings.

Secret # 3 – Follow a spiritual guide: While we outwardly learn self-knowledge from genuine spiritual masters, we inwardly acknowledge that universal truth itself is the ultimate guide to greater wisdom. In other words, a guru on the spiritual path is indispensable, but the ultimate guru is god, Brahma.

Secret # 4 – Mental balance: Feelings of inferiority and superiority, fear, arrogance, selfishness, etc., are all human complexes that slow spiritual progress. To overcome these complexes, we cultivate fearlessness, humbleness, tolerance, respect and love for the divine consciousness present within all.

Secret # 5 – Self-restraint: Scientific studies have found that self-discipline among children is indispensable to success as an adult. Success on the spiritual path is no exception.

Secret # 6 – Balanced diet: The food we eat nourishes our bodies and affects our emotions and thoughts. The food must be vegetarian or vegan, primarily sattvic and never tamasik. And don't eat too much.

Secret #7 – There is no seventh secret: If you practice these six secrets, you will definitely be successful, so why, said Shiva jokingly, is there a need for a seventh secret?

Chapter Fourteen

The Personal Path of Divine Evolution

Follow Your Dharma

One of the reasons I travelled abroad to learn about tantra was to explore the exotic and ancient cultures of the East. I could have studied at an ashram in Sweden, but instead of seeking refuge in the familiar pine forests of Scandinavia, I decided to go on an adventure to India and Nepal. It turned out to be a spiritual and cultural quest beyond my wildest dreams – a journey into the mysterious world of the spirit that I will never forget.

Like the protagonists in Jack Kerouac's classic book, *The Dharma Bums*, I was seeking a simpler, more exuberant life. Like them, I was also searching for enlightenment; yet, unlike them, I was not looking for cool jazz, psychedelic drugs or casual sex. I was looking for a different way of life, the simple and detached lifestyle of a wandering monk. Indeed, I would soon don the saffron robes of an Eastern holy man, but unlike Buddhist monks, I would, in the tradition of Shiva tantra, keep a beard and my hair long .

My journey to the East was sparked by excitement and longing. Before I joined the monastery, I wanted to experience the crazy, colourful, urban hustle of Kolkata and Kathmandu, behold the serene beauty of the Taj Mahal, ascend the snow-covered Himalayas, and hang out with the wild and eccentric sadhus along the Bagmati and the Ganges.

Travel and adventure was in my blood. Since an early age, I had led an untraditional life. Before the age of 24, I had lived in an organic eco-village in Norway, received a degree in agronomy, co-founded an organic agricultural course that would later become one of the first organic agricultural colleges in Europe, hitchhiked through Europe several times, travelled through Scandinavia as an actor with a multimedia troupe of musicians, actors and artists, published a book of poetry and written articles for several prestigious journals, and, finally, I had lived on an organic farm in Finland which eventually became that country's pre-eminent organic herb farm. So, before I embarked upon that faithful flight to India, I had already fulfilled many of my dreams. But now I longed for something else, something deeper but less tangible – peace of mind and spiritual bliss. I wanted to learn the ancient techniques of how to quench my inner thirst for happiness.

There was also a third reason for my uncommon journey. I wanted to be of service to the poor. I had heard that many ordained yogic monks and nuns were doing social service work in poor countries. Since I had grown up in a rich country, I felt compelled to serve those less fortunate than myself. Thus, in contrast to many of my peers, who were looking forward to getting married and receiving high pay cheques, I opted out of the 'rat race'. Thus my own 'career move' was rather downwardly mobile: travel, meditation and service to the poor. Moreover, the salary would be zilch and the hours long. Still, I felt happy and sure that I had made the right choice.

Before I left for India, I did not know that the three reasons that inspired me to go – to expand my horizon, seek inner peace and do social service – are, according to tantra, inherently part of the innate, spiritual nature or characteristic of all human beings. These three drives – and not merely sex, drugs and rock and roll, which so many in my generation were hooked on – are indeed our natural dharma, our true spiritual inclination. In Sanskrit these human yearnings are called *vistara, rasa* and *seva* respectively. And, of course, you need not become a monk or a nun to practice these expressions of our human nature or dharma.

Dharma – this ancient Sanskrit word so casually uttered by many spiritual seekers today – what does it actually mean? Dharma simply means 'the innate characteristic of something'. The dharma of fire is to burn. The dharma of the universe is growth and balance. The spiritual dharma of human beings is to seek enlightenment. Dharma is often also referred to as righteousness. Thus to lead a dharmic life means to be both ethical and spiritual. Dharma practice, then, simply means the practice of spirituality, the practice of spiritual ethics, yoga and meditation.

That the dharma of life in the universe is both growth and balance can be observed by the growth and bio-diversity of natural evolution and by the stable equilibrium of nature over millions of years. It is this insight that led scientist James Lovelock to postulate that our 'blue planet' and the life on it is not two separate systems but one. He named this delicate biological and ecological system of our planetary biosphere after the Greek Goddess Gaia. Thus all of life in the Brahmachakra, in the cosmic cycle, all of life on our planetary home, Gaia, has two inherent characteristics: growth and balance.

The growth principle in human psychology is our innate urge to expand our mind. We want to learn new things. We want to travel to exotic places. We want to embark upon shamanic or yogic journeys in our own minds and spirits. Consciously, or unconsciously, we also want unlimited happiness and peace. Ultimately, this search, this spiritual expansion of mind, is our search for union with Brahma or God. This expansion through the spiritual panoramas within is called *vistara* in tantra.

The balance or harmony principle in human psychology is experienced as an urge to be courteous, ethical and caring for others. That this psychological urge is a universal phenomenon has been confirmed by modern psychology. Best-selling author and psychologist Mihaly Csikszentmihalyi has spent a life time researching this subject and terms it *flow*. When reaching a state of inner harmony and flow, we are focused. We lose sense of time. We feel exhilarated and transcendent. Another famous psychologist, the late Abraham Maslow, describes this flow as a *peak experience*. Other apt terms are ecstasy and rapture. When flow is experienced on a purely spiritual level, the Sanskrit term for it is *rasa*, which actually translates as *flow* in English. Thus the ultimate experience of flow in human life is when our mind merges with the spiritual flow of cosmic consciousness. In tantra this state is achieved through meditation, and in particular through the practice of *dhyan*, which is also the

THE PERSONAL PATH OF DIVINE EVOLUTION

seventh stage of Patanjali's asthanga yoga. Patanjali defines dhyan as 'an unbroken flow of mind towards the supreme goal'. The term dhyan, which in tantra represents a visualization practice without the use of a mantra, became known as *chan* in China, *chen* in Korea and *zen* in Japan.

I learnt the practice of dhyan on the banks of the Bagmati River a few weeks into my monastic training in Nepal. I remember vividly my teacher, Acarya S., asking me, prior to the instruction, to practice meditation with him for a while. After some time of deep meditation – for I found it exceedingly easy to concentrate – I was overwhelmed by the feeling that I had lived in this area of Nepal in a previous life. The feeling was so strong that after a while it was nearly impossible to focus on my meditation practice, so I opened my eyes. Acarya S. sat serene as an orange candle in lotus position in front of me. Obviously in a deep ecstatic trance, his head tilted backwards; his lips formed a subtle, inward smile; his slow breath was barely noticeable. Behind his shoulders, the snow covered peaks of the Himalayas shone bright against a turquoise sky. To our right, the Bagmati River flowed dark and sleepily. Further up stream two young boys washed some buffaloes in the cool, shallow water. Suddenly, as if awakened from another world, the great yogi in front of me opened his eyes and said: 'Yes, it is true, I also feel you have lived in this part of the world before.'

I was stunned by his remark. Overwhelmed by emotion and by the synchronicity of our insights, especially his accurate 'reading of my mind', tears started to roll down my cheeks; tears of awe and gratitude. Then, as if on cue, we both started to laugh. The tantric explanation for this incident is that both my teacher and I had accessed the deep psychic flow of the atimanas kosha, or supramental mind. In this state, one gains access to the expanded mind which the pioneering psychologist Carl Jung termed the 'collective unconscious'. This all-knowing mind has the capacity to transcend the bondage of time, space and person. Sometimes, in this state, one simply experiences a sense of timelessness and bliss, at other times one may have deep, creative or intuitive insights, including memories of past lives, mystical visions or clairvoyant insights. It is from this state of mind that great visionary art, poetry and music are created and from where some of the world's greatest scientific inventions have been conceived.

The ultimate goal of dhyan meditation, Acarya S. instructed me, is not to 'get caught up' in these visions or insights, but to soar even higher than the atimanas kosha, into the subliminal and causal level of the vijanamaya and hiranmaya kosha. Finally, one will soar even higher, into the state of the atman, into the purely spiritual flow of the infinite soul beyond our individual mind. To achieve that sublime flow, tantrics skilfully adopt a seemingly contradictory practice: to meditate on a sublime form or image in order to gain insight and devotion deep and strong enough to transmute our mind into the divine flow of formlessness. Just as a Zen Buddhist Koan consists of a story, dialogue, or question which is not rationally understood but only conceived by intuition or lateral thinking, the dhyan practice uses form to transcend the mind to experience the consciousness beyond rationality and form. This practice, to contemplate a sacred form – a geometric yantra, or the guru – in order to achieve divine formlessness or a state of non-dualism is, in a nutshell, what tantric dhyan is all about. The attainment of this flow, this sweet, spiritual rasa, says tantra, is the goal of human dharma, the goal of all perennial, spiritual practice.

A few months after I learnt this meditation from Acarya S., I started reading Andrew Harvey's book A *Journey in Ladakh: Encounters with Buddhism*. Since this book described Harvey's many encounters with Tibetan lamas, some of whom practised Buddhist tantra, it made me wonder if some of their meditation practices were similar to mine. In particular, I had heard that the guru yoga practice in Vajrayana Buddhism was similar to the tantric dhyan that I had learnt, which would confirm the deep tie between Hindu tantra and Buddhist tantra. So, a few days after starting to read the book, I meditated for several hours. During meditation, I developed a deep desire to confirm these anecdotes and hunches. After meditation, I casually opened Harvey's book on a random page. To my great surprise, it opened on page 232 where Harvey describes how Thuksey Rinpoche instructs him in guru yoga. On the following pages, he outlined an esoteric, tantric visualization technique that was practically identical to the one I had recently learnt on the banks of the Bagmati River from Acarya S. This technique, which for the superficial observer may resemble idolatry, teaches us, through deep devotion and strong concentration, to gradually transcend form, then the mind itself, and to experience the non-dual consciousness beyond rationality and form. This paradoxical practice is very powerful and subtle, and it represents the very heart and essence of tantric transmutation and awakening. [62]

Creating a Tantric Lifestyle

Tantric Philosophy: *Bhaktirbhagav Adbhavana Na Sthutirnarcana* – Devotion is ideation on god; not praise or ritualistic worship.

Daily Contemplation: It is said that, 'Devotion is the fruit and rituals are the flower. The flower drops off as soon as the fruit appears.' Attraction for god is the highest form of love. Attraction for god is bhakti yoga, to dance and sing the name of God.

Daily Acts of Sacredness

One: Ask yourself, 'Do you express your love for God in words and song?'

Two: If not, it is time to start expressing your love for God in words and song!

EPILOGUE

The Reasons Why I Love Tantra

- I love tantra because it is about walking your spiritual talk.
- I love tantra because it is a comprehensive body–mind–spirit tradition that includes the practice of physical yoga exercises, devotional dancing, mantra meditation and chanting, breathing exercises, visualization techniques, sacred cosmology and even alchemy and holistic medicine.
- 'The techniques of yoga have their source in tantra and the two cannot be separated, just as consciousness, Shiva, cannot be separated from energy, Shakti.' – Swami Satyananda Saraswati
- In other words, when you practice a contemporary yoga studio version of a more ancient version from the hatha yoga pradipika, or sit in lotus position, or simply cross-legged at home, reciting a mantra flowing like water over your silent tongue, you are a tantrika.
- I love this comprehensive tradition of dual mind–body energies entwined like lovers in a tight embrace, entwined like the ida and pingala nadis of your esoteric spine, entwined like a oneness-flower in each chakra of your sacred body. I love this body–positive practice which they refer to as tantra yoga.
- In this microcosmic architecture of my own body–mind, I also see the architecture of the whole macrocosm. I always see my own dance, whether in the shade or in the light, or in the mirror of reality.
- Hence it is said in the Vishva–Sara–Tantra: 'What is here is elsewhere, what is not here is nowhere.' Hence the alchemists of Europe were also tantrikas when they said: 'As Above, so Below.'

- I love tantra because when we practise our asana in harmony with our breath, we are the whole universe moving in one tantric flow. So when we meditate knowing that the breath we are breathing is the cosmos breathing through us, then we know we are in the rasa, the cosmic flow.
- I love tantra because it is hardly just about sex. Indeed, it's about making love to the Universe.
- Since health is not gained by gorging on organic food and true wealth is not found in the desire for more money, tantra is not the path of indulgence, tantra is not the path of mere sensual gratification.
- I love tantra, because tantric yogis embrace both unity and duality, both wholeness and opposites. They have realized that these opposites dissolve in Brahma, in spirit, and that the inner essence of all life and all things is bliss and love.
- That is why tantra is often called the path of ecstasy, or the path of love.
- I love tantra because of its notion that everything is divine. This essential realization – that every form, particle, atom, or rock in this universe has an inherent capacity to reveal the divine.
- I love tantra for boldly claiming that not just everyone, but everything, even this book, is at its core, God.
- I love tantra because it understands there is no free spiritual lunch. So, jump into action, engage in a sustained spiritual effort (sadhana) in order to realize this inherent divinity. Do it now! Because it is highly unlikely that the weekend seminar you are looking forward to in a few months will give you instant enlightenment!
- Tantric spirituality means that in order to experience sacredness in everyday life, we must practice spirituality – hatha yoga, meditation, prayer, chanting, dancing – diligently and with total abandon. We must walk (or dance) our spiritual talk. It's that simple.
- In other words, daily spiritual practice is essential in achieving results on the path of tantra. Indeed, all sacred paths worthy of its mala beads would agree.

- I love tantra because it signifies a spirituality that is vigorous and fearless, a spirituality that encourages and enables us to overcome limitations, phobias, worries and egotistical tendencies head-on. Just do it! (Tantra said that thousands of years before the Nike advertisement made the slogan popular.)
- I love tantra because of its alchemical use of energy, its ability to transform desire into bliss, and violence into peace.
- For the tantric understands that all dualities, all conflicts and opposites, all forms and energies are different expressions of God that ultimately dissolve in a state of non-dual unity and peace. That is, if you compost all your shadow stuff in a tantric way. In other words, if you do as the Spanish poet Antonio Machado did: he let the bees in his heart make honey out of all his past mistakes, all his past samskaras. That's tantric psychology in action.
- I love tantra because it's more science than religion, more art than science, more spiritual practice than doctrine.
- 'Tantra is 99 per cent practice and 1 per cent theory.' – Shrii Anandamurti
- I love tantra for its adherence to non-dualistic dualistic non-dualism – the understanding that the one created the many and that we, the many, are all part of the one. This ability to see the oneness of everything is the essence of tantra.
- In India, both tantrics and vedantists are non-dualists – they both believe in the oneness of existence – however, when the vedantists say the world is really an illusion, the tantrics say the world is really divine.
- It is perhaps this holistic and practical attitude – that divinity is everywhere and that sacredness can be realized anywhere – which makes tantra so appealing to contemporary seekers. At least that is why I love tantra.

Creating a Tantric Lifestyle

Tantric Philosophy: *Tasminupalabde Parama Trisnanivritti* – When we realize Brahma, all our thirst is quenched.

Daily Contemplation: It is our thirst for the limitless, for infinite happiness that lies behind all our desires, even our desires for more wealth, power and fame. We imagine that these limited goals will quench our limitless desires. How foolish! Once we make more money, we want even more! Only the limitless entity can truly quench our limitless thirst. Only the ocean can make the drop become an ocean.

Daily Acts of Sacredness

One: Feel satisfied with what you have for the moment. Feel that your life is infinitely fulfilled from within through the grace of infinite Brahma.

Two: Feel that Brahma surrounds you, always. Feel that Brahma is within you, always.

Notes and References

1. Huston Smith, as quoted by Ken Wilber, *Sex, Ecology, Spirituality: The Spirit of Evolution*, 2nd edition, Shambhala, Boston, 1996.
2. Ken Wilber, *One Taste: Daily Reflections on Integral Spirituality*, Shambhala, Boston, 1999.
3. Georg Feuerstein, *The Encyclopedia of Yoga and Tantra*, Shambhala, Boston, 2011.
4. Robert Bly, *The Soul Is Here for Its Own Joy*, Ecco Press, New York City, 1995, p. 78.
5. Alain Daniléou, *Shiva and the Primordial Tradition: From the Tantras of the Science of Dreams*, Inner Traditions, Rochester, 2006.
6. David Crow, *In Search of the Medicine Buddha: A Himalayan Journey*, Tarcher, USA, 2003.
7. N. N. Bhattacarya, *History of the Tantric Religion*, South Asia Books, Columbia, 2006.
8. Georg Feuerstein, *Tantra: The Path of Ecstasy*, Shambhala, Boston, 2008.
9. Ibid.
10. N. N. Bhattacharya, *History of the Tantric Religion*, South Asia Books, Columbia, 2006.
11. Swami Abhayananda, *The History of Mysticism: The Unchanging Testament*, Atma Books, Olympia, 1996.
12. Alain Daniélou, *Shiva and the Primordial Tradition: From the Tantras of the Science of Dreams*, Inner Traditions, Vermont, 2006.
13. Alain Daniélou, *A Brief History of India*, Inner Traditions, Vermont, 2003.
14. N. N. Bhattacharya, *The History of the Tantric Religion*, South Asia Books, Columbia, 2006.

15. Shrii Shrii Anandamurti, *Discourses on Tantra*, Vol. 2, Ananda Marga Publications, Calcutta, 1994.
16. Max Müller, as quoted by Georg Feuerstein, Subash Kak and David Frawley, *In Search of the Cradle of Human Civlization*, Quest Books, Chennai, 1996.
17. Arvind Kumar, 'Women and the Vedas: Limiting Women Limits All of Society,' *India Currents*, September, 1994.
18. Dr Spencer Wells in an interview in Rediff magazine. See: http://www.rediff.com/news/2002/nov/27inter.htm
19. Ibid.
20. Michael Bamshad, Lynn Jorde et al., *Genetic Evidence on the Origin of Indian Caste Populations*, Genome Research, June 2001, www.ncbi.nlm.nih.gov/pmc/articles/PMC3
21. Robert Cooke, 'History of Aryan Conquest of India told in Modern Genes', *San Francisco Chronicle*, 26 May, 1999.
22. Shrii Shrii Anandamurti, *Discourses on Tantra*, Vol. 2, Ananda Marga Publications, Calcutta, 1994.
23. Christopher Isherwood, *Ramakrishna and His Disciples*, Nesma Books, Chennai, 2002.
24. St Theresa of Ávila, *The Interior Castle*, Dover Publications, Mineola, 2007.
25. Shrii Shrii Anandamurti, *Subhasita Samgraha*, Vol. 4, Ananda Marga Publications, Calcutta, 1982.
26. Christopher Isherwood, *Ramakrishna and His Disciples*, Nesma Books, Chennai, 2002.
27. Shrii Shrii Anandamurti, *Discourses on Tantra*, Vol. 2, Ananda Marga Publications, Calcutta, 1994.
28. Lex Hixon, *Coming Home: The Experience of Enlightenment in Sacred Traditions*, Larson Publications, San Francisco,1995.
29. Ibid.
30. Ibid.
31. Christopher Isherwood, *Ramakrishna and His Disciples*, Nesma Books, Chennai, 2002.
32. The Dalai Lama, *The Art of Happiness: A Handbook for Living*, 10th edition, Riverhead Books, New York City, 2009.

33. Georg Feuerstein, *The Yoga Tradition: Its History, Literature, Philosophy and Practice*, Hohm Press, Chino Valley, 2001.
34. Ken Wilber, *Sex, Ecology, Spirituality: The Spirit of Evolution*, 2nd edition, Shambhala, Boston, 1996.
35. Shrii Shrii Anandamurti, *Ánanda Vacanámrtam*, Vol. 14, Ananda Marga Publications, Kolkata, 2009.
36. Coleman Barks, *The Essential Rumi*, HarperOne, San Francisco, 2004.
37. Robert Bly, in conversation with the author.
38. Paul Davies, *The Mind of God: The Scientific Basis for a Rational World*, Simon & Schuster, New York City, 1993.
39. Vasant Lad, *Ayurveda: The Science of Healing*, Lotus Press, New Delhi, 1985.
40. David Frawley, *Ayurveda and the Mind: The Healing of Consciousness*, Lotus Press, New Delhi, 1997.
41. John Gribbin in Ken Wilber, *Sex, Ecology, Spirituality: The Spirit of Evolution*, 2nd edition, Shambhala, 2001.
42. George Seielstad, *At the Heart of the Web: The Inevitable Genesis of Intelligent Life*, Harcourt, San Diego, 1989.
43. Brian Swimme, *The Universe Is a Green Dragon: A Cosmic Creation Story*, Bear & Company, Rochester, 1984.
44. Lex Hixon, *Coming Home: The Experience of Enlightenment in Sacred Traditions*, Larson Publications, Burdett, 1995.
45. These stories were sent to the author in an e-mail shortly before Kirtanananda Swami passed away.
46. http://www.universal-mind.org/Chakra_pages/ProofOfExistence.htm
47. Ibid.
48. Dr Candace Pert, *Molecules of Emotion: The Scientific Basis Behind Mind-Body Medicine*, Scribner, New York City, 1997.
49. Avadhutika Ananda Mitra Acharya, *The Spiritual Philosophy of Shrii Shrii Anandamurti: A Commentary on Ananda Sutram*, Ananda Marga Publications, Calcutta, 1998.
50. Dr Candace Pert, *Molecules of Emotion: The Scientific Basis Behind Mind-Body Medicine*, Scribner, New York City, 1997

51. Avadhutika Ananda Mitra Acharya, *The Spiritual Philosophy of Shrii Shrii Anandamurti: A Commentary on Ananda Sutram*, Ananda Marga Publications, Calcutta, 1998. All information on chakras and vrittis from my study with tantra masters in India.

52. Shrii Shrii Anandamurti, *Discourses on Tantra*, Vol. 1, Ananda Marga Publications, Calcutta, 1998.

53. Shrii Shrii Anandamurti, *Namah Shivaya Shantaya*, Ananda Marga Publications, Calcutta, 1998.

54. John of the Cross, Selected Writings, Paulist Press, Mahwah, 1988.

55. Ibid.

56. Dannion Brinkley, *Saved by the Light*, HarperOne, San Francisco, 2008.

57. Lama Thubten Yeshe, *Introduction to Tantra: The Transmutation of Desire*, fifth edition, Wisdom Publications, Somerville, 2005.

58. Robert Bly, from a poetry reading at University of North Carolina Asheville, May 2007.

59. Coleman Barks and John Moyne, *The Essential Rumi*, HarperOne, San Francisco, 2004.

60. Peter Thmopkins and Christopher Bird, *The Secret Life of Plants: A Fascinating Account of the Physical, Emotional and Spiritual Relation Between Plants and Man* , Harper and Row, USA, 1989.

61. http://en.wikipedia.org/wiki/Vegetarianism_by_country

62. Andrew Harvey, *A Journey in Ladakh: Encounters with Buddhism*, Mariner Books, 2000.

ACKNOWLEDGEMENTS

The initial impetus to write this book came from conversations with and support from my friend and fellow tantric yogi Jake Karlyle. My writer friend Donald Devashiish Acosta was also an important part of these early conversations, as well as my yogi friend Premamurti, who gave me support and encouragement during various stages of the manuscript. While all of them inspired me to write on tantra, especially Jake Karlyle gave me important feedback on various drafts of the manuscript; none of them are responsible for any shortcomings or mistakes the manuscript may contain.

Acclaimed poet and friend Robert Bly has infused my life with the poetic vision of bhakti yoga through his fresh interpretations of the works of Kabir, Mirabai and Rumi, and wherever the book dips into those sweet waters, his spirit and inspiration hopefully shines through. Many teachers and scholars have gifted me with important insights related to the practice, philosophy and history of tantra over the years, especially Georg Feuerstein, Lalan Prasad Singh, Alain Daniélou, N. N. Bhattacharyya and Swami Satyananda Saraswati, and of course all of the personal teachers mentioned in the pages of this book.

None have been more important than my guru, Shrii Shrii Anandamurti, however, whose teachings are characterized as both 'universalist' and 'tantric' by prominent yoga scholar Georg Feuerstein. Whatever spirit and wisdom of authentic tantra is found in these pages are due to the teachings and guidance of Anandamurti, who, according to many, was contemporary India's most enigmatic master and eminent philosopher of yoga and tantra.